Studies in Economic Ethics and Philosophy

Springer-Verlag Berlin Heidelberg GmbH

Studies in Economic Ethics and Philosophy

P. Koslowski (Ed.)
Ethics in Economics, Business, and Economic Policy
(out of print)
X, 178 pages. 1992, ISBN 3-540-55359-2

P. Koslowski · Y. Shionoya (Eds.)
The Good and the Economical
Ethical Choices in Economics and Management
(out of print)
X, 202 pages. 1993, ISBN 3-540-57339-9

H. De Geer (Ed.)
Business Ethics in Progress?
IX, 124 pages. 1994, ISBN 3-540-57758-0

P. Koslowski (Ed.)
The Theory of Ethical Economy in the Historical School
XI, 343 pages. 1995, ISBN 3-540-59070-6

A. Argandoña (Ed.)
The Ethical Dimension of Financial Institutions
and Markets
XI, 263 pages. 1995, ISBN 3-540-59209-1

G.K. Becker (Ed.)
Ethics in Business and Society.
Chinese and Western Perspectives
VIII, 233 pages. 1996, ISBN 3-540-60773-0

P. Koslowski
Ethics of Capitalism and Critique of Sociobiology.
Two Essays with a Comment by James M. Buchanan
IX, 142 pages. 1996, ISBN 3-540-61035-9

F. Neil Brady (Ed.)
Ethical Universals in International Business
X, 246 pages. 1996, ISBN 3-540-61588-1

P. Koslowski and A. Føllesdal (Eds.)
Restructuring the Welfare State
Theory and Reform of Social Policy
VIII, 402 pages. 1997, ISBN 3-540-62035-4

G. Erreygers and T. Vandevelde
Is Inheritance Legitimate?
Ethical and Economic Aspects
of Wealth Transfers
X, 236 pages. 1997, ISBN 3-540-62725-1

P. Koslowski (Ed.)
Business Ethics
in East Central Europe
XII, 151 pages. 1997, ISBN 3-540-63367-X

P. Koslowski (Ed.)
Methodology of the Social Sciences, Ethics,
and Economics in the Newer Historical School
From Max Weber and Rickert
to Sombart and Rothacker
XII, 565 pages. 1997, ISBN 3-540-63458-4

Andreas Føllesdal
Peter Koslowski (Eds.)

Democracy and the European Union

Springer

Dr. Andreas Føllesdal
ARENA, Advanced Research on the Europeanisation of the Nation State
P.O. Box 1143, Blindern
N-0317 Oslo
Norway

Prof. Dr. Peter Koslowski
The Hannover Institute of Philosophical Research
Centre for Ethical Economy and Business Culture
Gerberstraße 26
D-30169 Hannover
Germany

ISBN 978-3-642-08333-4 ISBN 978-3-662-03622-8 (eBook)
DOI 10.1007/978-3-662-03622-8

Cataloging-in-Publication Data applied for
Die Deutsche Bibliothek - CIP-Einheitsaufnahme
Democracy and the European Union / Andreas Føllesdal ; Peter Koslowski (ed.). - Berlin ; Heidelberg ; New York ; Barcelona , Budapest ; Hong Kong ; London ; Milan ; Paris ; Santa Clara ; Singapore ; Tokyo : Springer, 1997
(Studies in economic ethics and philosophy)

Originally published by Springer-Verlag Berlin Heidelberg New York in 1998.
Softcover reprint of the hardcover 1st edition 1998

Hardcover Design: Erich Kirchner, Heidelberg

SPIN 10643517 42/2202-5 4 3 2 1 0 - Printed on acid-free paper

Preface

The volume at hand contains invited papers addressing the normative issues of democracy and the European Union. Most papers were first discussed at the conference "Democracy and the European Union", held in Oslo on August 8-10, 1996, with the support of the Norwegian research programme Advanced Research on the Europeanisation of the Nation-State (ARENA).

The editors wish to thank the organisers and participants of the Oslo conference. They are grateful to Kristin Johansen and Simen Bræin for managing the conference, to Anna Maria Hauk and Victoria Pogosian for professional assistance with the manuscript, and to Andreas Holm Bakke and Torstein Buggeland for generating the index.

Hannover, Germany, and Oslo, Norway, May 1997

Peter Koslowski Andreas Føllesdal

Contents

CONTENTS

Part D

Conclusion

Chapter 13

Democracy and the European Union: Challenges

ANDREAS FØLLESDAL

The "great question", as John Locke put it, is not whether there should be political power in the world, nor whence it came, but who should have it. For domestic institutions, these three questions of normative political theory may well be separable and ordered. However, the legitimacy of trans-state institutions can hardly be determined without keen regard for whether and why they should exist, and whence they arose.

The characteristics and constraints of sovereign states have shaped the parameters for democratic answers to Locke's question. Just domestic government must be accountable to the governed. That is: the power to make laws and secure compliance should ultimately reside with citizens generally, securing coincidence of the affected and the electorate. This general and equal distribution of political rights gives expression to the equal worth of all citizens, and is the best institutional arrangement in light of the effects both on popular will formation and for collective decision-making.

Theories of democracy have not only endorsed universal suffrage, but also justified more specific details. The commonplaces include constitutionally specified procedures and constraints, including the division of legislative, executive and judicial powers; transparency; accountability of elected representatives to the electorate; and majority rule.

The European Union is a new subject for theories of legitimacy, and poses fundamental challenges to the established concepts and principles of democratic theory. The mere existence of the EU proves that the sovereign state cannot remain the sole focus of normative reflection. Indeed, the very conception of sovereignty is at stake in current disputes about the proper scope and legal powers to be transferred to central European institutions, without divesting traditional member states of all powers (see below the contributions by Jachtenfuchs and by Koslowski).

I. Democratic Deficit?

Formally, the "democratic deficit" of the EU may be taken to refer to "the gap between the powers transferred to the Community level and the control of the elected Parliament over them, a gap filled by national civil servants operating as European experts or as members of regulation and management committees, and to some extent by organized lobbies, mainly representing business" (Williams 1991, p. 162). Pivotal parts of the decisions of the EU are subject to neither watch nor control by the citizens of member states, neither directly nor by their representatives. Furthermore, what control and accountability there is runs counter to received democratic theory.

The current Intergovernmental Conference realizes that the emerging political institutions at the European level require a new answer to Locke's question (Nentwich). Popular worries about a democratic deficit partly stem from the perennial fear of absolutism, which in earlier times gave rise to democratic checks on monarchs and emperors, and in turn to constitutional checks on majority rule. The specters of unchecked, diffuse and dispersed power rear their heads again. But these worries about a democratic deficit in the EU are not the exclusive concern of fearful philosophers. General compliance and popular acceptance and respect for European law is at stake.

In addition to popular unrest, there are two further causes for modifying the European institutions which may entail reduced powers for small member states. One central issue is whether and how to deepen the EU, vesting its institutions with further supra-national powers transferred from its member states. Secondly, institution must be redesigned to prepare for a possible widening of the EU to include many new small states to the east. The legislative powers of states are circumscribed in the union, yet they retain the power to act and block through qualified majority voting or unanimity requirements of unanimity. The powers of existing and future member states must be specified in light of two conflicting threats. Small states with effective political powers can threaten effective governance in some areas, contrary to the interests of a majority of the citizens of Europe. But several small states may also promote actions contrary to the interests of the current, larger state members.

To understand the present dilemmas the historical aims of the EU must be remembered. Indeed, the question whence the Union raises important normative issues, Locke's claim notwithstanding: The European institutions have been created by formally free and sovereign states, and this genesis is central for explaining and assessing the allocation of powers among the member states. Securing peace and economic prosperity in a global economy have been paramount goals, coupled with the recognition by most governments that increased interdependence reduce the value and efficacy of formal state sovereignty.

The question of legitimate governance is raised anew, regarding the exercise of legal powers in Europe. The legitimacy of such transnational institutions born by political integration has so far received some, but scant attention (Hanson). The task of normative political theory is to offer concepts, arguments and criteria that further these debate, addressing problems of principle.

The peoples of Europe, weaned on democratic institutions at home, are alarmed by the transfer of powers out of their reach: "the notion that government must rest on the consent of the governed has become an article of political faith, a conviction that much contemporary political philosophy labours to secure" (Flathman 1993, p. 528). Thus several responses consist in unsuccessful grafts of this issue onto traditional democratic theory.

Some have appealed exclusively to the pedigree of European institutions. While processes of European integration defies easy classification, they basically transfer legislative, executive and judicial powers from the member states of the European Union to transnational institutions. These institutions are the fruits of intra-governmental bargains among democratic states. This genesis is sometimes said to suffice for their legitimacy. The EU institutions enjoy powers willfully surrendered. On the assumption that legitimacy transmits by consent, whatever democratic governments agree to, must be democratic and legitimate. However, this approach fails (Pogge). Consent is not, as a rule, legitimacy-preserving. In particular, domestic government power is limited. The authority to legislate, execute and adjudicate are limited and listed. Notably, governments are not as a rule authorized to transfer these powers to others (Gustavsson). The powers entrusted to national governments are not for governments to give away.

Nor can the question of criteria for just European governance be regarded as domestic democratic theory writ large. European institutions are not designed to replace domestic nodes of governance, but instead turn Europe into a system of multi-level governance (Jachtenfuchs). The EU was introduced to enhance and complement domestic sovereignty in recognition of discrepancies between state borders, electorates, and the range of affected parties. Thus any insights to be garnered from democratic theory would likely hark from theories of multi-level democracy and federalism (Midgaard, Hanson, Van Parijs, Føllesdal).

The democratic deficit may be permanent. One must then ask whether European integration can find legitimate institutional expression at all. Current tendencies in the Europeanisation of the nation-state suggest a Grotian or neo-Medievalist world order with overlapping loyalties (Schmitter, Koslowski). We must ask whether non-democratic modes of government may be justified to the citizens of Europe. In any case, the received conceptual grid of democratic theory cannot easily be brought to bear on this polity at the supra-state level. It remains to be determined whether concepts such as the constitutional division of powers, transparency, accountability of representatives, and majority rule can play a role at all in assessing European institutions. The role of democratic decision procedures and consent must be rethought, both for domestic and multi-level governance, to consider why and in what sense legitimate government must rest on consent of the governed. A central issue must then be the proper scope of democratic decision procedures at the EU level.

II. EU Institutions

To bring home the theoretical challenges for a democratic theory for Europe, a brief sketch of central institutions of the European Union is in order[1]. Power is distributed among four main bodies: the Council of Ministers, the European Parliament, the Commission, and the Court of the Euro-

1 For further development of the topics of sections II and III see MALNES (1995), to which these remarks are indebted.

pean Union. At issue is the legitimacy of the existing distribution of authority and functions between these bodies.

The *Council of Ministers* has legislative power, with the final word on legal matters. It is intergovernmental, composed of representatives of the governments of all member states, and reaches its decisions by voting. 76 votes are distributed among countries according to size. The Council actually consists of various councils, each of which represent specific domestic departments. It determines the pace and course of further integration and generally acts as the "ultimate locus of ... decisionmaking on all major issues" (Wessels 1991, p. 133). While the Treaty of Rome demanded unanimity for every decision, the Single European Act of 1987 opened the door to legislation by qualified majority (54 or more votes) on many issues.

The Council is a forum for inter-governmental bargaining and coalition making. Every member state has considerable leeway in protecting national interests. National governments can control decisions by veto or blocking minorities under qualified majority voting. These mechanisms, coupled with its hitherto powerful role, ensure that the European Union falls short of a European federation. However, the scope of qualified majority voting as well as the distribution of votes are on the agenda of the IGC, to prevent decision paralysis.

The democratic deficit is illustrated by the position of the Council of Ministers and its mode of operation. With the exception of Denmark and Austria, member states do not allow their national parliaments to exact commitments from ministers before Council meetings, consult them during sessions or hold them answerable afterwards.

Moreover, considerable secrecy surrounds its work. Debates and voting take place behind closed doors, and no proceedings are available. Even the political leadership of member states lack information about preparations for the Council's sessions. The only "effective though not necessarily democratic watch mechanism is the network of well-informed lobbies" (Wessels 1991, p. 150).

Direct elections of the members of the *European Parliament* were initiated in 1979. Originally the Parliament had a marginal role, but from 1975, it has shared authority on budgetary appropriations with the Council of Ministers. Nevertheless, its old right of "consultation" before the adoption of new legislation has been supplemented by rights to readings of certain kinds of law, as well as power to amend draft legislation. Thus the power of the Parliament is ascending, even though it still does not have sovereign legislative competences. The Maastricht Treaty empowers the Parliament to ask the Commission for legislative initiatives, thus increasing its role vis-a-vis the Council of Ministers (Mancini 1991, p. 179). The concrete stakes are budgetary and legislative competences. An enhanced role for the directly elected Parliament at the expense of the intergovernmental Council augments the federal components of the union.

The *Commission* is the major source of legal and political initiative in the EU. It has exclusive right of initiative regarding legislation, and its drafts of laws and regulations are the only basis for decisions in the Council. It is also the guardian of the Treaty, ensuring that the provisions are applied. Due to its appointment and mixed powers, the Commission is perhaps that body of the EU which fits least easily with traditional democratic theory (Matlary).

The Commission has the appearance of a representative bureaucracy, numbering at least one national of every member states and two from the largest ones. Nevertheless the commissioners are expected to act as professional civil servants, loyal only to the Union as custodians of the "European interest" (Ludlow 1991, p. 122). The Commission spearheaded major leaps forward in the European integration process, including the Maastricht Treaty of 1992 (Sandholtz and Zysman 1989).

The *Court of Justice of the European Communities* seeks to maintain the rule of law, and shall ensure uniform interpretation of Community law. Its 15 judges and 9 advocates are appointed by common accord by the Member States for renewable terms of six years. In federations and other non-unitary systems the jurisdictions of the central body and sub-units are carefully demarcated. Not so for the EU, where the European Court of Justice has gradually eroded the jurisdiction of Member States through processes of Direct Effect, Supremacy and the enforcement of fundamental human rights (Weiler 1995).

The European Court will also be the arbiter of the Principle of Subsidiarity, which was introduced to limit the competence of central institutions. The Principle of Subsidiarity, as elaborated at the meeting of the Council of Ministers in Lisbon in June 1992, says that "the Union shall only act to carry out those tasks which may be undertaken more effectively in common than by the members States acting separately". Given contested and conflicting visions of the proper aims of the union, this principle is so far of little impact, but can be used in far-reaching ways to increase the scope of Community action.

The cumulative effects of expanded Community jurisdiction are pervasive, so that today the European Court and national courts contest the material limits to Community jurisdiction. These disputes may lead us to question whether the European Union indeed has a final legal order.

III. Precepts of Democratic Theory

A central normative issue is the legitimacy of the quasi-constitutional distribution of authority and functions between the main bodies of the EU. Accountability and control over the political agenda may be strengthened by enhancing the power of the European Parliament or subjecting the Council to closer scrutiny by national parliaments. At the same time, the power of directly elected bodies must be checked to secure individual rights and the rule of law. However, such *constitution-like constraints* may stiffle the requisite political debate and will formation, and put undue restrictions on the political agenda - now a privilege of the Commission (Bellamy and Castiglione).

A necessary precondition of legitimate and accountable government is that its structure is *transparent* to the citizens. Thus the opacity of the present political system of the European Union raises immediate doubts about its legitimacy. The poor reception of the Maastricht Treaty at the Danish and French plebiscites can partly be explained by its nearly incomprehensible text, which accurately reflect the decision making procedures. Thus the Council of Ministers operates according to a perplexing set of procedures involving majority, unanimity, qualified majority and so forth — as well as "co-decision" procedures specifying how authority is shared with the Parliament. Such worries were well expressed by the American Anti-Federalists, who opposed the constitution of 1787 because vagueness and indeterminacy allows for unchecked abuse of power. (Manin 1994, pp. 44-45).

Accountability towards the citizens of Europe must be increased within more democratic European institutions. Currently, citizens are ill-equipped for well-informed assessment of their representatives, and citizens enjoy few formal mechanisms for withdrawing and replacing representatives. Neither the European nor national Parliaments appoint commissioners or civil servants of "comitology". The Parliament can only dismiss the entire Commission *en bloc* — a threat so close to mutual destruction as to be politically futile.

Accountability is of course impossible when minutes are secret, and when voting rules are complex, as in the Council. Only in Denmark and Austria is there even a semblance of indirect accountability, with national parliaments controlling national ministers.

Majority rule is sometimes said to be central to the democratic ideal (Dahl 1989, chs. 10, 11). Decisions which accrue the largest number of votes should prevail. To be legitimate, majority rule must operate on the basis of informed public deliberation about the interests and alternatives available, as well as information about the candidates' performance and promises. These procedures thus allow well-founded preference aggregation among citizens. Furthermore, will formation is also fostered. Public deliberation allows for the development of solidarity, a shared understanding of political culture, as well as a recognition that under majority rule among a fixed set of individuals, most members can expect to be in the majority most of the time.

Such assumptions are less plausible at the European level (Alvira). Conceptions of the good life and preferences generally diverge even more broadly across state borders than within them. In addition to the opacity of EU institutions, the lack of a European public space and European political parties reduce the informational bases and range of choices. Segments of citizens, for instance those of small states harbor reasonable fears of becoming permanent minorities under majority rule. In addition, the proper role of states is increasingly brought to the fore in debates about majoritarian voting systems: should decisions secure the equal influence of citizens, or of states?

The European institutions must respond to the dual challenges of democratic deficit and efficiency, with increased stress due to the prospects of further enlargement. To be sure, there is more to legitimacy that political participation and just rule. Efficiency is also required, since a paralysis — democratically induced or otherwise — hardly commands respect and compliance. The reallocation of powers, increased accountability and adjusted voting procedures must thus both secure citizens' participation, and secure joint decisions where such are appropriate. Some hold that a major impediment to the smooth working of the EU is the current power of national governments. The slowest participant determines the speed of the convoy. However, as long as the goals of the European Union are unclear or contested, it is impossible to determine whether the blocking ability of member states prevents or promotes the proper working of the union.

The project of European integration may be only the latest fain attempt at embodying the ancient ideals of democratic rule in polities far from the Greek *polis*. John Dunn (1993, p. 29) points to the paradox that "we have all become democrats in theory at just that stage of history at which it has become virtually impossible for us in practice to organize our social life in a democratic fashion any longer". But the democratic deficit of the European Union need not herald tragic choices among incompatible values. For the issue of designing political institutions of Europe, it is simply too early to tell. Creative and politically astute research and negotiations may increase the range of institutional alternatives. And careful and well-informed deliberations in normative political theory must be brought to bear on the range of alternatives. The present volume contributes to this important task.

References

DAHL, ROBERT: *Democracy and Its Critics*, New Haven, Conn. (Yale University Press) 1989.

DUNN, JOHN: *Western Political Theory in the Face of the Future*, Cambridge (Canto) 1993.

FLATHMAN, RICHARD E.: "Legitimacy", in: ROBERT E. GOODIN and PHILIP PETTIT (Eds.): *Companion to Contemporary Political Philosophy*, Oxford (Blackwell) 1993, pp. 527-533.

LUDLOW, PETER: "The European Commission", in: ROBERT O. KEOHANE and STANLEY HOFFMANN (Eds.): *The New European Community*, Boulder (Westview Press) 1991, pp. 85-132.

MALNES, RAINO: "Europeanisation and the Transformation of Political Structures and Institutions", in: ERIK O. ERIKSEN, ANDREAS FØLLESDAL and RAINO MALNES: *Europeanisation and Normative Political Theory*, ARENA 95/1, Oslo (ARENA) 1995, pp. 21-32.

MANCINI, G. FREDERICO: "The Making of the Constitution of Europe", in: ROBERT O. KEOHANE and STANLEY HOFFMANN (Eds.): *The New European Community*, Boulder (Westview Press) 1991, pp. 177-194.

MANIN, BERNARD: "Checks, Balances and Boundaries: The Separation of the Powers in the Constitutional Debate of 1787", in: BIANCAMARIA FONTANA (Ed.): *The Invention of the Modern Republic*, Cambridge (Cambridge University Press) 1994.

SANDHOLTZ, WAYNE and JOHN ZYSMAN: "1992: Recasting the European Bargain", *World Politics*, 42, 1 (1989), pp. 95-128.

WEILER, J. H. H.: "Limits to Growth? On the Law and Politics of the European Union's Jurisdictional Limits", in: *State and Nation: Current Legal and Political Problems Before the 1996 Intergovernmental Conference*, Centre for European Law, University of Oslo, No. 15, Oslo (Scandinavian University Press) 1995, pp. 1-32.

WESSELS, WOLFGANG: "The EC Council: The Community's Decisionmaking Center", in: ROBERT O. KEOHANE and STANLEY HOFFMANN (Eds.): *The New European Community*, Boulder (Westview Press) 1991, pp. 133-154.

WILLIAMS, SHIRLEY: "Sovereignty and Accountability in the European Community", in: ROBERT O. KEOHANE and STANLEY HOFFMANN (Eds.): *The New European Community*, Boulder (Westview Press) 1991, pp. 155-176.

Part A

EU Institutions

Chapter 1

Is it Really Possible to Democratize the Euro-Polity?

PHILIPPE C. SCHMITTER

My root assumptions in this essay are the following and, if they seem implausible, do not bother to read further since all of the subsequent argumentation is contingent upon their, at least, superficial plausibility:

1. The emerging Euro-polity has not yet acquired its definitive institutional configuration, either in terms of its territorial scale, its functional scope or its level of political authority.[1]

2. The Euro-polity in its present, provisional, configuration is not a democracy and will not become one unless and until its member states decide explicitly to endow it with new rules and rights.[2]

---

1 I have substantiated this in "Examining the Present Euro-Polity with the Help of Past Theories", to be published in GARY MARKS, FRITZ SCHARPF, PHILIPPE C. SCHMITTER and WOLFGANG STREECK: *Governance in the European Union*, London (Sage) 1996.

2 The literature on the so-called "Democracy Deficit" of the EU is enormous — and, by-and-large, substantiates the observation that its existing institutional configuration falls considerably short of being democratic. As one wag put it, "since the EC requires that its member be democratic, if the EC were ever to apply to join itself, it would have to turn itself down."
What is also (if less overtly) presumed is that there is no "indirect" or "functionalist" strategy that can fill this deficit. Hence, its members will have to agree "formally and intergovernmentally" — if and when it becomes imperative to address the issue.

3. The conjunctural forces affecting its configuration are currently pushing the Euro-polity in contrary directions toward diverse outcomes with no stable equilibrium likely to emerge in the near future.[3]

4. Nevertheless, its most likely outcome within the medium-term (say, 20 years) is a form of non-state, non-national polity or stable political order which is novel, i.e. will not resemble either an inter-governmental organization or a supra-national state or any of the possible points along this institutional continuum.

5. If, eventually, its member states decide to transform this novel polity into a democracy, they will have to experiment with new forms of citizenship, representation and decision-making in order to be successful. Merely copying the institutions of existing national democracies, even federal ones, will not suffice — and could even have counter-productive effects.[4]

6. No matter how reluctant they may be and how ill-informed about what to do, the member states of the Euro-polity will eventually have to democratize it, or risk the loss of what they have already attained (i.e. a high level of economic interdependence and a reliable degree of security community) through declining legitimacy with mass publics.[5]

---

3 Elsewhere, I have explored the four factors that seem (to me) to be pushing the EU in such contrary directions: (1) the problem of enlargement — especially to the East, (2) the increase in the politicization of integration issues, (3) the growing implementation deficit, and (4) the rising need to deal with issues of European security after the Cold War.
NB the tacit implication that the democratization deficit alone has (so far and for the foreseeable future) **not** been of sufficient magnitude to compel the member states to make a serious good faith effort to eliminate it — even though some of the impetus behind the rising controversiality and wider public attention to EU affairs (politicization) probably has something to do with a general increase in questioning the democratic legitimacy of EU procedures and policies. "The Future Euro-Polity and Its Impact upon Private Interest Governance within Member States", *Droit et Société*, No. 28 (1994), pp. 659-676.

4 For my first effort at addressing this issue, see my "Alternatives for the Future European Polity: Is Federalism the Only Answer?", in: MARIO TELÓ (Ed.): *Démocratie et construction européenne*, Bruxelles (Editions de l'Université de Bruxelles) 1995, pp. 349-361.

5 It should be observed that, if the EC/EU had not already expanded beyond the limits of intergovernmental cooperation, the issue of its democratization would be moot. There is no compelling reason why citizens would expect

I. What Would a Euro-Democracy Have to Have?

In principle, an eventual Euro-democracy would have to satisfy the generic/minimal qualities of any modern political democracy, which Terry Karl and I have defined elsewhere as:

> "Modern Political Democracy" *is a regime or system of governance in which rulers are held accountable for their actions in the public realm by citizens, acting indirectly through the competition and cooperation of their representatives.*

Note that, according to this definition, democracy does not consist of any particular configuration of institutions and it is not confined to any specific level of aggregation. It is a property that emerges from the relationship of three distinctive sets of actors, regardless of their size, scale or scope: rulers, citizens and representatives. Let us, however, examine briefly each of the concepts in the above definition in terms of the present practices of the EC/EU.

> 1. A *regime* (or *system of governance*) is an ensemble of patterns that determines (1) the forms and channels of access to principal governmental positions; (2) the characteristics of the actors who are admitted to or excluded from such access; (3) the resources or strategies that these actors can use to gain access; and (4) the rules that are followed in the making of publicly binding decisions. To produce its effect, the ensemble must be institutionalized, i.e. the various patterns must be habitually known, practiced and accepted by most, if not all, of the actors. Increasingly, this has involved their explicit legalization or constitutionalization, but many very stable regime norms can have an implicit, informal, prudential or precedential basis.

By these criteria, the EC/EU is definitely a regime, although not a democratic one. The characteristics of the actors (i.e. citizens) who are permitted direct access to its institution are not fully defined (or are contingent upon specifications established by its national member-states) and the absence of

---

such an arrangement to be accountable — provided that their own democratically accountable rulers could either veto its actions or withdraw from its jurisdiction with little or no effort.

anything like an explicitly constitutional bill-of-rights means that which resources or strategies are legitimate are also largely defined at the national level or left to the vagaries of practice at the supra-national level. Finally, the modifications embedded in the Single European Act and the Maastricht Treaty on European Union (TEU) concerning qualified majority voting do not constitute a definitive statement of the decision rules that actors expect to live with for the indefinite future.

> 2. The *rulers* are those who occupy dominant positions in the formal structure of governance. Democracies are not anarchies. They are not voluntarily or spontaneously coordinated, but depend upon the presence of persons who occupy specialized roles and can give legitimate commands to others. What distinguishes democratic rulers from non-democratic ones are the norms that determine how they become rulers and the practices that hold them accountable for what they do once they have become rulers.

Here, the key issue is whether the supra-national authorities of the EC/EU have sufficient capacity for giving direct commands legitimately and effectively. Not only are there relatively few Eurocrats and not only do they dispose of vastly less resources than the rulers of their member-states, but also they devote most of their effort to giving commands to these national rulers who remain directly responsible for the actual acts of governance. As the mounting complaints testify, the compliance of these more numerous and more resourceful authorities at the national and sub-national levels cannot be taken for granted.

Moreover, the EC/EU's rulers are only accountable *en bloc* to the directly elected representatives of citizens. They cannot be refused or dismissed as individuals responsible for specific tasks. Although the data are not clearly apposite, the public opinion surveys of *Eurobaromètre* do suggest that most of the EC/EU's subjects/citizens do not feel directly obligated by or identified with its commands and they have increasingly raised serious doubts about the legitimacy of some of its highly secretive and technically obscure decision-making practices. Finally, the opt-out, opt-in provisions of several EC/EU policy arenas (e.g. EMS and the Schengen Agreement) and the subsequent sanctification of this sort of variable geometry in several clauses of the TEU would seem to indicate that countries (and, hence, their citizens) that do not agree with certain measures will not be bound by the decision of the majority - whether qualified or not.

> 3. The *public realm* involves that part of the collective choice process in which norms binding on the society as a whole and backed by the coercive force of the state are made. This realm can vary a great deal across democracies depending upon how previous decisions have drawn distinctions between the public and the private, between state and society, between legitimate coercion and voluntary exchange, between collective needs and individual preferences. Differences of opinion over the optimal mix of the two provide much of the substantive content of political conflict within established democracies.

There is no question that these issues involved in delimiting the public realm have been debated extensively in the EC/EU — but they have not been definitively resolved. The notion that the SEA had definitively opted for a narrowly "liberal" conception has been denied by subsequent developments. While its nature has changed substantially, regulation of economic exchanges has increased not decreased with the implementation of the SEA. *Pace* the provision of regional funds, however, the arrangement has yet to engage in any substantial deliberate re-distribution of funds within its class and territorial borders — other than the sectoral welfare state it has created for agriculture.

> 4. *Citizens* provide the most distinctive element in democratic regimes. All types of regime have rulers of some sort and a public realm of some dimension; only democracies have citizens.

The EC/EU has only just recently begun to specify the distinctive rights and obligations of its individual citizens and, so far, they are far inferior in quality and quantity to those defined and protected by its national member-states. Nevertheless, the Treaty of European Union signed at Maastricht in 1992 formally specifies in its Arts. 8, 8a, 8b, 8c, 8d and 8e a set of rights, involving such items as the enfranchisement of residents of other EC/EU member states to vote and run as candidates in local elections — which could be the first step in extending the right to all Euro-citizens to vote in all elections in the constituencies where they permanently reside regardless of their national citizenship; the reaffirmation of the rights of all individuals, nationals and resident foreigners, to petition the European Parliament; the creation of an Ombudsmans-office at the EC/EU level; and a pledge to make the proceedings of EC/EU institutions more "transparent" in the future. The last of these articles (8e) even invites the Council of Ministers "acting unanimously" and only on a proposal from the Commission and after consulation with the European Parliament to strengthen or to add to this list in the future. When one combines these newly founded aspects of *political* citizenship with the "four freedoms" of *economic* citizenship already promised by the Single European Act of 1986, i.e. free movement of trade, capital, services and persons, one has the potential basis for the development of a varied and consequential "Euro-citizenship" above and beyond existing national citizenships guaranteed by its member-states.

It should be noted, however, that Euro-citizenship differs in one fundamental aspect from national citizenship. While it conveys equal rights and opportunities upon individuals (and firms), their *political* weight in EU decision-making is highly unequal, given the complex formulae that systematically overcompensate the smaller countries, and relatively marginal, given the weakness of the European Parliament in the process as a whole. Granted that overrepresentation of rural districts and other peculiarities of malapportionment and gerry-mandering are never completely absent from national democracies, the EU's weightings across member states is of a qualitatively different magnitude.

> 5. *Competition* has not always been considered an essential defining condition of democracy. The classical Greek conception presumed decision-making through consensus. The assembled citizenry was expected to agree unanimously (or, at least, overwhelmingly) on a common course of action after listening to the alternatives and deliberating their merits and demerits. This tradition of hostility to "faction", "adversarial action" and "particular interests" persists in democratic thought, but at least since the *Federalist Papers* it has become widely accepted that competition among factions is a "necessary evil" of all democracies that operate on a more than local scale.

The most widely diffused conception of democracy makes it virtually synonymous with the presence of regular, fairly conducted and honestly counted elections of uncertain outcome. Without denying their centrality for democracy, these contests between candidates are held sporadically and only allow citizens to choose between the highly aggregated alternatives offered by political parties. In between, however, individuals can compete to influence public policy through a wide variety of other intermediaries: interest associations, social movements, locality groupings, clientelistic arrangements, and so forth. *Modern democracy, in other words, offers a variety of competitive processes and channels for the expression of interests — associational as well as partisan, functional as well as territorial, collective as well as individual. All are integral to its practice.*

Nor is there agreement on the appropriate rules of competition. There is certainly a commonly accepted image of democracy that identifies it exclusively with majority rule. The problem, however, arises when *numbers* meet *intensities*, when a perfectly properly assembled majority (especially a stable majority) produces decisions that negatively affect some minority (especially a threatened cultural or ethnic minority). In these circumstances, the actual practice of successful democracy tends to displace one of its central principles and to recognize and protect the rights of minorities.

The most common, insidious and effective way of protecting minorities lies in the everyday operation of interest associations and social movements. These reflect (some would say, amplify) the different intensities of preference that exist in the population and bring them to bear on those chosen directly or indirectly according to the majority principle. Another way of putting this intrinsic tension between numbers and intensities would be to say that "in modern democracies, votes may be counted, but influences are weighted".

On these grounds, the democratic status of the EC/EU is highly ambiguous. Partisan competition is recognized and enshrined in the elections to the EP and in its internal legislative operations, even if the lines of cleavage and aggregation are often inconsistent from country to country and change frequently at the European level. Voters in Euro-elections are simply not offered an opportunity to choose between rival partisan elites presenting alternative programs at that level of aggregation. In any case, this principle of party-structured competition does not govern the formation of the Commission or its policy deliberations. Nomination by national governments according to fixed quotas prevails and those who are subsequently appointed are explicitly not supposed to represent the interests of their respective governments. Most importantly, there is virtually no way that individual citizens voting in free, equal, fair and competitive Euro-elections could influence the composition of Euro-authorities, much less bring about a rotation of those in office.

Votes are taken by simple majority in the EP but they are not generally binding or determinant, even if they have been increased in importance through the cooperation procedures of Maastricht. It remains impossible to translate a majority produced by the European electorate at large into an effective and predictable change in government or policy. The best one can expect is an indirect expression through a qualified majority of the member-states which themselves all have majoritarian governments — at least on that range of issues which is subject to this decision rule. The closest analogy might be German democracy with only the Bundesrat and no Bundestag.

Otherwise, the EC/EU is a rather extreme case of a type of democracy that weighs intensities, especially those intensities that are aggregated and expressed as "national interests". Not only are small countries overweighted in the voting formula of the Council of Ministers, but on a wide range of important issues unanimity is still required. To a limited extent, the new cooperation procedures resemble a confederal system of concurrent majorities. The absence of statutory guarantees for the powers of national, provincial and/or local governments — *pace* the recent references to subsidiarity — means that a federalist consensus on the distribution of powers has not yet been established. One could describe the process of forming the Commission as a sort of consociational arrangement in that all member-states are included and, by tradition, those with more than one commissioner tend to nominate them from opposing both the government and the opposition. Repeated efforts by the Eurocracy (and, most recently, by the former President of the European Commission) to create a viable "Social Dialogue" between capital, labor and themselves have yet to produce any regularized channeling of class-based interest intensities. The advisory Economic and Social Council has never made a serious contribution since its founding in the late 1950s.

Supplementing the institutionalized expression of national -- and, hence, allegedly majoritarian -- interests through the Council of Ministers, is the less visible but nonetheless pervasive expression of minority interests through interest associations. From its founding, the Eurocracy has attracted (and, occasionally, sponsored) organizations representing specialized class, sectoral and professional interests. Especially since the SEA, Bruxelles has been literally invaded by an increasing variety of "Euro-lobbies" — not just formal interest associations, but also social movements, individual enterprises and law firms. While all this is entirely appropriate for a modern democracy, the normative issue is whether these channels are freely and fairly available to all minorities with intensive preferences. So far, the evidence suggests a mobilization of bias in favor of business and systemic problems in adjusting to the expanded scale of genuinely European interaction.[6]

6 FRANZ TRAXLER and I have discussed this at some length in our "The Emerging Euro-Polity and Organized Interests", *European Journal of International Relations*, Vol. 1, No. 2 (June 1995), pp.191-218.

> 6. *Cooperation* has always been a central feature of democracies. Actors must combine with each other by some voluntary process to make collective decisions binding on the polity as a whole. Most obviously, they must cooperate in order to compete. They must be capable of engaging in collective action through parties, associations and movements that can select candidates, articulate preferences, petition authorities and influence policies.

But beyond this unavoidably "adversarial" aspect to democracy, its freedoms should encourage citizens to deliberate among themselves, to discover their common needs and to resolve their possible conflicts without relying on centralized political authority. The "classical" conception of democracy stressed these qualities and they are by no means extinct — despite repeated efforts by contemporary theorists to stress the analogy with behavior in the economic marketplace and to reduce all its operations to competitive interest maximization.

As mentioned above, no viable party system has yet emerged at the level of the Community/Union as a whole. To a limited extent, members of national parties do cooperate under supra-national labels within the legislative process of the EP, but candidates for Euro-deputy are neither nominated nor funded through supra-national parties. On the contrary, their selection by national party oligarchies and election by proportional representation within a single national constituency (except for Great Britain) more or less ensure that the winning candidates will be unknown to the citizens who have elected them. In any case, none of this effort at partisan cooperation has been translated into cooperation in the formation of governing coalitions or cabinets.

Moreover, the sheer scale of the Euro-Polity — not to mention its *potpourri* of languages and traditions — seems to have inhibited the sort of deliberation among individual citizens that Tocqueville regarded as so crucial. With the exception of academic cooperation and the proliferation of European policy centers and think-tanks, there are very few sites at which its practices and purposes can be discussed. During the difficulties that surrounded the ratification of the TEU, this sense of alienation from Bruxelles became manifest. Individuals proved willing to accept almost any rumor presented to them about arbitrary behavior on the part of Eurocrats — in large part because they were ill-informed and unable to discuss these issues reasonably with their peers.

7. The principal agents of modern political democracy are *representatives.* Citizens may elect them or choose to support the parties, associations or movements they lead, but representatives do the real business of governing. Moreover, most of these persons are not amateurs but professionals. Without individuals who invest in democracy to the extent that they orient their life's career around the aspiration to fill its key roles, it is doubtful that any democracy could survive. The central question is not whether or not there will be a "political elite" or even a "political class", but how that group of representatives will be composed and subsequently held accountable for its actions.

The EC/EU is indeed surrounded by representatives, but these are hardly representative of the citizenry as a whole. At the functional level, they are overwhelmingly skewed to favor business interests. With the increased importance of the EP, there is some evidence of a shift of attention and greater access for social movements, consumer groups and environmental constituencies — but they have a long way to go before they have redressed the imbalance. At the territorial level, representatives owe their allegiance almost exclusively to national constituencies. Recently, the Maastricht TEU officially opened up an opportunity for the representation of sub-national polities with the creation of an advisory Committee of Regions, but this may have no more effect than the preceding establishment of an Economic and Social Council.

What is missing are the professionals. With the exception of the relatively unknown Eurocrats that labor away in its core bureaucracy, there are few persons who identify exclusively with the Euro-Polity. The careers of the politicians-*cum*-technicians who are momentarily active in its Commission or who are elected to its Parliament continue to be much more affected by what is happening in their countries of origin. Very few lose an election or fail to gain a promotion for something they have done in Bruxelles or Strasbourg — and many are sent there after their real careers are over. The composition of Europe's emerging "political class" may be more varied and less predictable than that of its component parts, but it is much less coherent and capable of defending its distinctive practices and purposes.

* * *

Simplifying considerably, an eventual Euro-democracy would have to be a regime with a public realm of its own in which *citizens* from the polity as a whole would have to be capable of ensuring the accountability — *via* the competition and cooperation of their political *representatives* — of those *rulers* entitled to make and implement those decisions that are binding on all members of that polity. This presents us with three key sets of actors: citizens, representatives and rulers whose behavior has to be regularly and reliably patterned in such a way that *accountability* is ensured.[7] In most modern settings, the regularity and reliability of these relationships requires that they be (at least, in part) protected by formal legal norms. Given both the nature of the contracting parties and the process whereby their bargaining over these norms takes place, it is highly likely that this would eventually have to involve the negotiating, drafting and ratifying of an explicit European Constitution.[8]

II. What Dilemmas Would a Euro-Democracy Have to Face?

Let us now take a quick look at several difficult choices — dilemmas, if you will — that would have to be resolved during the process of democratizing and eventually constitutionalizing the Euro-polity:

First, let us set aside the usual convenient "theoretical" devices for constituting an acceptable democratic polity.[9] No impartial outside *législateur* is going to appear providentially and produce a solutions based on such com-

7 It would be more accurate to say that "accountability appears to be ensured in a way that satisfies the legitimate expectations of the citizenry," since this can vary rather considerably from one political culture to another. Needless to say, in the context of contemporary Europe, national differences over such things as "parliamentary sovereignty", "party government", "transparency in the actions of public officials", etc. will make it all the more difficult to arrive at a consensual perception of what is involved in accountability.

8 Hence, it is very unlikely to emerge from the interpretive procedures that the European Court of Justice has resorted to in order to convert the Treaty of Rome into a quasi-constitution. Indeed, it is resistance to the further expansion of these norms that mat provide one of the strongest incentives for explicit constitutionalization.

9 I am indebted in the following section to DARIO CASTIGLIONE: "Contracts and Constitutions", in: BELLAMY, BUFACCHI and CASTIGLIONE: *Democracy and Constitutional Culture in the Union of Europe*, London (Lothian Foundation Press) 1995, pp. 59-79.

pelling abstract principles that the design of the Euro-democracy will be recognized by all as an obvious emanation of the General Will of Europe (Rousseau 1762). No charismatic leader is likely to so mesmerize the diverse populations of Europe that they will enthusiastically welcome his or her message and routinize it into a new set of magically legitimated institutions.[10] No opaque "veil of ignorance" is going to descend and obscure the vision that actors have of how various configurations of scale, scope and rules will affect their self-interest (Rawls 1972). No extraordinary "window of opportunity" is likely to open which will allow the participants to suspend their mundane concerns with "low politics" — to be superseded by a unified devotion to the "high politics" of meta-rule-making (Ackerman 1992). No "*herrschaftsfreier Diskurs*" or "perfect speech situation" awaits those who would dare to produce a fair set of procedures and rights for the citizens of Europe (Habermas 1990).

If and when the Euro-polity gets down seriously to the task of filling its democracy deficit, it will be a much messier affaire with a rather more prosaic purpose. These *pouvoirs constituents* (NB the plural) will not deliberate learnedly and try to persuade each other intellectually in the manner of the famous founding fathers of the United States of America; they will negotiate in secret and haggle their way to a mutually acceptable set of rules increasing the accountability of rulers to citizens *via* representatives. Moreover, they will only be founding a regime — not a polity or, least of all, a nation. For better or worse (and admittedly on a much smaller scale), "Europe" was founded as a polity in 1957 at Messina. "Europe" as a nation has yet to ap-

10 *Pace* KEN JOWITT who has argued that the European Community is already a "charismatic project" and only likely to advance further under the inspiration of more charisma. "No More Normans in Europe", talk given to the Seminar/Forum on Sovereignty and Governance, Institute of International Studies, Stanford University, 19 January 1996. Nothing in my view is less likely to lead to the re-founding or revising of EU institutions. Even should a charismatic leader or movement emerge and even if he (or she?) would attempt to create more democratic institutions at the level of Europe, my supposition is that the effort would be as dismal a failure as all the preceding efforts by national charismatics at consolidating democracy - from Sekou Touré, Kwame Nukrumah and Nassar to Alain Garcia, Fernando Collor and Alberto Fujimori. For the original version of this notion, see - not Max Weber - but DAVIID APTER: *Ghana in Transition*, New York (Atheneum Press) 1963.

pear and no treaty or constitution is going to establish it *ex ante*. At best, it may emerge *ex post*.

Moreover, whatever "refounding" of this polity occurred at Maastricht and might occur again in the near future, it is highly unlikely that such actions will definitively fix the external limits or establish the overriding identity of those involved. The eventual Euro-constituents will be asked to design a democratic regime for a territory and a citizenry whose future boundaries and identities are unknown.

If and when this daunting (if prosaic) task is attempted, the participants are going to have to resolve some rather formidable practical dilemmas in the process — without the help of any enlightened outside leverage or very much reasoned inside deliberation. Two of these dilemmas are generic to the consolidation of democracy in any context;[11] two are more specific to the difficult choices that will have to be made within Europe.

> 1. The consolidation or constitutionalization of democracy involves resolving a complex double game in which politicians/representatives must first reach agreement on a viable set of rules for cooperation and competition among themselves and, then, convince the relevant citizenry that these rules are fair and appropriate for rendering rulers accountable.

The challenge for democratic *constituents*, therefore, is to find a set of institutions that embody contingent consent among politicians, i.e. are regarded as fair and feasible among the principal players, and are capable of invoking the eventual assent of citizens, i.e. are considered as legitimate by their fans-*cum*-audiences. Even if both groups do not necessarily have to agree upon a set of goals or substantive policies that command widespread consensus at the same time, it may still be difficlut to find mutually acceptable procedures. Not only are the choices *intrinsically conflictual* — with politicians grouped into different parties preferring rules that will best ensure their own re-election or eventual access to office, and citizens aggregated into different social groups wanting rules that will best ensure the accountability of their representatives — but they are also *extrinsically consequential*. Once they are

11 And, hence, have been discussed in greater detail in my forthcoming *Essaying the Consolidation of Democracy* which deals exclusively with the processes of recent democratization at the national level in Southern Europe, Latin America and Eastern Europe.

translated, *via* the uncertainties of elections and influence processes into governments that begin to produce public policies, the rules and practices applied will affect rates of economic growth, willingness to invest, variation in the value of currency, competitiveness in foreign markets, access to education, perceptions of cultural deprivation, racial balance and even national identity. To make things worse, even if these substantive matters are not explicitly embedded in the initial constituent agreement, they will be anticipated by the actors involved and incorporated in the compromises they are willing to make with regard to specific rights and procedures.

Fortunately, this basic "democratic bargain", to use Robert Dahl's expression,[12] can vary a good deal from one society to another, depending on objective inequalities and cleavage patterns, as well as such subjective factors as the degree of mutual trust, the standard of fairness, the willingness to compromise and the cultural legitimacy of different decision rules.

In the case of a prospective Euro-democracy polity, however, there are two quite serious further complications:

> *1.1. The politicians involved at the European level are much more entrenched (and, in the contemporary context, vastly more professionalized) within their respective national systems. Hence, they have greater resources and higher incentives to resist any possible threats to their tenure or re-electability than do the politicians involved in consolidating democracy in post-1974 neo-democracies.*

> *1.2. The citizens potentially involved are much more confident of their rights and entitlements at the national level and much less conscious of their identities at the supra-national level. They are also vastly less articulate and organized at the later level. Hence, they are going to be more difficult to sell on a new system of accountability (and there is potentially much less to offer them) than are the citizens of neo-democracies in Southern/Eastern Europe and South/Central America — and, even if they were to become aware of its advantages, they would be much less capable of pressing for them.*

Both features strongly suggest that playing the double game of consolidation/constitutionalization will not be easy for those who would democratize the Euro-polity. The temptation to settle for a restrictive, mutually benefi-

12 *After the Revolution: Authority in a Good Society*, New Haven (Yale University Press) 1970.

cial arrangement among politicians which "in the national interest" would discriminate against an uncertain and unconscious Euro-citizenry seems almost irresistible. And, it is unavoidable that the first steps in this direction will have to be gradual, cautious and "retractible". Whether such petits pas will be sufficient to contain the rising doubts about the legitimacy of the present decision-making procedures remains to be seen.

> *2. Support for democracy (at whatever level of aggregation) is based on popular expectations for an improvement in existing conditions, usually, in the direction of greater equality; yet, the successful consolidation of such a regime requires that politicians pay attention in its design to existing inequalities if they are to avoid significant defections or alienation of particular minorities.*

Everywhere, this translates into a struggle over the rules between haves and have-nots and, more specifically, between the mobilization of majorities and the protection of minorities (between numbers and intensities in my jargon). Again, Europe adds some significant complications beyond the obvious likelihood that, given its size and diversity, the heterogeneity of preferences and tolerances for inequality is very great to begin with:

> *2.1. The existing pattern of inequalities to be addressed by an emerging Euro-Democracy involves not just individuals and classes of individuals but well-entrenched historical collectivities, i.e. states, which themselves are significantly different in terms of their size, development, competitiveness, consumption levels, etc. and, hence, are even more sensitive to political disparities and policy distributions at the point of institutional departure than would be individuals or social classes within a given pre-existent society.*

> *2.2. The popular expectations of individuals about improvements at the Euro-polity level are much more vague and "projective" than are the corresponding expectations at the national level. Until and unless the former become be more firmly fixed in the calculations of individuals (and organized into European scale units of action), it seems unlikely that entrenched national politicians can be outbid for support.*

> 2.3. Since the Treaty of European Union enshrined it, these very same politicians can often plausibly invoke the principle of subsidiarity to protect the local or national *status quo* from "unwarranted" intrusions by a prospective Euro-democracy that would equalize rights and regula-

tions for the Euro-polity as a whole — and, thereby, override national peculiarities in the name of a more general public interest.

In the absence of some manifest collapse of the *anciens régimes nationaux*, as sometimes occurred within the authoritarian regimes of Southern Europe and Latin America and even more dramatically in Eastern Europe, it is not clear whether these two generic dilemmas can be sufficiently overcome to allow for any substantial progress toward Euro-democratization. Perhaps, the gradual accumulation of firmer popular expectations of equality, security and recognition at that level will suffice, but it is more likely that an intervening crisis of legitimacy in existing EU institutions will preempt that slow and uneven process. Mere mal-performance and declining policy competence in the member states are not likely to be sufficient to compel actors to shift their allegiances, *pace* David Mitrany (1943) and Ernst B. Haas (1958).

The two Euro-specific dilemmas are no less daunting. Both have to do with the unprecedented nature of the enterprise:

> 3. If, as I have hypothesized above, the non-state Euro-polity will have to come up with novel institutions in order to democratize itself, then both politicians and citizens may have considerable difficulty in recognizing these novel rules and practices as "democratic."

While there is already a considerable range of variance within member states in what they consider democratic, the shift to a much larger scale and, in all probability, diminished scope of public authority is bound to mean experimenting with forms of representation, citizenship and accountability of rulers that do not yet exist and whose consequences are rather unpredictable. The more novel (and, perhaps, functionally appropriate) these citizen rights and decision-rules are, the greater the initial obstacles to their being accorded legitimacy. On the other hand, following the "time-tested" ways of a federal or confederal nature, will only be ineffectual or counter-productive — if my non-state hypothesis holds. Admittedly, Publius in *The Federalist Papers* was fully aware of this dilemma and did a masterful job of overcoming it, but will the more diverse, distracted and, perhaps, skeptical publics of contemporary Europe prove so easy to persuade?

> 4. Filling the Euro-polity's democracy deficit with novel rights and rules will not only have to satisfy the already diverse set of actual member states, but it will also have to be sufficiently flexible, open

and "acceptable" to incorporate an indeterminate number of future members over an, as yet undefined, territory.

Moreover, the Eastern and Southern (Mediterranean) countries in which this expansion will have to take place have even greater levels of diversity in development and culture, and are much less settled in terms of their domestic regime characteristics. Those founding fathers of the United States faced a roughly analogous situation in that they certainly envisaged that their constitution would be applied to a Westward expanding population and set of new units, but it is doubtful that they envisaged anything like the economic, social, cultural and political diversity that the Euro-polity will have to absorb![13]

III. How Should a Euro-Democracy Be Configured?

My first assumption is that — because, in the immediate future, the Euro-polity is headed toward becoming a non-state non-nation — it would be inappropriate and even counterproductive to define its citizens, representatives and rulers in the usual manner for a large-scale, socially heterogenous, advanced capitalist nation-state, i.e. as a federal polity.

The core of the emerging Euro-polity's novelty lies in *the growing dissociation between territorial constituencies and functional compétences.* In the classic model of the state (if not invariably in their praxis), the exercise of public authority in different functional domains is coincident or congruent with a specific and unique territory.[14] When one arrives at its physical borders, the legitimate exercise of coercion in all these domains ends. The poli-

13 And the one issue of diversity which these American founding fathers tried to finesse — slavery — proved to be unresolvable within the framework of their constitution. I doubt if the founding fathers of Euro-democracy would be willing even to contemplate anything as horrendous at the U.S. Civil War as a way of eventually resolving those issues of diversity which could not be initially dealt with.

14 And, in the **nation**-state model, these domains are supposed to be co-terminous with a distinctive and unique national identity based on a common language, culture, descent group or "community of fate" (*Schicksalsgemeinschaft*).

ty on the other side has, in principle, no right to command obedience in any domain on one's own side — and there presumably exists no superordinate entity exercising authority over both sides.

Not even the initial contours of such an institutional coincidence can be detected in the Euro-polity as presently constituted. Instead, the distribution of territorial and functional powers has remained indeterminate and inconsistent in decisive respects (Schmitter 1992a, 1992b). Examining the territorial organization of the EC/EU makes clear that the boundary between insiders and outsiders remains uncertain and/or follows no unitary criterion. This is especially the case with monetary unification, a core area of the TEU. For instance, it is foreseen that those member states who do not fulfill the convergence criteria will be suspended from participation in Stage III of Economic and Monetary Union (Art. 109j). Moreover, Great Britain and Denmark reserved the right to decide whether they would eventually participate in it.

Great Britain also remains explicitly exempt from the commitments to a common social policy. Article 198a empowers local and regional sub-units to participate in an advisory Committee of Regions. While the relevant clauses fix the number of committee members for the individual member states, they leave the conception of local and regional units unspecified. Nor is there a clear and uniformly binding distribution of functional *compétences* among the territorial units of the EU. Whereas the treaty declares that "decisions are taken as closely as possible to the citizen" (Article A) and that the goals of the Union are to be realized "respecting the principle of subsidiarity" (Article B), the concrete implications of this principle are left to subsequent intergovernmental agreements (and eventual judgements of the European Court of Justice).

The functional distribution of *competénces* has also become even more diffuse through the creation of new European organizations and coordinating mechanisms. This is, for instance, apparent in the establishment of a joint conference of the national parliaments and the European Parliament which can form and meet "as necessary" (Declaration on the Conference of the Parliaments); in the exceedingly complex co-decision procedure of the European Parliament, the Council, and the Commission on a broad range of issues (Article 189b, 189c); and in the proto-corporatist procedures outlined for the area of social policy, according to which the Commission can call on the "Social Partners" to draft relevant measures, which could even pre-empt Community action and lead to independent private contracts implemented either through the member states or through the European Union itself (Agreement on Social Policy, Article 3 and 4).[15] On questions of foreign and security policy, a political committee was created as a sort of embryonic foreign office, but with compétences in relation to the other organs of the EU that are only vaguely delineated. In defense policy, the WEU is named as an "integral part of the development of the European Union" (Art. J4), but its relationship to existing Community bodies is left indeterminate. Moreover, the TEU makes it clear that there will be no necessary coincidence between membership in the EC/EU and in the WEU. The latter will be open to all present and future members of the EC/EU, but there is no obligation to join.

So, in the emergent Euro-polity, the functional and the territorial domains of authority have become less rather than more congruent over time. What seems to be asserting, and even consolidating, itself is a plurality of polities at different levels of aggregation — national, sub-national and supra-national — that overlap in a multitude of domains. Moreover, the EU authorities have few exclusive *compétences*, and have yet to assert their hierarchical control over member states -- except *via* the limited jurisprudence of the European Court of Justice and in such limited functional domains as competition policy. Instead, these multiple levels negotiate with each other in a continuous way in order to perform common tasks and resolve common problems across an expanding range of issues. Without sovereignty — without a definitive center for the resolution of conflicts or for the allocation of public goods — there is only a process and, hence, no definite person or body that can be held accountable for its actions in the public realm. Moreover, the participants in this process are not just a fixed number of national states, but

15 The Maastricht Accord contains no specific criteria for the recognition of associations as "social partners". In their response, the three most important Euro-associations of business and labor (i.e. the UNICE, the CEEP and the ETUC) presented a proposal for applying very restrictive criteria for recognition. Above all, this proposal would have excluded all sectoral Euro-associations from participation in drafting and implementing social policy. The Commission, however, has chosen to adopt rather loose criteria which recognize as "social partners" virtually all associations operating at the EU level (BUDA 1994). Hence, the highly pluralistic structures of the European system of associations that have been emerging *de facto* have now been recognized *de jure* by the Commission. This seems likely to cripple any effort to exploit these provisions of the Maastricht Accord for proto-corporatist purposes.

an enormous variety of sub-national units and networks, supra-national associations and transnational firms.

To make the point clearer, I ask the reader to try to imagine a polity that did *not* have the following:

(1) a locus of clearly defined, unchallengeable supreme authority;

(2) an established, central hierarchy of public offices;

(3) a pre-defined and distinctive sphere of competence within which it can make decisions binding on all;

(4) a fixed and contiguous territory over which it exercised authority;

(5) an exclusive recognition by other polities, membership in international organizations and capacity to conclude international treaties;

(6) an overarching identity and symbolic presence for its subjects/citizens;

(7) an established and effective monopoly over the legitimate means of coercion;

(8) a unique capacity for the direct implementation of its decisions upon intended individuals and groups; and

(9) an exclusive capacity for controlling the movement of goods, services, capital and persons within its borders —

but *did* have the capability to take decisions, resolve conflicts, produce public goods, coordinate private behavior, regulate markets, hold elections, respond to interest pressures, generate revenue, allocate expenditures, and even declare and wage war! If you can do this, you will have succeeded in at least mentally superseding the limits imposed by the nation-state upon our habitual ways of thinking about politics, although it may still be difficult for you to imagine how such a "post-sovereign, poly-centric, incongruent, neo-medieval" arrangement of authority could possibly be stable in the longer run.

Elsewhere, I have argued that the EU is likely to become something qualitatively different, neither an intergovernmental *confederatio* nor a supra-national *stato/federatio* — but one of two novel forms of political domination I have called a *consortio* or a *condominio*.[16]

As an ideal-type, the *consortio* assumes a fixed and irreversible set of member states within defined territorial boundaries, but with varying policy responsibilities ("*L'Europe à la carte*" seems to capture this property well). Sub-sets of members would pool their capacity to act autonomously in domains that they could no longer govern at their own level of aggregation, but would be free to determine — either at the moment of joining or when subsequent revisions were made — which specific common obligations they were willing to accept. Presumably, they would form a singular and relatively contiguous spatial bloc, but they would arrange their common affairs within a multitude of distinctive functional authorities, only some of which would be coordinated from a single center or secretariat.

The emergence of something resembling an ideal-type *condominio* would be an even more unprecedented outcome, i.e. the one that least resembles the pre-existing Euro-state system. In it, both territorial as well as functional constituencies would vary. Not only would each member country be able to select from a menu of potential common tasks, but each European institution would be composed of a different (although presumably overlapping) set of members. Instead of a single Europe with recognized and contiguous boundaries, there would be many Europes: a trading Europe, an energy Europe, an environmental Europe, a social welfare Europe, even a defence Europe *et ainsi de suite*. Instead of one "Eurocracy" which coordinated all the distinct tasks involved in the integration process, there would be multiple regional institutions acting autonomously to solve common problems and produce

16 I have subsequently discovered that I am not alone in concluding that the EC/EU may be heading for novelty. BEN ROSAMUND, for example, has suggested that "integration may be coaxing (or perhaps even is) the evolution of new state forms which are not nation-states." "Mapping the European Condition: Theory of Integration and the Integration of Theory", *European Journal of International Relations*, Vol. 1, No. 3 (Sept. 1995), p. 403.
My presumption is that the EC/EU is not becoming either a nation or a state. In addition to my "Imagining the Future of the Euro-Polity with the Help of New Concepts", cited above in FN 4, see my "If the Nation- State Were to Wither away in Europe, What Might Replace it?", paper prepared for presentation at the Colloquium on The Future of the Nation-State, Uppsala University, 22-25 March 1995, which should be appearing shortly in a volume edited by Axel Hadenius to be published by Cambridge University Press.

different public goods. Given its formidable coordination problems -- not to mention, its unprecedented nature — one can hardly imagine the deliberate establishment of such a cumbersome arrangement. It could only emerge in an improvised and incremental fashion from successive compromises among members with divergent interests and institutional legacies.

If either of these models better describe the medium-term outcome than those that lie on the more orthodox continuum connecting the intergovernmental organization with the supra-national state — something that admittedly is a matter of conjecture — and if democratization cannot be indefinitely postponed, then it seems reasonable to me to presume that the Euro-Polity will have to invent and implement new forms of ruler accountability, new rights and obligations for citizens and new channels for territorial and functional representation. For all existing conceptions of democracy — with the limited exception of those involving small-scale, highly localized forms of direct democracy — presume the existence of a political unit with the minimal properties of a state. Only if there is a ruling person or body with a legitimate command of legitimate violence can it be made accountable to citizens through the appropriate channels of representation. Without such a prior coincidence between external and internal sovereignty, the most that one can expect is a *confederatio* or intergovernmental arrangement that does not itself have to be democratic.

My assumption is that the process of European integration has irrevocably crossed the threshold of intergovernmentalism, but is still far removed from reaching that "indispensable" coincidence of territorial and functional authority that is the foundation of stateness — not to mention the even more elusive property of a common identity that is the foundation of nationhood.

The main strategic implication I have drawn from this is that the democratization of the EU can be postponed, but not indefinitely. At the present moment there is no grassroots movement clamoring for greater participation and access in order to make its rulers more accountable — just a diffuse (but growing) public dissatisfaction with its remote and opaque *modus operandi*. Nevertheless, the EU has made itself sufficiently omniscient, controversial and indispensable in the lives of Europeans that its "real-existing" practices cannot simply be tolerated or ignored.

To those who, recognizing the dilemma, claim that the answer lies in revising and reinforcing the capacity of national democracies to control what is going on within the EU, I would reply that not only is this not likely to be sufficient but it might also deprive the integration process of its dynamic ability to resolve conflicts and generate the sort of public goods to which Europeans have become increasingly accustomed.

To those who, welcoming the prospect of the EU's losing its integrative dynamic, argue that it is high time to reign in this increasingly obtrusive organization, I would respond that it is not clear whether this can be accomplished without endangering what has already been accomplished — that famous *acquis communautaire.* And that *acquis* consists not just of the four freedoms for the movement of goods, services, capital and persons with all the private benefits that accrue to them, but it may also include an even more important acquisition — namely, the transformation of the European state system into what Karl Deutsch has called a "pluralistic security community" within which all participants are confident that their conflicts will never be resolved by the use of force, or even the threat of it.

Proponents of integration like to rely on the analogy of a *bicycle* to describe it: unless it continues to move forward or even when it begins to lose momentum, it risks toppling over and throwing its riders back where they came from. Its opponents presumably believe that the analogy should be that of a *tricycle* that can be parked safely whenever and wherever one wishes. Frankly, there is no way that we can know which is the proper analogy for the EU in its present condition,[17] but even the remotest prospect that the Europe conveyance might tip over — and, after all, even tricycles do this occasionally — should be regarded with alarm. Reverting to its *statu quo ante integratio* of pervasive anarchy, constant threats of violence and unstable balances of power punctuated by international war would most certainly be against the interests of everyone.

So, if I am also correct in assuming that the strategy that has guided integration since its origins in the European Coal and Steel Community: the Monnet Method with its reliance on functional interdependence, indirection, unintended consequences, spillovers from one issue area to another and package-deals that increase the scope and level of common institutions is no longer capable of providing further momentum to the process — *pace* the prospect of monetary unification — then a more directly political strategy based on democratization might be able to take up the slack. However, if and

17 The often-remarked-upon institutional stagnation of the mid-1960s to the mid-1970s was only a relative matter that disguised a good deal of forward, if less visible, momentum (especially in the field of European jurisprudence), so that it does not constitute a fair test between the competing analogies.

when this happens, its promoters are going to have to invent novel forms of citizenship, channels of representation and rules for decision-making that are specifically appropriate for the emerging Euro-polity. I shall have more to say about that in subsequent articles/chapters.

References

APTER, D.: *Ghana in Transition,* New York (Atheneum Press) 1963.

DAHL, R.: *After the Revolution: Authority in a Good Society,* New Haven (Yale University Press) 1970.

MANSBRIDGE, J.: *Beyond Adversarial Democracy,* New York (Basic Books) 1980.

MARKS, G., SCHARPF, F., SCHMITTER, P.C. and STREECK, W.: *Governance in the European Union,* London (Sage) 1996.

ROSAMUND, B.: "Mapping the European Condition: Theory of Integration and the Integration of Theory", *European Journal of International Relations,* Vol. 1, No. 3 (Sept. 1995), p. 403.

SCHMITTER, P. C.: "Future Euro-Polity and Its Impact upon Private Interest Governance within Member States", *Droit et Société,* No. 28 (1994), pp. 659-676.

SCHMITTER, P. C.: "Alternatives for the Future European Polity: Is Federalism the Only Answer?", in: MARIO TELÓ (Ed.): *Démocratie et construction européenne,* Bruxelles (Editions de l'Université de Bruxelles) 1995, pp. 349-361.

TRAXLER, F. and SCHMITTER, P. C.: "The Emerging Euro-Polity and Organized Interests", *European Journal of International Relations,* Vol. 1, No. 2 (June 1995), pp. 191-218.

Chapter 2

Democracy and Governance in the European Union*

MARKUS JACHTENFUCHS

I. Introduction

The link between internationalization, governance and democracy is a central problem for politics as well as for political science. Even if clear empirical evidence on the nature of this link is not yet available, the literature seems to support the view that internationalization both undermines the capacity for governance and puts into question traditional forms of democracy. This phenomenon has two dimensions. On the one hand, it is a process taking place in political reality which can be studied scientifically. On the other hand, it constitutes a challenge for a number of concepts and theories in the

* This paper is strongly inspired by discussions during the preparation of a research programme of the German Science Foundation on ,Governance in the European Union' and by an empirical research project on party images of a legitimate European political order. My thanks go particularly to Thomas Diez, Sabine Jung, Beate Kohler-Koch and Michael Zürn for stimulating discussions and comments.

social sciences as well as in law. In their reasoning, these disciplines often assume the existence of the externally and internally sovereign, democratic nation-state. It is therefore difficult to even consider the possibility of the erosion of this very model.

Because of this deep-rooted difficulty to think about a model of democratic governance different from the democratic nation-state, it seems reasonable to discuss this problematique not by abstract reasoning but by focusing on a concrete case. The best case available is the European Union which in recent decades has developed into a new type of political system with enormous consequences on democracy and governance in its member states. Despite repeated attempts for major institutional reforms, this system is arguably likely to persist in its basic structures for a foreseeable future and is unlikely to develop into a federal state or to disintegrate into a classic international organization. The present state of democracy and governance in the EU is therefore worth to be analyzed as it is not a mere transitory phenomenon.

In the following, I will first present an analytical perspective on this political system which by its choice of concepts and theoretical tools allows for an open view on possible tendencies and problems with respect to democracy and governance in the EU. In the third part, I discuss those features of the EU's political system which are most important for an understanding of its present state and its prospective development. The fourth part presents two highly stylized, ideal-typical system models, each of which embodies different mixtures and forms of democracy and governance. Both could be permanently stable but none of them can be reduced to the traditional forms of either ‚state' or ‚international organization'. The final part consists of an overall assessment of the EU's possible development.

II. The EU as a Dynamic Multi-Level System

The frequent qualification of the European Union as an institution ‚sui generis' reflects the difficulties in science as well as in the political debate to find an appropriate analytical or normative approach to the European Union. The reason for this is that scientific as well as political thought is deeply marked by the idea that modern societies organize themselves in the form of nation-states.

Not only in political science but also in legal science, sociology and economics basic concepts and theories rely on a traditional concept of the state. In this view, the state is organized internally as a hierarchy and externally in an anarchical system. In this reasoning, there are national political systems which take the form of a universally competent state as a powerful central organ on the one hand and international relations taking place in the absence of central authority on the other hand; there is public law on the one hand and public international law or private international law governing the collisions of domestic legal systems on the other hand; there is national society as the level of social integration and world society as the level of system integration; there are national economies which allow for an intentionally created order on the one hand and the world market which is governed at best by ‚spontaneous order' (Hayek) on the other hand (Kohler-Koch/Jachtenfuchs 1996 p. 540).

This dichotomic characterization of social and political order runs through the entire social sciences. It is increasingly inappropriate for the analysis of present politics and society. This is particularly true for the analytical as well as for the normative assessment of the European Union. If already by the choice of fundamental theoretical notions the member states on the one hand and the European Union on the other hand are considered as two separate political systems which are only linked in the Council of Ministers, changes in this dichotomy easily disappear from the analyst's view and even from the scientific agenda. As a consequence, analytical models of the integration process consider the question of whether it overcomes (Haas 1964) or strengthens the nation-states (Hoffmann 1966; Moravcsik 1994) as the most important issue of integration research. The same applies for normative models which on this conceptual basis can only consist of variations of the ideal-types of ‚federal state' or ‚international organization'. From this perspective, political discourse and actual European policy-making are usually perceived as a dramatic fight between these two poles in which the respective players more or less succeed to push the reality of European integration in one of these two directions. This does not only apply to the numerous ‚plans for Europe' but also to theories *in* the political system (Luhmann 1981, 1991), i.e. theories which guide and justify political action. The 1993 judgment of the German constitutional court on the Maastricht Treaty is a striking example of the political importance of the analytic and normative separation of member states and European Union.

This zero-sum logic misses the essence of the integration process as well as the true challenge for science and politics. Almost fifty years after the creation of the first European institution it makes less and less sense to understand and judge the European Union by reference to one of these two ideal-typical models. One possibility to deal with the present state of the EU without loosing its particular features out of sight is to regard it as a ‚dynamic multi-level system' (Jachtenfuchs/Kohler-Koch 1996). ‚Dynamic' refers to the permanent process of institutional change, ‚multi-level system' indicates that the EU includes its member states in an encompassing system while at the same time, national political, economic or legal system continue to exist. The concept itself already precludes the notion of two distinct levels and the resulting normative as well as analytical implications. Such a concept takes account of the wide-spread feeling of unease with the application of state-bound concepts to the analysis of the European Union (Schuppert 1994 p. 53). It also directs the analytic attention to the dynamic character, i.e. to the constantly changing division of competencies and the permanent state of institutional change within the system which result in numerous tensions, cleavages and pathologies.

Obviously, a concept is not yet a theory. However, other attempts to grasp the ‚sui generis' character of the European Union (Schmitter 1992; Ruggie 1993; Bogdandy 1993) show to what considerable extent the choice of appropriate terms and concepts can open up analytical possibilities which remain constrained by the terminological orthodoxy of integration research and policy-making. Speaking of the EU as a dynamic multi-level system is still more a conceptual approach, a particular way of looking at reality rather than a developed analytical model. It is useful, however, to overcome the intellectual ties with the idealized model of the modern state which increasingly appears as an analytical hindrance not only in integration research (Ellwein 1992).

Instead of regarding the EU as being in a permanent state of transition, it is analytically, normatively and practically more fruitful to look at the present state of the EU not in terms of its organizational structure but in terms of a general *problematique* which is not confined to the EU. One such possibility is to ask about actors, processes, means and results of governance in the European Union. In other words, it seems less fruitful to analyze and assess the organizational structure of the EU and the relationships of different actors within this structure but more promising to ask in which particular way and with what consequences the EU solves the problem of governance. By ,governance' I understand the adoption of generally binding decisions.

Unfortunately, the term ,governance' in political science as well as in law is often without further qualification reserved for the activities of a state government. This is less so in the Anglo-Saxon as compared for instance to the German tradition because in the former it is at least semantically possible to distinguish between ,governance' and ,government' whereas this is not the case in German. But even in English-speaking social science, the conceptual link between ,governance' and ,state' is very strong. In recent years, this link has come under empirical as well as theoretical criticism from very different angles. On a very general level, it may be said that both internationalization (Zürn 1995) and functional differentiation (Mayntz et al. 1988) make it increasingly difficult to associate governance unequivocally with the state.

In the European Union, there is a strong degree of both internationalization and functional differentiation. It is thus a particularly well-suited object for asking for the conditions and possibilities of responsive and responsible governance under modern conditions. This question by far transcends integration theory in the narrow sense but makes it possible for integration research to contribute to a more general issue of major importance. Analyzing the European Union from a governance perspective denies that it is a ,sui generis' institution which by its very nature precludes to arrive at general conclusions. On the contrary, such a perspective also allows for comparisons of the EU with the most diverse kind of governance systems in the sense of a ,most different systems design' (Przeworski/Teune 1970), thus opening up a whole range of possibilities for comparative research which remains as yet largely unexplored. The position held by parts of integration research that the EU was unsuitable for comparative research because there was nothing to compare it with is thus untenable. Politically, however, this thesis is important because it has the function to prevent from the outset comparisons with ,mere' international organizations on the one hand and with the democratic structures of modern states on the other hand.

If the European Union is regarded as a dynamic multi-level system from a governance perspective, it is possible to study central problems of the integration process from a more general point of view and at the same time acknowledge the possibility that the EU has developed into a unique and new type of political system. In this sense, the EU is a political system ,sui generis' but could well be compared with other political systems and their solutions to the problem of responsible and responsive governance from an analytic as well as from a normative standpoint.

III. Central Features

In the following, I will discuss those features of the EU's political system which seem to be most important for its possible development as well as for the possibilities of responsible and responsive governance. These features are not meant to be a comprehensive list. I merely wish to highlight those properties indicating that the EU is neither a state nor an international organization and will not develop in either direction. The discussion is not concerned with details but focuses on persistent lines of conflicts and problems which have existed for decades and will most likely remain important in the years to come. The background of the discussion is the general question to which extent political institutions are dependent on particular features of society and to which extent they can create these preconditions by themselves.

1. Uneven Europeanization

By this term I understand the fact that functional subsystems of society are europeanized to largely different degrees and that the action capacity of politically relevant actors on the European level and with regard to European affairs differs widely. This is not a new insight but it seems to me that the consequences of this trend for political responsibility and governance both within the member states and of the EU are not yet sufficiently discussed.

The Europeanization of functional systems does not proceed in parallel to the Europeanization of the actors in these systems. Despite remaining deficits in the implementation of the ‚four freedoms' of the internal market, the Europeanization of the economy is the most advanced. As a result, economic transactions can take place in the entire EU without any significant difference to the domestic context. It does not mean that a homogeneous economic area with an even distribution of economic activity had emerged, that borders do not create additional transaction costs or that economic agents can act on the European scale independently of their seize. It means, however, that the possibility of capital owners to move freely in the entire EU constrains national governments in their economic policy.

The Europeanization of the economy is made and institutionalized by a rapidly developing European economic law. Even if again there is no homogenous European legal space and probably there will never be one, the importance of the dynamics of European economic law for the restructuring of political relationships can hardly be underestimated. European law does not only consist of constitutional provisions in the classical sense, and the agenda of European law-making is not only concerned with the elaboration of a constitution for the European Union and the issue of whether and to which degree the national democratic legal order is compatible with the European legal system, as stated vigorously by the Maastricht-decision of the German constitutional court (Bundesverfassungsgericht 1994). Whereas the emergence of a European constitution mainly by the jurisprudence of the European Court of Justice and its impact are increasingly discussed in the literature (Weiler 1981, 1982, 1991; Burley/Mattli 1993; Garrett/Weingast 1993), this is much less the case for the Europeanization of economic law and its impacts. However, economic law is not a technical subject and of interest only for specialized lawyers but is of utmost political importance even if (or better: precisely because) it is not on the agenda of intergovernmental reform conferences (Joerges 1993, 1994, 1996). The analysis of European economic law is a striking illustration of the degree to which the Europeanization of the economy is not a ‚natural' process but created and sustained by political actors and even more by allegedly unpolitical experts. One major issue in this respect are the social consequences of economic integration caused and institutionalized by economic law. A second, and probably even more important issue is whether the institutionalization of a particular ‚criterion of rationality' (Lepsius 1995), namely that collective welfare was increased by market enlargement and market liberalization can also legitimate the disintegrative effects of economic integration.

Contrary to the far-reaching Europeanization of the economy and the legal system, politics and society largely remain organized within nation-states. This is even more the case for society than for politics. Despite a general and long-term trend towards conversion in the Western world, ambiguous as it may be (Kaelble 1987; Therborn 1995), social cleavages, political culture, social structures and political identities are to a large extent national ones. European societies have many similar but few common problems (Flora 1993: 756). A large number of institutions understood in a larger sense emerged as the result of long and fierce fights over conflicting values that took place within nation states. Among these are party systems, democracy and the welfare state in their respective national versions.

These institutions cannot be easily europeanized because of this path-dependent development and the necessity to link them to a societal base. Political parties are the most well-known example. High expectations of the emergence of a European party system on the occasion of the first direct elections of the European Parliament were largely disappointed. Even parties of the same ideological orientation but from different member states had great difficulties to agree even on minimal common programmatic guidelines. As their organizational and electoral basis remains within the member states, they follow the imperatives of the national political game instead of showing solidarity, and be it only programmatic solidarity, with a party in a different country.

Similar limits to Europeanization apply to social movements which usually are even deeper rooted in small-scale social relationships. Contrary to popular criticism of an overwhelming influence of interest groups on European policy-making, this also applies to interest groups. Already in the national context, interest groups have to balance the ‚logic of membership' and the ‚logic of influence' (Schmitter/Streeck 1981). On the European level, heterogeneity is much stronger and decision-making much more complicated. For this reason, European umbrella associations have a very limited capacity for action. Only representations of single multinational enterprises are capable of effective targeted action. As a result, Commission and European Parliament are not faced with a few homogeneous actors representing economic interests as expected in the early years of the integration process but with a multitude of European peak associations, national associations and representatives of single enterprises. On the whole, the limits to the Europeanization of interest groups strengthen rather than weaken the executive, although this very general statement should not lead one to overlook the existing asymmetries, for instance between trade unions and industrial associations (Grande 1996; Kohler-Koch 1994, 1996).

Thus, on a very general level the economy and economic law are largely europeanized in the European Union whereas politics and society but also constitutional law largely remain national. In particular large enterprises and parts of the political executive are able to act effectively on the European level whereas this is only to a much lesser degree the case for political parties, social movements, trade unions and to some degree interest groups. Because of the structural nature of this asymmetry, the EU will have to live with it for a considerable time to come.

2. Permanent Institutional Change

In western societies, governance usually takes place in a rather stable institutional context. Both formal and informal institutions such as government, parliament, intermediary institutions, democracy, rule of law, the welfare state, as well as the relationship between rulers and ruled are more or less stable. This situation changes only in cases of intentional reform (e.g. federalization in Belgium) or in cases of severe system crises (e.g. Italy). The European Union on the other hand is characterized by a decade-long process of institutional change which is both incremental and deep. This process of change does not only concern the institutions of the EU but also those of the member states. The latter process is being perceived only slowly (Héritier/Knill/Mingers 1996).

This type of institutional change has never been on the agenda of intergovernmental reform conferences. On the contrary, it is a phenomenon which is only to a small degree the result of intentional political engineering. Instead, it is the result of non-intended but politically important consequences of numerous single decisions which seem unimportant if taken alone but the cumulative effects of which are substantial. Institutional change within the member states is not restricted to spectacular and highly politicized measures to make these states ‚fit' for the European Union, such as new constitutional articles or the creation of specialized parliamentary and governmental bodies dealing with European politics. More importantly, a general process of disintegration and change of political structures is taking place at member state level. Interest groups and political parties are most concerned by this process. Both do not only have to mediate between the interests of their members or their electorate on the one hand and the political system on the other. In addition, their margin for action is often severely constrained or transformed by European law or by the pressure of competition in an open European market. Because of their embeddedness in national traditions very different national from each other, Europeanization is only possible to a limited extent. In the case of political parties, what is at issue is the capacity to mobilize political support, in other words, a decisive element of the stability of national political systems.

This transformation also concerns institutions in a broader sense, e.g. the particular national versions of the welfare state, democracy, rule of law and labor relations. Examples include the competencies of the German constitutional court, the central role of the British parliament and the financing of the Danish welfare state. The problem is not that these institutions are being abolished by the EU. At stake is the intended or unintended pressure exerted by the integration process which might lead to modifications in these institutions changing their core. This breaking up of institutionalized solutions to past and present conflicts does not have to be bad as such. It may also help to overcome long-established impasses and blockades of reform (e.g. Eichener 1993). It also does not necessarily need to lead to manifest conflicts. The politically decisive point is, however, that changes induced by Europeanization have to be dealt with in *national* political systems.

The transfer of authority to private or semi-public institutions on the European level is another element in this general process of institutional change. Depending on the political preferences of the respective government or on national traditions, governance by private or semi-public institutions can also be found in member-states. This tendency is, however, systematically favored by the structure of the EU because it takes issues defined as technical ones out of the difficult process of consensus formation in the Council of Ministers. One result of this process is ‚comitology', a unique but relatively unexplored phenomenon both empirically and normatively (Winter 1994; Joerges/Neyer 1996). The creations of ‚regulatory agencies' is another. Although the emergence of regulatory agencies is still in an embryonic stage compared to the United States, it is a clear example of how political decision-making bodies are relieved of complicated issues by expert bodies.

The processes of institutional change discussed above take place in a political system with clear outlines. Practically unknown in nation-states and hardly understood in its consequences for efficient and responsible governance is a phenomenon which figures under various headings and which shall be referred to here as ‚variable geometry' (for an overview c.f. Stubb 1996). In such a system, participants and possibilities for participation as well as decision-making rules change depending on the issue at stake. Variable geometry is not a minor issue of institutional design for the EU but has to do with basic questions of large-scale polities which emerge due to a large variation in territorial and functional units and a strong coupling of these units. On an even more abstract level, it has to do with the relationship between unity and diversity.

With some exceptions (e.g. Schmitter 1992), variable geometry in political science as well as in the political debate is considered to be a pragmatic and temporary derivation from the ideal of uniformity (e.g. Grabitz 1984). However, such a view downplays the quasi permanent character of the ‚exception' by pointing to the unattainable ideal. The other alternative, namely to consider variable geometry (e.g. in the form of ‚functional federalism', c.f. Straubhaar 1993) as an adequate solution to a large number of highly different problems of regulation may convince from an efficiency point of view but leaves out the issue of the political responsibility of such a number of overlapping and variable regimes with considerable impact on their members.

Already the ‚Single' European Act consisted of three separate and distinct parts. The Maastricht Treaty officially partitioned the EU into three pillars, without counting the other sub-systems of the EU (Schengen, the European Monetary System, the Western European Union) and the differentiation contained in the Maastricht Treaty itself (social protocol). Faced with further enlargements and hence larger heterogeneity, variable geometry is likely to increase. At present, it is doubtful whether conventional constitutions for a polity, even federal ones, are able to deal with such a degree of interdependent heterogeneity. Thinking about this problem should not be made even more difficult by looking for non-existing ways of overcoming heterogeneity.

3. Democracy and Legitimacy

Democracy is understood here as the institutionalization of a set of procedures for the control of governance which guarantees the participation of those who are governed in the adoption of collectively binding decisions. Legitimacy means a generalized degree of trust of the addressees of these decisions towards the political system. From this definition, it follows that democracy does not necessarily and exclusively have to be synonymous with parliamentary government. It also follows that the legitimacy of a political system is not exclusively linked to democracy and certainly not to parliamentary democracy. Such a statement does not imply an agreement with old and new technocratic visions of the EU (Ipsen 1972; Majone 1994a, 1994b; Andersen/Burns 1996). It does imply, however, that models of democracy developed in the national context cannot be easily transferred to the European Union and that a political strategy based on such a transfer would not necessarily lead to a more democratic EU and to an increase in its legitimacy.

The necessity of democracy in the EU can be justified on normative grounds. Each system of governance takes collectively binding decisions and thus at least potentially intervenes massively into the lives of people. For this reason, the latter have to have voice in the system and a realistic chance to change the course of events. A more pragmatic reason is also possible: Even in hierarchically structured systems it is impossible to govern against a substantial resistance of citizens or organized groups. This is even more true for the highly decentralized system of the EU where decisions are frequently taken by unanimous decision and where capacities for implementation and sanctions are weak. In such a situation, democracy increases system stability and problem-solving efficiency.

Rejecting claims for a democratization of the EU is therefore questionable both for normative and for practical reasons. At the same time, asking for a full parliamentarization of the EU is equally unrealistic. Whereas the public debate in most member states turns around the *desirability* of a European Union organized as a (strongly decentralized) federal state with a two-chamber system representing the ‚European people‘ and the member states, the scientific debate in recent years has gradually become more critical against the *possibility* of democracy in the EU. The reason given are structural ones. It is argued that democracy cannot simply be installed by a constitutional act (Kohler 1978) but that it is linked to particular social preconditions which are only partially existent in the EU and which cannot be created by political intervention (Habermas 1992; Lepsius 1991; Scharpf 1993; Kielmansegg 1996). Democracy requires the existence of a collective identity which does not exist on the European level.

In particular, democracy requires a functioning political infrastructure which mediates between decision-makers and citizens. In the member states, this function is performed by political parties and by media-based public discourse. The function of these institutions is to transform even complicated issues into distinguishable alternatives for decision along clearly defined conflict lines. However, parties and the media belong to those institutions which are most strongly linked to the historical development of the respective states. The limits to a Europeanization of political parties have been discussed above; with regard to the media, it is clear that linguistic barriers prevent the emergence of a European public discourse. As a result, it is difficult if not impossible to achieve an EU-wide politicization of issues, in other words to bring issues on the European political agenda and discuss them along ideological instead of national cleavages. Thus, politicization usually takes place in a national context. What is politically important and discussed controversially in one member state does not have to be so in any of the other. As a result, even a political debate in Germany as the biggest member state would not have much impact on the European scale. Influence could only be exerted by the intergovernmental channel which follows, however, a completely different logic than public discourse. For this reason, the problem cannot be solved by a reform of decision-making procedures.

The problems of how to organize political responsibility in a system of variable geometry are even more severe. In the present Union, only the Community pillar is subject to some parliamentary responsibility whereas the two other pillars as well as the subsystems existing outside the Maastricht Treaty are not controlled by a parliament at all. A substantial increase in overlapping functional areas would lead to a multiplication of specialized parliaments and thus even further decrease the possibility of politicization of particular issues.

Does this mean that those are right who make a plea for a renationalization of the European Union in the name of democracy? Even if one does not reject renationalization on the grounds of the general benefits of European integration, this seemingly easy solution is at best a partial one. Despite all justified criticism of the immense hunger for competencies of the Brussels institutions, one has to admit that some decisions have to be taken on the EU-level if the common market is to be preserved or if gains from economic policy coordination are to be realized. Renationalization is not an answer to the question of how these decisions shall be made accountable.

In sum, the EU is faced with a dilemma between efficiency and democracy. The political decision to create a European market requires at least some political decision-making competencies at the European level. Their democratic control, however, is hampered by structural problems of the Europeanization of democracy and its social preconditions. Insisting on the virtues of national democracy in turn risks to defend an increasingly empty set of formal participation rules while the impact of the European market dictates political choices.

IV. Which Type of Polity?

How is it possible to grasp the present state of the European Union and which future developments are conceivable on the basis of this conceptualization? Whereas the political debate focuses on whether the EU should or is likely to become either a federal state or an association of states, it seems to me that this conception of the EU's prospective development in terms of opposing alternatives misses essential features of the present state of the EU or downplays them to transitory phenomena. The normative debate in particular should not restrict itself to comparing the sad reality of European democracy to the bright ideals of the democratic nation-state. At the same time, the argument that there was no real problem of democracy because democratic nation-states kept firm control over the integration process is not very convincing either.

For this reason, it is necessary to develop models of political organization which are not conceptually based on the image of the state in order to provide a guidepost for the analytical as well as for the normative discussion of governance in the European Union. Two such models will be briefly presented here. They are based on theoretical resonings and empirical investigations within the framework of a research project on the legitimation of the European Union (Jachtenfuchs/Diez/Jung 1996). In the first place, these models are provisional attempts to grasp the rapidly changing and confusing reality of governance in the EU. In addition, however, they are more than abstract scientific models because they can also be found in the conceptions of political parties in some member states about a legitimate political order for the EU. Thus, they are not only theories *about* but also theories *in* the political system of the EU. They symbolically express desired political orders and thus have a legitimizing or delegitimating function.

The distinction of theories about and theories in the political system also applies to the concept of the democratic nation-state. This concept is not only an analytical one but also a normative theory about the appropriate organization of the state which serves as a reference point for political actors in their assessment of political reality. As the model of the democratic nation-state has been the only successful one historically, it is the most influential normative theory in the political system. As a consequence, the EU is being compared to this very normative model, irrespectively of whether it is a state or not. The model of the democratic state structures the debate about the future of the European Union and has an influence on the proposals made in order to diminish the ,democratic deficit' or create a ,Europe of the citizens'. If the ideal of a European state is unattainable, as has been argued previously, this becomes problematic. If the entire endeavor of European integration is not put into question, the only remaining alternative is either to accept the discrepancy between democratic ideal and European reality (and possibly try to legitimize it) or to look for different models of political organization. These models must at the same time match reality more adequately than the model of the state and meet the requirements of political efficiency and responsibility.

1. Economic Community

This model is closely linked to the German theory of a neoliberal ,economic constitution' for the EU (Mestmäcker 1994a; Petersmann 1993; Scherer 1970; Streit/Mussler 1995). Although it is strongly influenced by particular German ways of thinking about the relationship between politics, law and the economy and is most influential politically only in Germany, its more abstract features can be combined to a model of the EU which is not linked to particular national traditions of thinking about institutions and society. In fact, empirical analysis shows that it is a prescriptive model how a legitimate political order for the EU could look like which is shared by several political parties in Britain, France, and Germany throughout the history of the EU (Jachtenfuchs/Diez/Jung 1996).

The most important feature of the model is the separation of the market and the state, in other words the co-existence of a single European market together with a number of distinct states on the same territory without a degree of political control equivalent to the degree of economic integration. In the framework of this model, economic integration is not only a necessary reaction to the requirements of a natural process of economic globalization but also an explicit normative goal. The underlying argument refers to the existence of a number of possible economic orders which have different consequences on economic efficiency and individual liberty. Both economic efficiency and individual liberty are best served by the institutionalization of a market economy which among other factors assures free competition, a strong respect of private property and a strict anti-cartel legislation. This type of market economy represents an optimum type of order for society both for efficiency and for normative reasons (respect of individual liberty). On the other hand, it is constantly threatened by organized rent-seekers trying to gain extra benefits at the expense of the well-being of society. Because of its superiority as a societal order and the risk of erosion by rent-seekers it must and can legitimately be sheltered from political influence. One means for achieving this is to codify the basic principles of the economic community into a constitution which has high majority requirements for change.

The model of the economic community should not be confused with the one of a free and self-regulating market. It is a normative order which is constituted by a number of legal rights and which must be protected against the egoistic interests of market participants. Because only a particular type of market economy best balances economic efficiency and individual liberty, the number of allowed interventions into the market is limited. For individuals and corporate actors (i.e. for enterprises), rights and obligations on the European level exist only within a relatively restricted economic domain. Individual social rights should not exist on the European level but remain restricted to the domain of the nation state, together with political rights.

As the citizen has only economic rights and obligation on the EU level, and these are conferred upon him by a constitution embodying principles of an optimal economic organization, there is no need for democracy at the EU level. Legitimation of the economic community is achieved by efficiency and liberty (Mestmäcker 1978, 1994b). It does not require democratic legitimation because the latter is only relevant for the political realm but not for the economic one. There is thus a sharp division between politics which has to be subject to democratic control but remains the exclusive domain of the member states and economics which is unpolitical and thus beyond the need for democracy and has to be organized on the European level (and possibly on an even larger geographical scale) due to the internationalization of economic activity. This division is seen as a natural one based on the properties of the respective functional systems.

Democracy and pluralism are a threat to this type of order because both favor particular individual interests which in the long run would undermine the efficiency of such a liberal economic order. The competition of different interests in the framework of democratic rules, mediated by political parties and interest groups in this view does not increase collective welfare, at least not if the latter is defined in purely economic terms. In this perspective, parliamentarians are considered as actors which are easily at the service of interest groups and other particularistic interests. Thus, a constitution must contain mechanisms which protect it even from the elected representatives of the people.

For this reason, the economic community should be institutionalized in a constitution as a constitution offers the best protection against opportunistic interests. This is particularly true for the European constitution (i.e. the EC Treaty) which can only be changed by unanimity and is thus even more immune to changes than a national constitution which can usually be changed by a two-thirds majority or something alike. The implementation of the constitutional provisions of the EU (or, more precisely, in its EC part) is controlled by the politically independent European Court of Justice. Thus, in the ideal case, a societal order which is considered optimal by scientific experts is institutionalized in a form which is difficult to change and its implementation conferred to an organ which is not subject to political control. At the same time, decisions are often made in the form of directly applicable and binding European law.

Because of the separation of the economy from politics, internal and external security are tasks of the state and thus irrelevant for the EU. The decisive domain for the latter is welfare understood in the sense embodied in the constitution. As the economic community is not a political one, it does not require whatever kind of collective identity and no symbolic integration.

This model of an economic community exists in various types also in the scientific literature. One example is Hans-Peter Ipsen's characterization of the EU as a ‚Zweckverband funktioneller Integration' (Ipsen 1972, 1985, 1987a, 1987b, 1993). Although Ipsen also distinguishes between the national state and the European market, he does not base this distinction upon quasi-objective necessities of an efficient and liberal economic order but on the need to cope with the consequences of economic liberalization. For this purpose, Ipsen argues, the member states had created the EU. This purpose legitimates the activity of the EU in a number of functional areas and at the same time limits the extension of EU competencies to what is necessary for coping with economic interdependence. According to Ipsen, the resulting activities are of a technical and organizational nature and can for this reason be carried out by experts without democratic legitimation. Only within these narrow margins, the legitimacy of the EU is guaranteed by the legitimacy of its member states. Broadening the scope of EU competencies would require democratic control which the European Parliament cannot provide because it is a representation of different national peoples rather than of one European people. In other words, the EU cannot become democratic, and an increase of the competencies of the European Parliament thus undermines rather than increases democracy (Ipsen 1985).

Another variant of the economic community model is Giandomenico Majone's ‚regulatory state' (Majone 1994a, 1994b, 1994c). Again, the economy and politics are organized on different geographical scales. However, the reasons given for this separation and the instruments used are different compared to the ones discusses above. Majone stipulates the existence of market failures and the need to correct them. This is best done by efficiency-oriented and independent regulatory agencies which are dominated by sectoral technical experts. The model of the regulatory state is politically more neutral than the model of the economic community because it explicitly allows the correction of market failures in areas of social regulation (e.g. environmental policy, health and safety at work) which are regarded critically or even rejected by the proponents of the economic community in the narrower sense. Correcting transnational market failures requires strong supranational powers but in limited sectors. For their democratic legitimation, the European Parliament is sufficient despite its deficiencies. Regulatory authorities draw their legitimation from the distinction between efficiency-oriented and redistributive policy. The former has to be based on expertise as long as society is willing or forced to avoid paying the price of inefficient policy resulting in times of internationalized markets. Only redistributive policies need democratic legitimation.

In sum, the separation of politics and the economy yields a number of criteria for assessing the legitimacy and efficiency of the EU and for constructing prescriptive models. Although the models discussed above differ in their institutional setup and in their political implications, they all allow at least in principle the co-existence of a European market together with national states and weak European governance. Whether such institutional models would be sustainable in practice depends, however, not only on the parsimony of the theoretical construction but also on the empirical question of whether it is possible to legitimate the division between state and market and the ensuing consequences.

2. Network

Whereas the model of the (federal) state (which will not be discussed here) is characterized by territorial congruence of those who govern with those who are governed, the model of the economic community is characterized by the separation of a European market and the national states. Both models thus have a clear structure with regard to the territorial scope of their different components. This does not apply to the network model which is characterized by a multitude of institutions, participation channels and actors. The social scientific literature has used the term ‚network' for capturing a particular type of social order. In contrast to the type of a ‚state' with the structuring principle of hierarchy and of a ‚market' with the structuring principle of anarchy, the particular feature of networks is the loose coupling of its components (Mayntz 1993). To some writers, they appear as the organizational form which fits best to the division of society into increasingly autonomous functional subsystems (Willke 1995). They neither have a fixed organizational structure nor a constant number or type of participants.

In the political debate, the network as a model of political organization has mainly been put forward by green parties. This usage of the network model insists on the necessity to increase citizen participation in decision-making which is of relevance to them and on the preservation of small-scale identities. The result is a bundle of different functional and territorial constituencies with overlapping and variable membership and without a clearly distinguishable center or geographical scope. Such a model is based on a particular concept of politics which reaches back to the ideas of ‚integral federalists' (Marc 1979; Roemheld 1978) and ideas of Jean-Pierre Proudhon about radical democracy to the ‚societal federalism' of Johannes Althusius (c.f. Hüglin 1991). It is based on the idea that the power of a unitary and hierarchical state with a center which is usually far away from the concrete live-world of the citizens prevents rather than furthers the development of individuals and groups. As this problem cannot be dealt with be means of majoritarian democracy in large and heterogeneous societies, this line of thinking stresses the need to grant far-reaching rights to people on the local and the regional level and with regard to those areas which are of direct relevance to them.

In the political debate, this concept is often referred to under the label of a ‚Europe of the regions' (Borras-Alomar/Christiansen/Rodriguez-Pose 1994). The main political unit would thus be a region, however it may be defined. Different regions would cooperate to different degrees and in varying ways in order to solve problems perceived to be common. By its proponents, the network concept is meant to be a possibility to separate participation from its link to the territorial organization of politics (Brock/Albert 1995; Ruggie 1993) which always implies practices of inclusion and exclusion (Connolly

1995). In this view, political organization does not necessarily require a strong and powerful center but can as well work in such an open and fluid structure, given in particular the opportunities provided by modern communication technology.

In the political science literature, networks are mainly discussed with regard to their ability for governance (Scharpf 1994) whereas the problems of democracy and legitimacy of and in networks are largely unexplored. The open structure of networks suggests, however, that legitimation cannot be achieved by classical means of democratic control because the institutional preconditions of democracy are lacking if the territorial congruence of rulers and ruled are not given. In the literature, it has been proposed to cope with this problem by creating a number of quasi-parliamentary bodies for particular problem fields. Their composition does not have to be determined by general elections but can follow other criteria, e.g. statistical representation or the representation of particular groups (Held 1991, 1995). The political proponents of the network model suggest that legitimation is mainly achieved by broad participation. Networks can become legitimate because they offer opportunities for participation which non-participants do not have. Whether this is sufficient to assure the legitimacy of a European Union constructed as a network or whether such an EU would in fact exclude large and distinguishable groups from the political process, is not yet clear. However, legitimation by participation bears the possibility that non-participants might become politically active as adversaries of the integration process instead of fighting for participation.

In sum, pluralism – understood in a comprehensive way as a mode of governance and participation – is a distinctive feature of the network model. State and societal actors of the most diverse kind participate in varying combinations in the decision-making process. Another particular feature is the preservation of small-scale identities. As a consequence, the network model is not only not very demanding with respect to a common European identity for the Euro-polity but on the contrary insists that a ‚substantial‘ identity of the EU would run counter to the very idea of organizing the EU as a network. At best, ‚procedural‘ identities (e.g. openness for varying forms of participation, mutual respect, respect of diversity) might be necessary.

As the notion of the network has developed at the margins of the political discourse and in a rather fragmented way, and also because it is a most innovative form of political design, its contours are not very clear. However, ignoring the network type means ignoring a number of models for the EU which exist in the political discourse and which cannot be captured by other models.

V. Perspectives for Polity Development

I have tried to characterize the EU by three trends: uneven Europeanization, permanent institutional change and structural problems of democracy. The overall image gained by such a view is a political system in which the principle of territorially organized and responsible politics is at stake. The decisive difference of this system with regard to the problems of internationalization and interdependence which touch most Western states consists in the fact the system is formally and factually highly immune to change. Should it turn out that some types of political decisions taken by the EU cannot be controlled democratically *as a matter of principle*, the EU would be a manifestation of a transformation of a fundamental principle of statehood.

From the two models discussed above, the economic community seems to reflect the present state of the integration process and its development options in the near future. This type also highlights the political problems caused by the integration process. The state as a normative or analytical model can only by considerably conceptual stretching be applied to a polity characterized by a variable geographical scope and structural problems of democracy. The network model takes these features into account and tries to build a normatively acceptable political order on this basis but overlooks the fundamental asymmetry between the European market and the national state.

The economic community as a normative and an analytical model of the EU is not politically neutral. Whereas the idea of a federal state is politically indifferent and the network is inspired by ‚green' thinking, the economic community is a conservative project. It precludes the developments of strong policies to cope with market failures and merely allows the EU to turn in to a ‚regulatory state'. This does not necessarily imply a dismantling of national welfare states but also allows for a positively joint sovereignty (Leibfried 1994). However, state intervention into the economy has to rely exclusively on market-correcting policies because it lacks the legal authority as well as the financial means to do anything different. An analysis of party programs in Britain, France and Germany shows, however, that the asymmetry between market-creating and market-correcting policies is widely accepted by political parties, and even by some parties on the left (Jachtenfuchs/Diez/Jung 1996). Does this imply that the EU is the institutionalization of the end of social-democratic visions for the change of society and the victory of neoliberalism?

The European internal market is widely accepted in most political camps. In addition, it is not only institutionalized in a kind of economic constitution (Joerges 1996) but also stabilized by a particular constellation of interests in the EU which favors ‚negative integration', i.e. the abolishment of barriers to economic transactions and hence ‚market making' at the expense of policies of ‚positive integration', i.e. market correction (Scharpf 1996). Democratic policy-making mainly takes place within the nation-state. Whether such an asymmetrical political order can become permanently legitimate in the eyes of citizens depends in particular on how disintegrative effects of the integration process and relative deprivations are perceived and attributed. A stable system in which the distributive consequences of market processes are regarded as unpolitical and not as the result of conscious and revisable political decisions is perfectly conceivable. Despite the turbulence created by the Maastricht debate, this seems to be by and large the case at present. The introduction of a common currency and the actions of a democratically uncontrolled European Central Bank could be the decisive test for showing whether an effective restructuration of normative expectations of citizens and thus a factual acceptance of binding European decision including their possible negative effects on individuals as legitimate and appropriate has taken place.

The true problem of the integration process does not reside in cumbersome decision-making processes. On the contrary: insisting exclusively on an even further increase of political and economic efficiency and the exclusive institutionalization of this idea of rationality could turn out to be a threat to the integration process. The neglect of other criteria of rationality such as ‚autonomy' or ‚democracy' could lead to the formation of political movements against integration which are stronger and more persistent than the ones that appeared during the referenda on the Maastricht Treaty. The perception of negative consequences of integration and the possible formation of political movements responding to this perception is, however, not directly linked to the ‚real' strength of such negative consequences but strongly shaped in the political discourse by political parties and the media.

Institutional reforms and increasing possibilities for citizen participation in EU decision-making are necessary but certainly not sufficient for permanently legitimating the EU in the eyes of the citizens. What is lacking are political programs containing normative criteria as well as concrete action proposals for the present state of integration. The increasingly widespread criticism of the EU is not a result of political manipulation which can be corrected by neutral information but stems mainly from the discrepancy between the prevailing normative model of political organization (i.e. the democratic state) and perceived deficits of the EU with reference to this model. If it is true that the EU is for structural reasons unlikely to develop into a state thus meeting the requirements of the prevailing normative model and if at the same time a renationalization of the EU is also unlikely, the public political debate is in desperate need for models of the European polity which give a realistic analytical image of the EU and at the same time serve as normative guideposts for feasible reforms balancing democracy and governance.

References

ANDERSEN, SVEIN S. and TOM R. BURNS: „The European Union and the Erosion of Parliamentary Democracy: A Study of Post-parliamentary Governance", in: SVEIN S. ANDERSEN and KJELL ELIASSEN (Eds.): *The European Union – How Democratic Is It?*, London (Sage) 1996, pp. 227-251.

BOGDANDY, ARMIN VON: „Supranationale Union als neuer Herrschaftstypus: Entstaatlichung und Vergemeinschaftung in staatstheoretischer Perspektive", *Integration*, 16 (1993), pp. 210-224.

BORRAS-ALOMAR, SUSANA, THOMAS CHRISTIANSEN and ANDRES RODRIGUEZ-POSE: „Towards a ‚Europe of the Regions'? Visions and Reality from a Critical Perspective", *Regional Politics & Policy*, 4:2 (1994), pp. 1-27.

BROCK, LOTHAR and MATHIAS ALBERT: „Entgrenzung der Staatenwelt. Zur Analyse weltgesellschaftlicher Entwicklungstendenzen", *Zeitschrift für Internationale Beziehungen*, 2 (1995), pp. 259-285.

BUNDESVERFASSUNGSGERICHT: „Urteil zum Maastricht-Vertrag", *Entscheidungen des Bundesverfassungsgerichts*, 89 (1994), pp. 155-213.

BURLEY, ANNE-MARIE and WALTER MATTLI: „Europe Before the Court. A Political Theory of Legal Integration", *International Organization*, 47 (1993), pp. 41-76.

CONNOLLY, WILLIAM E.: „Democracy and Territoriality", in: WILLIAM E. CONOLLY: *The Ethos of Pluralization*, Minneapolis/London (University of Minnesota Press) 1995, pp. 135-161.

EICHENER, VOLKER: *Social Dumping or Innovative Regulation? Processes and Outcomes of European Decision-Making in the Sector of Health and Safety at Work Regulation*, Firenze (EUI Working Paper No. SPS 92/28) 1992.

ELLWEIN, THOMAS: „Staatlichkeit im Wandel. Das Staatsmodell des 19. Jahrhunderts als Verständnisbarriere", in: BEATE KOHLER-KOCH (Ed.): *Staat und Demokratie in Europa (18. Wissenschaftlicher Kongreß der Deutschen Vereinigung für Politische Wissenschaft)*, Opladen (Leske + Budrich) 1992, pp. 73-82.

FLORA, PETER: „Europa als Sozialstaat?", in: BERNHARD SCHÄFERS (ed.): *Lebensverhältnisse und soziale Konflikte im neuen Europa (Verhandlungen des 26. Deutschen Soziologentages in Düsseldorf)*, Frankfurt a.M./New York (Campus) 1993, pp. 754-762.

GARRETT, GEOFFREY and BARRY R. WEINGAST: „Ideas, Interests, and Institutions. Constructing the European Community's Internal Market", in: JUDITH GOLDSTEIN and ROBERT O. KEOHANE (Eds.): *Ideas and Foreign Policy. Beliefs, Institutions, and Political Change*, Ithaca (Cornell University Press) 1993, pp. 173-206.

GRABITZ, EBERHARD (Ed.): *Abgestufte Integration. Eine Alternative zum herkömmlichen Integrationskonzept?*, Kehl am Rhein/Strasbourg (N.P. Engel) 1984.

GRANDE, EDGAR: „The State and Interest Groups in a Framework of Multi-Level Decision-Making. The Case of the European Union", *Journal of European Public Policy*, 3 (1996), pp. 318-338.

HAAS, ERNST B.: *Beyond the Nation-State. Functionalism and International Organization*, Stanford (Stanford University Press) 1964.

HABERMAS, JÜRGEN: „Citizenship and National Identity. Some Reflections on the Future of Europe", *Praxis International*, 12 (1992), pp. 1-19.

HELD, DAVID: „Democracy, the Nation-State and the Global System", *Economy and Society*, 20 (1991), pp. 138-172.

HELD, DAVID: *Democracy and the Global Order. From the Modern State to Cosmopolitan Governance*, Cambridge (Polity Press) 1995.

HÉRITIER, ADRIENNE, CHRISTOPH KNILL and SUSANNE MINGERS: *Ringing the Changes in Europe. Regulatory Competition and the Transformation of the State. Britain, France, Germany*, Berlin/New York (de Gruyter) 1996.

HOFFMANN, STANLEY: „Obstinate or Obsolete? The Fate of the Nation-State in the Case of Western Europe", *Daedalus*, 95 (1966), pp. 862-915.

HÜGLIN, THOMAS O.: *Sozietaler Föderalismus. Die politische Theorie des Johannes Althusius*, Berlin/New York (de Gruyter) 1991.

IPSEN, HANS PETER: „Die Bundesrepublik Deutschland in der Europäischen Gemeinschaft", in: PETER-CHRISTIAN MÜLLER-GRAFF and MANFRED ZULEEG (Eds.):

Staat und Wirtschaft in der EG (Kolloquium zum 65. Geburtstag von Prof. Dr. Bodo Börner), Baden-Baden (Nomos) 1987a, pp. 9-15.

IPSEN, HANS PETER: „Europäische Verfassung – nationale Verfassung", *Europarecht*, 22 (1987b), pp. 195-213.

IPSEN, HANS PETER: „Zum Parlamentsentwurf einer Europäischen Union", *Der Staat*, 24 (1985), pp. 325-349.

IPSEN, HANS PETER: „Zur Exekutiv-Rechtsetzung in der Europäischen Gemeinschaft", in: PETER BADURA and RUPERT SCHOLZ (Eds.): *Wege und Verfahren des Verfassungslebens. Festschrift für Peter Lerche zum 65. Geburtstag*, München (Beck) 1993, pp. 425-441.

IPSEN, HANS PETER: *Europäisches Gemeinschaftsrecht*, Tübingen (Mohr) 1972.

JACHTENFUCHS, MARKUS and BEATE KOHLER-KOCH: „Regieren im dynamischen Mehrebenensystem", in: MARKUS JACHTENFUCHS and BEATE KOHLER-KOCH (Eds.): *Europäische Integration*, Opladen (Leske + Budrich) 1996, pp. 15-44.

JACHTENFUCHS, MARKUS, THOMAS DIEZ and SABINE JUNG: *Regieren jenseits der Staatlichkeit? Legitimitätsideen in der Europäischen Union* (Paper Presented at the Conference of the Arbeitskreis Integrationsforschung, Deutsche Vereinigung für politische Wissenschaft, November 1-2, 1996, University of Mannheim) 1996.

JOERGES, CHRISTIAN and JÜRGEN NEYER: *The Law's Potential of Transforming Strategic Interactions into Deliberative Political Processes. An Interdisciplinary Analysis of the European Comitology-Complex in the Foodstuffs Sector* (Paper Presented at the Conference ‚Problem-Solving Capacity of Transnational Governance Systems', Max-Planck-Institute for the Study of Societies, Cologne, November 8-9) 1996.

JOERGES, CHRISTIAN: „Legitimationsprobleme des europäischen Wirtschaftsrechts und der Vertrag von Maastricht", in: GERT BRÜGGEMEIER (Ed.): *Verfassungen für ein ziviles Europa*, Baden-Baden (Nomos) 1994, pp. 91-130.

JOERGES, CHRISTIAN: „Taking the Law Seriously. On Political Science and the Role of Law in the Process of European Integration", *European Law Journal*, 2 (1996), pp. 105-135.

JOERGES, CHRISTIAN: „Wirtschaftsrecht, Nationalstaat und der Vertrag von Maastricht", *Leviathan*, 21 (1993), pp. 493-516.

KAELBLE, HARTMUT: *Auf dem Weg zu einer europäischen Gesellschaft?*, München (Beck) 1987.

KIELMANSEGG, PETER GRAF: „Integration und Demokratie", in: MARKUS JACHTENFUCHS and BEATE KOHLER-KOCH (Eds.): *Europäische Integration*, Opladen (Leske + Budrich) 1996, pp. 47-71.

KOHLER, BEATE: „Der Abgeordnete als Vertreter des europäischen Volkes? Die Demokratietheorie vor der Bewährungsprobe", *Europarecht*, 13 (1978), pp. 333-350.

KOHLER-KOCH, BEATE and MARKUS JACHTENFUCHS: „Regieren in der Europäischen Union. Fragestellungen für eine interdisziplinäre Europaforschung", *Politische Vierteljahresschrift*, 37 (1996), pp. 537-556.

KOHLER-KOCH, BEATE: „Changing Patterns of Interest Intermediation in the European Union", *Government and Opposition*, 29 (1994), pp. 166-180.

KOHLER-KOCH, BEATE: „The Evolution of Organized Interests in the EC: Driving Forces, Co-Evolution or New Type of Governance?", in: HELEN WALLACE (Ed.): *Participation and Policy-Making in the European Union*, Oxford (Oxford University Press) 1996.

LEIBFRIED, STEPHAN: „The Social Dimension of the European Union. En Route to Positively Joint Sovereignty?", *Journal of European Social Policy*, 4 (1994), pp. 1-24.

LEPSIUS, M. RAINER: „Institutionenanalyse und Institutionenpolitik", in: BIRGITTA NEDELMANN (Ed.): *Politische Institutionen im Wandel (KZfSS Sonderheft 35/1995)*, Opladen (Westdeutscher Verlag) 1995, pp. 392-403.

LEPSIUS, M. RAINER: „Nationalstaat oder Nationalitätenstaat als Modell für die Weiterentwicklung der Europäischen Gemeinschaft", in: RUDOLF WILDENMANN (Ed.): *Staatswerdung Europas? Optionen für eine Europäische Union*, Baden-Baden (Nomos) 1991, pp. 19-40.

LUHMANN, NIKLAS: „Theoretische Orientierung der Politik", in: NIKLAS LUHMANN: *Soziologische Aufklärung 3. Soziales System, Gesellschaft, Organisation*, Opladen (Westdeutscher Verlag), 2nd ed. 1991, pp. 287-292.

LUHMANN, NIKLAS: *Politische Theorie im Wohlfahrtsstaat*, München/Wien (Olzog) 1981.

MAJONE, GIANDOMENICO: „The European Community. An ‚Independent Fourth Branch of Government'", in: GERT BRÜGGEMEIER (Ed.): *Verfassungen für ein ziviles Europa*, Baden-Baden (Nomos) 1994a, pp. 23-43.

MAJONE, GIANDOMENICO: „The Rise of the Regulatory State in Europe", *West European Politics*, 17: 3 (1994b), pp. 77-101.

MAJONE, GIANDOMENICO: *Independence vs. Accountability? Non-Majoritarian Institutions and Democratic Government in Europe*, Firenze (EUI Working Paper SPS No. 93/3) 1994c.

MARC, ALEXANDRE: „New and Old Federalism: Faithful to the Origins", *Publius* 9: 4 (1979), pp. 117-130.

MAYNTZ, RENATE, BERND ROSEWITZ, UWE SCHIMANK and RUDOLF STICHWEH: *Differenzierung und Verselbständigung. Zur Entwicklung gesellschaftlicher Teilsysteme*, Frankfurt a.M./New York (Campus) 1988.

MAYNTZ, RENATE: „Policy-Netzwerke und die Logik von Verhandlungssystemen", in: ADRIENNE HÉRITIER (Ed.): *Policy-Analyse. Kritik und Neuorientierung (PVS-Sonderheft 24)*, Opladen (Westdeutscher Verlag) 1993, pp. 39-56.

MESTMÄCKER, ERNST JOACHIM: „Politische und normativ-funktionale Legitimation der Europäischen Gemeinschaft", in: ERNST JOACHIM MESTMÄCKER: *Recht und ökonomisches Gesetz*, Baden-Baden (Nomos) 1978, pp. 82-99.

MESTMÄCKER, ERNST-JOACHIM (1994a): „Zur Wirtschaftsverfassung in der Europäischen Union", in: ROLF H. HASSE, JOSEF MOLSBERGER and CHRISTIAN WATRIN (Eds.): *Ordnung in Freiheit. Festgabe für Hans Willgerodt zum 70. Geburtstag*, Stuttgart (1994), pp. 263-292.

MESTMÄCKER, ERNST-JOACHIM (1994b): „On the Legitimacy of European Law", *Rabels Zeitschrift für ausländisches und internationales Privatrecht*, 58 (1994), pp. 615-635.

MORAVCSIK, ANDREW: *Why the European Community Strengthens the State. Domestic Politics and International Cooperation*, Cambridge (Harvard University, Center for European Studies, Working Paper No. 52) 1994.

PETERSMANN, ERNST-ULRICH: „Grundprobleme der Wirtschaftsverfassung der EG", *Aussenwirtschaft*, 48 (1993), pp. 389-424.

PRZEWORSKI, ADAM and HENRY TEUNE: *The Logic of Comparative Social Inquiry*, New York (Wiley-Interscience) 1970.

ROEMHELD, LUTZ: *Integraler Föderalismus. Modell für Europa. Ein Weg zur personalen Gruppengesellschaft* (Vol. 1: Geschichtliche Entwicklung, Vol. 2: Philosophie, Staat, Wirtschaft, Gesellschaft), München (Ernst Vögel) 1978.

RUGGIE, JOHN GERALD: „Territoriality and Beyond: Problematizing Modernity in International Relations", *International Organization*, 47 (1993), pp. 139-174.

SCHARPF, FRITZ W.: „Politiknetzwerke als Steuerungssubjekte", in: HANS-ULRICH DERLIEN, UTA GERHARDT and FRITZ W. SCHARPF (Eds.): *Systemrationalität und Partialinteresse. Festschrift für Renate Mayntz*, Baden-Baden (Nomos)1994, pp. 381-407.

SCHARPF, FRITZ W.: „Politische Optionen im vollendeten Binnenmarkt", in: MARKUS JACHTENFUCHS and BEATE KOHLER-KOCH (Eds.): *Europäische Integration*, Opladen (Leske + Budrich) 1996, pp. 109-140.

SCHARPF, FRITZ W.: „Versuch über Demokratie im verhandelnden Staat", in: ROLAND M. CZADA and MANFRED G. SCHMIDT (Eds.): *Verhandlungsdemokratie, Interessenvermittlung, Regierbarkeit. Festschrift für Gerhard Lehmbruch*, Opladen (Westdeutscher Verlag) 1993, pp. 25-50.

SCHERER, JOSEF: *Die Wirtschaftsverfassung der EWG*, Baden-Baden (Nomos) 1970.

SCHMITTER, PHILIPPE C. and WOLFGANG STREECK: *The Organization of Business Interests. A Research Design to Study the Associative Action of Business in Advanced Industrial Societies of Western Europe*, Berlin (Wissenschaftszentrum, Arbeitspapier IIMV dp 81-13) 1981.

SCHMITTER, PHILIPPE C.: „Representation and the Future Euro-Polity", *Staatswissenschaften und Staatspraxis*, 3 (1992), pp. 379-405.

SCHUPPERT, GUNNAR FOLKE: „Zur Staatswerdung Europas. Überlegungen zu Bedingungsfaktoren und Perspektiven der europäischen Verfassungsentwicklung", *Staatswissenschaften und Staatspraxis*, 5 (1994), pp. 35-76.

STRAUBHAAR, THOMAS: *Zur optimalen Größe eines integrierten Wirtschaftsraumes. Das Konzept des funktionalen Föderalismus*, Hamburg (Universität der Bundeswehr, Institut für Wirtschaftspolitik, Diskussionsbeiträge zur Wirtschaftspolitik Nr. 23) 1993.

STREIT, MANFRED E. and WERNER MUSSLER: „The Economic Constitution of the European Community. From ‚Rome' to ‚Maastricht'", *European Law Journal*, 1 (1995), pp. 5-30.

STUBB, ALEXANDER C.-G.: „A Categorization of Differentiated Integration", *Journal of Common Market Studies*, 34 (1996), pp. 283-295.

THERBORN, GÖRAN: *European Modernity and Beyond: The Trajectory of European Societies, 1945 - 2000*, London (Sage) 1995.

WEILER, JOSEPH H.H.: „Community, Member States and European Integration: Is the Law Relevant?", *Journal of Common Market Studies*, 21 (1982), pp. 39-56.

WEILER, JOSEPH H.H.: „The Community System: the Dual Character of Supranationalism", *Yearbook of European Law*, 1 (1981), pp. 267-306.

WEILER, JOSEPH H.H.: „The Transformation of Europe", *Yale Law Journal*, 100 (1991), pp. 2403-2483.

WILLKE, HELMUT: *Systemtheorie III: Steuerungstheorie. Grundzüge einer Theorie der Steuerung komplexer Sozialsysteme*, Stuttgart (Ehmke) 1995.

WINTER, GERD: „Drei Arten gemeinschaftlicher Rechtsetzung und ihre Legitimation", in: GERT BRÜGGEMEIER (Ed.): *Verfassungen für ein ziviles Europa*, Baden-Baden (Nomos) 1994, pp. 45-71.

ZÜRN, MICHAEL: „The Challenge of Globalization and Individualization. A View from Europe", in: HANS-HENRIK HOLM and GEORG SØRENSEN (Eds.): *Whose World Order? Uneven Globalization and the End of the Cold War*, Boulder (Westview) 1995, pp. 137-163.

Chapter 3

Democratic Legitimacy and the Role of the Commission

JANNE HAALAND MATLÁRY

When viewed with the conventional lenses of the separation of powers in national Western political systems, the Commission is an anomaly. It is neither an executor of government policy nor a government accountable to a parliament. It is clear that both its formal and informal roles warrant discussion in terms of democratic theory.

Although it was not much studied until the Single Market was launched in 1985, by now we possess a good number of empirical studies of the role of the Commission. These draw on developments after 1985, and investigate various issue areas of policy as well as stages in the decision-making process. Two important anthologies provide important analyses of the Commission: Nugent's edited volume *At the Heart of the Union: Studies of the European Commission* (1997) and Edwards and Spence' edited volume entitled *The European Commission* (1994). In addition, there are many case-studies that document various influences of the Commission in policy-making.

This chapter seeks to systematise some of the most salient findings from this literature and to evalute them in terms of democratic legitimacy. The empirical discussion is ordered around the themes of formal and informal roles played by the Commission, and a discussion of the empirical findings from various recent studies of the actual importance of the Commission in the post-85 period. Then we proceed to a discussion of various criteria of democratic legitimacy in the face of this empirical evidence of the Commission's role.

I. The Structure and Setting of the Commission

It has been said that the work of the Commission can be likened to the mating of elephants - there is a lot of noise and it takes a long time before there are any results. This does however not imply that the results that obtain are insignificant. The Commission is a complex institution with a plethora of activities. Before we can assess the role of this institution we need to arrive at an understanding of it and of its environment:

The Commission is legally speaking only the *collegium* of 20 commissioners, but in practise one uses the term to refer to the entire staff as well. The bureaucratic level counts some 13.000 people in 23 DGs, many of whom are experts in their respective fields. Merit is the official criterium for recruitment, but there are unofficial national quotas. The President of the Commission is *primus inter pares* - formally nothing more. He however has the exclusive right to attend European Council meetings, and has since 1987 participated in the World Economic Summits. He also has the largest *cabinet* - which is a staff of personal advisors. Individual commissioners have *cabinets* as well, which in sum consist of several hundred people. These staffs are important policy-makers in the coordination of policy and in the development of e.g. the President's policy initiative. The Delors *cabinet* has been singled out as being especially powerful and efficient, and whose work stood in stark contrast to the ordinary work of the DGs, which largely resent the *cabinet* system (Peterson 1994). The commissioners are evolving in 5 year terms, and they are appointed according to different national quotas, not by the Commission president. Portfolies are fought over, and once assigned, the commissioner is responsible only to himself - there is no procedure for a 'vote of no confidence' for the individual commissioner, but only for the entire *collegium*. This has however never happened. It is the European Parliament (EP) which can unseat the Commission.

Metcalfe notes that "for an organization dedicated to integration, the Commission is not itself well integrated" (Metcalfe 1992, p. 119). There is an 'unofficial' ranking of importance between DGs - like national ministries - and there are many cases of a lack of efficient coordination between DGs.

The various DGs do not correspond sharply to functional areas, and in terms of bureaucratic culture there seems to be agreement that hierarchical management predominates along with a traditional legalistic culture. Metcalfe, who is not concerned with the political role of the Commission, but with how efficient it is in terms of management, has severe reservations about its ability to perform its tasks in the 1992-process: he argues that the Commission is "under-resourced, under-staffed in many areas, over-stretched and inadequately managed" (ibid, p. 121). But this is not the only problem, argues he: if we look at implementation, there is infinite possibility for the member states to sabotage the latter. These conclusions are subscribed to by Peter Ludlow, perhaps the keenest long-term observer of the Commission (Ludlow 1991).

The decision-making process is open, access for interest groups is easy, and national bureaucrats are increasingly interrelated with Commission officials in formal and informal working groups. This phenomenon, called *engrenage*, includes as much as about 25% of e.g. German cival servants. These are mainly interrelated with Commission officials at the regional, viz. *Lander* level. One can thus talk about networks of issue-specific decision-makers that are operating in close-knit and long-term units. There are about 500 expert groups of a certain permanence, where "nationale und Kommisionsbeamte wirken intensiv zusammen" (Wessels 1992, p. 46). There are innumerable working groups (Commission plus national bureaucrats), advisory committees (Commission plus outside experts), the formal COREPER committees (Commission plus national bureaucrats). In this partly informal, partly formal process, organised as horizontal networks which bridge the state-EU divide, Commission experts deal with the same national experts time and again. The policy 'language' is professional, cast in expert terms, not in interest terms. This does of course not preclude the advocacy of national or industry interest under a professional, expert-term guise - quite the contrary - but demands that participants in the process command the professional aspects of a quite often very technical problem.

The Commission is dependent on a close and cooperative working relationship with the Council of Minsters and the EP. Ludlow never tires of pointing to this interrelatedness: "A conflictual model of Commission-Council relations is ..totally misleading" (Ludlow 1991, p. 103). After the Single European Act (SEA), the mutual interdependence between the Commission and the EP is much stronger.

The Commission is thus part of the Community structure - which does not ressemble a parliamentary system - and it functions in an interrelationship with other Community institutions and member state ministries. Policy-making takes place in many fora before a proposal is launched. Proposals are cleared with other DGs, and the whole Commission must approve them. Only routine matters are delegated to individual commissioners. Weekly meetings only take care of the politically sensitive issues.

It is perhaps often overlooked that the Commission represents the 'Community interest' - in the treaties it is charged with promoting this interest, which could be called 'integration'. It thus is not surprising that the Commission develops strategies that aim at integrative outcomes. We do not have to assume a 'bureaucratic politics' intention of consolidating and enhancing own institutional powers - the task given to the Commission is to enhance integration. This is a political aim, set out in the Rome Treaty.

II. The Formal Powers of the Commission

The formal powers of the Commission are laid out in the Rome Treaty: It is the *guardian* of the treaties - it can intervene in cases of non-compliance with e.g. competition legislation, and indeed does this increasingly in the post 85-period. It can use the Court or intervene alone. It has the the *exclusive right - and obligation - to initiate and formulate policy* within the terms of the treaty, and importantly, in order to 'further integration'. Finally, it is the executive branch of the Council and obliged to *implement* its policies. Here much is left to the member states themselves. The issue of implementation is relatively understudied in the literature on the states-EU relationship, but is a very important one in assessing the importance of the Commission.

However, in this role as well as in its general role, the emphasis has been on cooperation with member states, not on confrontation. This is very clearly spelt out in the informal 'rules of the game' that obtain between the states and the Commission. Lindberg and Scheingold provided the most extensive inventory of such practises in their work from 1970 (Lindberg and Scheingold 1970, p. 96). Based on their own in-depth study of the Commission's first years up to the crises wrought by de Gaulle, they state that the 'rules of the game' regulating the interaction between the states and the Commission strongly emphasize cooperative behaviour. The Commission rarely challenges member states directly apart from instances where it has supra-national competence and can deal directly with the states, firms, or individuals without any political process at the EU-level.

"The Commission can exercise a good deal of discretion that it can use to expand the scope of integration" notes Lodge.(Lodge 1989, p. 40). The exclusive *right of policy initiation* is therefore in this analysis of substantial interest. This includes the *goal setting* and 'operationalisation' of policy - the key role of the Commission's leader. Both Hallstein and Delors - the two Commission presidents that are generally considered to be the most able leadership figures - have been able to combine political vision with practical types of strategy. This is also possible because of the President's place in the European Council. But lofty goals may be easily disclosed as empty rhetoric unless they are tied to a practical progamme of policy. This was the ingenious combination that Delors and Cockfield produced - the internal market slogan coupled with a concrete set of proposals for its realisation. I will return to the role of leadership in the Commission - only here point out that the right to develop policy goals with a general European interest as the only limitation allows for a *strong potential leadership* role for the president of the Commission.

But policy initiation can occur at many levels below the president, and does. Ludlow reports that "the function of *animateur* permeates the whole structure and ethos of the institution" (Ludlow 1991, p. 97). The Commission, notes he, was formed with the *Commissariat du plan* as the model - the point was to produce policy ideas on a large scale. Once a vision has been agreed upon, there is the great opportunity of formulating issue-specific policy under this aegis that still conforms to it, but which is highly technical and specific, involving experts in the many working groups and fora.

The point here is that when the Commission provides a general goal to which member states agree, then this goal is the *reference point* and *legitimation* for the development of issue-specific policy, which also can be interpreted quite freely. This means that issue-specific policy makers in the various DGs may be very important actors. When there is conflict with interest groups, the Commission invokes the general mandate of this goal as a legitimation for issue-specific policy. This is a very powerful tool because the policy style in the Commission is as stated earlier, one that is *not* based on interest argumentation but on legal-technical arguments.

Summing up, the Commission has important formal roles but it depends on the cooperation with both the states and other Community institutions. It is not a major force in implementing policy or supervising the treaty obligations within the member states, and is in many ways small, often ill-coordinated, and unable to monitor the competition policy in the member states because it lacks the resources. This would also be politically controversial. The role of leadership and member state legitimacy appear to be major factors in explaining when the Commission's policy-initiating role is activated.

III. The Informal Roles of the Commission

The formal roles of the Commission enable it to play also important informal roles. The importance of the Commission's many roles may be seen better if we distinguish between arena and actor roles:

An actor influences the output of policy in an independent way, as a standard understanding of the concept goes (Sjøstedt 1977; Underdal 1992). The criteria for defining someone to be an actor must as a minimum include that there exists an ability to act at the outset - some degree of autonomy, some independent resources, and so on. But also arenas may be politically important. Underdal argues that they may be important for different reasons, and not necessarily in less ways than actors (Underdal 1992).

The Commission's *arena* roles include its agenda setting power and the ability to regulate access of participants to a considerable degree. By setting the agenda the Commission may shape the states' own agenda. The states will take into account the EU level activity and likely strategy when they make their own *The Commission may on this logic shape states agendas and consequently, interest formation.*

States are interested in their reputation, and will want to be constructive participants in international problem-solving. Rittberger et al. found the reputational factor to be very important in the political calculus of Russia and Germany in their study of East-West regimes (Rittberger et al. 1993). In the EU case, we can expect there to be a high value attached to reputation in the sense that no member state will want to be seen as one that obstructs the policy- making process. This is particularly important in the post-85 period where qualified majority voting (QMV) ensures that states can eventually be outvoted. The general record on fulfilling expectations is important. After the introduction of QMV the laggards are visible - it is much more important to be active and cooperative, not try to stop new policies.

Further, by defining new problems and new solutions to them, by making wide-spread use of experts, the Commission may define solutions to new problems and induce *learning* on the part of the states. Ernst Haas has discussed the notion that 'knowledge is power' in his book by the same title (Haas 1990). The Commission may thus be an important arena for learning, and in some types of policy it may even be warranted to speak of 'epistemic communities' (P. Haas 1993). Its policy language is essentially technical-legal, about the 'objective' solutions to problems; that is, issues are always depolitisized.

Turning to the *actor* roles of the Commission, there exists as discussed above formal autonomous powers to act in certain policy areas. In competition policy the Commission has the formal autonomy to act in a way that also has direct applicability and thus effect in member states and on members states. DGIV does intervene very forcefully in cases of hindrances to competition. The European Court of Justice (ECJ) has been found to very often support Commission moves againt companies and member states. Together these two institutions act autonomously. Thus, like a state, the Commission has formal autonomous acting powers in selected policy areas. It can use para. 90 of the Treaty of Rome to pass directives without Council approval; it can fine companies suspected of cartelization or price fixing, and can intervene as an antitrust actor (Montagnon 1990; Jacobs and Stewart-Clark 1990; Louis 1990). These powers are clearly supra-national and autonomous, but they may be more able to be activated in some periods than in others. The formal powers are thus 'resource bases' for various informal roles.

Summing up, the Commission can *directly apply* policy in member states, and it can *issue binding directives* in some policy areas on its exclusive authority. It thus has formal actor capacity, and several occasions for using its formal powers. These serve to enhance its role in informal ways, for instance in the policy-making phase, the Commission can use its skills in *timing decision-making* and in presenting *better informed proposals* than member states. As any bureaucracy, it represents *profound knowledge* about the issue areas in question, although the importance of knowledge in policy-making is a contested one. Further, the Commission can utilise its skills as *broker between national styles* and interests to steer outcomes to its own preferences, yet the actual importance of this in terms of outcomes of policy is undetermined.

IV. Empirical Evaluation: How Important Is the Commission?

In areas where the EU shares competence with the states or has exclusive competence, we expect the importance of EU actors to be a major one. Where the EU has exclusive competence, such as in the common commercial policy (CCP) and common agricultural policy (CAP), as well as in the prospective Economic and Monetary Union (EMU), the formal role of the Commission is well-established. We are thus not concerned with these policy areas here, but discuss how the Commission uses its formal roles in such areas to extend its powers into new policy areas.

There is a growing literature which shows that the Commission and the ECJ both use formal and informal powers to make an impact and to enhance their institutional roles vis-a-vis the states. I will not discuss this literature here in any comprehensive way, but highlight the types of influence and the issue areas that are particularly important:

First, the story of the expansionism of the ECJ is well-documented. Throughout the 70es it has ruled to expand its role and implicitly that of the Commission by establishing legal supremacy over national legislation as well as so-called direct effect of EU legislation (Burley and Mattli 1993; Weiler 1991). This *inter_alia* entails that national courts often ask for a preliminary judgement from the ECJ, which in turn means that the ECJ is the sole interpreter of who is 'der Herr der Vertrage'. Lower national courts may thus circumvent higher national courts, creating direct links with the ECJ. The competence of the various EU institutions is not well established in the treaties, and the interpretation by the ECJ has not been contested until the *Bundesverfassungsgericht* contested the legality for Germany to accede to the TEU. However, in most instances the supremacy of the ECJ is not a contested one. The ECJ has often ruled in favour of the Commission's views in cases where the latter has been challenged. Heritier argues that the ECJ often employs a strategy which she calls 'testing the waters'-scheme which gradually widens the competence of ECJ rulings: First a general principle is established in one ruling, later it is applied specifically (1996, p. 30).

ECJ rulings have direct implications for member states, and the 'constitutionalisation' of the treaties is the basis for *polity*-building in the sense that firms and individuals can appeal directly to the Court, bringing cases before it. The 'mutual recognition' in the *Cassis de Dijon* case (1979) meant a tremendous increase in leverage to the Single Market project. *This evolution has enabled the Commission to act with the backing of the Court when there have been conflicts with member states over interpretations of competences.* The insitutional setting of the Commission is therefore a favourable one, not only in terms of formal powers, but also in relation to the Court.

As outlined above, the formal and informal roles of the Commission are manifold. It is the formal *agenda-setter* as the initiator of policy. Marks et al. remark that "in political systems that involve many actors, complex procedures and multiple veto points, the power to set the agenda is extremely important" (1996, p. 356). There is no consensus on the importance of this function in the literature or on how to measure the impact of agenda-setting. Several authors of case studies from the post-85 period however conclude that the Commission's agenda-setting was very important to the outcome of policy-making (Matlary 1997; Sandholz 1992 and 1993; Cowles 1995; Cameron 1992). Marks et al. conclude that "the Commission is a critical actor in the policy initiation phase, whether one looks at formal rules or practise" (1996, p. 361).

By setting the agenda, the Commission may succeed in creating new policies at the EU-level. In the telecommunications sector, the Commission *created a new policy* to which the states responded. Sandholz (1992) shows that all policy ideas and proposals consistently emanated from the Commission itself, and that even those states that had a national deregulatory policy in the sector, like the UK, were rather passive in the policy process. There was in most instances *however no national policy in the issue area* before the Commission proposed policy. We cannot assume that national positions are formulated *prior* to the policy-making process itself.

Sandholz's findings concur with my own. In energy policy, an issue area which, like telecommunications, had been characterized by state monopolies, it was the Commission and not the member states that formulated policy. There were no major policy ideas that came from the states, and in the case of the UK, which had already deregulated its energy sector, there was only *reactive, not proactive* policy behaviour (Matlary 1997).

Further, the role of the Commission in *linking up with sub-national actors* and enabling them to act vis-a-vis national governments is beginning to be well documented (Heritier 1996; Marks et al 1996; Hoogue 1996). Likewise, the Commission is the 'linking-pin' of large professional networks of state executives, but we know little about the importance of shared knowledge and expertise and the moulding of professional loyalties that can be assumed to take place in these networks. We know, however, that the proposals from the Commission are often more or less adopted as policy output, such as in the case of the Delors Report on EMU, which was largely transscribed into the TEU as was (see e.g. Dyson 1994).

The Commission has also been shown to *exert leadership*, such as under Delors (Ross 1994; Cowles 1995; Sandholtz and Zysman 1989; Camreon 1992). However, one might add that it has also been amply shown not to exert leadership; thus there is neither agreement on the conditions for such leadership in the literature, nor on the theoretical or empirical importance of it.

The degrees of formal-legal powers - competences - varies with issue areas. Sometimes a *weak or almost non-existing power to act in one issue area may successfully be coupled with competition policy by* defining the policy issues in competition terms. For instance, energy company structures in member states - often monopolies - were the subject of interventions from DGIV when energy policy became a sub-set of internal market issues. The Commission may thus redefine issue areas in ways that bend them towards the areas where it itself yields powers. This has happened in the post-85 period.

Sandholz' (1992) empirical findings are highly interesting in this respect: Arguing that the Commission played the leading role in creating an internal telecommunications market, he found that it initiated a tough deregulatory approach against the interests of the states in basing a controversial directive in 1988 on paragraph 90, which does not require Council approval. This directive, creating an open market in terminals and services, was based on paragraph 86, arguing that monopolies in the sector abused their dominant position. It was feared that in using paragraph 100a, the directive would be delayed by about two years and watered down considerably in the Council negotiations. The member states agreed with the policy objective of the directive, but they strongly disagreed about the use of paragraph 90 which would "set a precendent for Community activism" (Ibid., p. 263). Nontheless DGIV proceeded, and issued the directive. France filed a case with the ECJ immediately, challenging the Commission's use of paragraph 90. Germany, Italy, and Belgium supported the French case in the Court. But the Court ruled in favour of the Commission's use of paragraph 90.

Also in the electricity sector the Commission clearly intensified the application of the competition legislation in the post-85 period. There was thus an intelligent use of 'spill-over' here: since the Commission has no competence in energy policy, it *first used the competition legislation in obvious ar-*

eas where it applied, like transportation and telecommunications, in order to set a precedent for defining energy policy as essentially being about deregulation.

Summing up, in the post-1985 period, the Commission has been found to *inter alia exert leadership, set the agenda, define new policy programs, use the formal powers of the CCP in an expansionist manner, and enable new sub-national actors by inter-linkages and money transfers.* Its intangible, informal power resources may be less conspicous than its tangible resources, but this does not mean that they were less important. Thus, without discussing how the evidence of Commission power ought to be assessed and measured - a major question for empirical theory - it is a safe conclusion that the Commission used both its formal and informal powers in the post-85 period. How can this exercise of power be legitimated in terms of democratic norms?

V. Normative Evaluation: How Democratic?

There has not been much scholarly discussion of the role of the Commission in terms of democratic theory. Usually one has looked at the overall relationship between the EU institutions and concluded that as long as it neither ressembles an intergovernmental system nor a federation, it is not democratic. The democratic norms that one judges by are those of the nation-state's democracy: government accountable to parliament; parliament elected by the people; the separation of powers, and so on. The EU system of governance is in comparison a hybrid: The Commission is only accountable to parliament as a *collegium*, but it is not a government, it is an executive yet also a policy-maker with specific powers. It has formal supra-national powers in some issue areas given it by national governments. The Commission is a real political actor in many issue areas, but has little or no power in other areas. The ECJ's role is likewise instituted and accepted by the states, but its role has developed in ways that probably would not be accepted anew today. When seen in an evolutionary pespective, the Commission as well as the ECJ have roles that go beyond the ones envisaged for them by the states. In periods of much general legitimacy for EU-activity, these roles are enhanced.

In general, it would seem that there is little point in assessing the Commission's role in terms of democratic norms that derive from national political systems. Nontheless some of these norms must be judged as democratic 'minimum norms', but they have to be de-coupled from the way they have been institutionalised in national democracies.

The most important democratic norm is in our view accountability. Others include participation, formal political equality, some degree of economic equality, freedom of speech and association, and so forth. The chapter by Nentwich in this volume discusses proposals for democratic reforms ir the intergovermental conference (IGC-96). There is no agreement on the relative importance of these norms, but they are all present in modern democracies to some degree or other. Below we will confine our remarks to a discussion of accountability:

In the EU system of governance, democratic accountability can be argued to exist to the extent that it is essentially an intergovernmental system. One presupposes that the democratic political process has taken place at the domestic level; prior to EU-level policy-making; and that the states are the main actors, in control of the EU. However, this intergovernmental model of the EU is not true to facts for two reasons: One, the EU is a hybrid consisting of supra-national and intergovernmental elements; and two, an actor like the Commission plays both formal and informal political roles that cannot be accounted for on this intergovernmentalist view, which assumes away the political importance of the Commission. As we have seen, the Commission is a political actor in its own right - at times more important than at other times; but even its formal roles cannot be legitimated in terms of democratic theory based on the parliamentary model of governance.

Judged in terms of the norm accountability; how can the various roles of the Commission be justified? Accountability here will mean some way of recalling delegated powers, and in the EU it is the EP which can unseat the Commission, not the Council of Ministers. If the EU moves in a more federal direction, this role is becoming more important. In the intergovernmental conference 1996-97 the Commission itself proposes enhanced powers of control on the part of the EP (Commission Report for the Reflection Group, 1996). Accountability is also proposed increased by ensuring much more transparency in the Commission's work, by simplifying procedures for decision-making, and by ensuring that the principle of subsidiarity is adhered to. The latter has been sought implemented by the Commission since the TEU by its evaluation of the need for Community action each time it has proposed legislation.

Heritier (1996) has surveyed attempts by the Commission to institute forms of democratic participation and accountability in new ways. Arguing that "the Commission has taken a number of small, yet important steps to expand public support for existing Euroepan policies by increasing the accountability and transparency of European policy-making" (1996, p. 3), she calls these attempts 'substitute forms of democratic legitimation'. She notes that the Commission uses at least two strategies in enhancing its role: the 'Russian doll strategy' which starts with framework legislation for then to be followed by a large volume of specific rulings; and 'coalition-building' with sub-state actors as well as national bureaucrats, and argues that the Commission realises that its needs public support and legitimacy for these policies. Finding new ways of creating accountability and possibilities of participation is thus also of primary political interest to the Commission.

The Commission's strong insistence on transparency in the policy-making process in its opinion to the Reflection Group is also evident in its attempt to institute such transparency in actual directives (1996). In environmental directives which require national reporting, the Commission has added a clause which ensures the right of public access to information. Thus, it not only encourages transparency as a way of creating accountability and perhaps participation, but also strengthens the tie between Euroepan citizens and the EU. The former are encouraged to turn to the Commission to report lack of implementation of directives or policies.

Further, the Commission tries to institute new forms of participation by oppositional interests groups like environmental action groups, citizens' initiatives, etc. The point here is to reach a broad consensus about policy through this process, which is called 'concerted bipartite policy planning' (Heritier 1996, p. 23).

Majone has suggested that delegated powers to autonomous expert-based agencies at the national level or the Commission can be subjected to accountability if the mandate given is specific. If the delegee performs well; that is, fulfills its mandate, there is no need for recall, and the criterion of accountability is met (Majone 1994). However, this view rests upon the premise that it is possible to de-politisise policy-making, and that experts can be controlled by other experts. In the case of the Commission, there is clearly much political conflict involved at all stages and in all types of policy-making; and it is unlikely that independent experts will exist outside the national-EU networks that make up many working groups. The system of 'engrenage' would rather seem to create one inter-related system of experts where political generalists have little say in the actual formulation of policy.

In sum, the political resources of the Commission - expert knowledge, resources for networking, the command of timing to set an agenda and of how to define specific policies - all seem very difficult to subject to any kind of effective democratic accountability or popular participation. Further, it is entirely unclear on which principles such accountability or participation should be instituted as long as there is no institutional design for the EU-states relationship that takes into account its hybrid character. The Commission tries to develop such a design in a piecemeal manner by strengthening the federalist logic and its own ties to horizontal expert networks and regional actors, while the member states continue to adhere to the intergovernmental logic as a strategy of preserving EU policy-making as their own 'foreign policy prerogative'. The ECJ likewise builds its own supra-national legal basis which is increasingly incongruent with the role of national judiciaries and their institutional balance in the system of separation of powers. The IGC-96 seeks to make the EU 'democratic'. This is largely a vasted effort as long as political actors do not agree on a fundamental political design for the EU on which the institionalisation of norms such as accountability and participation must be based.

References

BURLEY, A.-M., WEILER, J.: "Europe before the Court: A Political Theory of Legal Integration", *International Organization,* 47 (1993).

CAMERON, D.: "The 1992 Initiative: Causes and Consequences", in: A. SBRAGIA (Ed.): *Europolitics: Institutions and Policy-Making in the 'New' European Community*, Washington (Brookings Institution) 1992.

Commission Report for the Reflection Group, 1996.

COWLES, M.-G.: "Setting the Agenda for a New Europe: The ERT and EC 1992", *Journal of Common Market Studies,* 33, No. 4 (1995).

DYSON, K.: *Elusive Union. The Process of Economic and Monetary Union in Europe,* London (Longman) 1994.

EDWARDS, G. and SPENCE: *The European Commission*, 1994.

HAAS, E.: *When Knowledge is Power*, Berkeley (U. of California Press) 1990.

HAAS, P.: "Epistemic Communities and the Dynamics of International Environmental Cooperation", in: RITTBERGER (Ed.): *Regimetheory and international relations.*

HERITIER, A.: *Policy-Making by Subterfuges: Interest Accomodation, Innovation and Substitute Democratic Legitimation in Europe*, paper, EUI, 1996.

HOOGHE, L. (Ed.): *Cohesion Policy and European Integration: Building Multi-Level Governance*, Oxford (Oxford U. Press) 1996.

JACOBS, D. and STEWART-CLARK, J.: *Competition Law in the EC*, London (Kogan-Page) 1990.

KEOHANE, R.: "Multilateralism: An Agenda for Research", *International Journal*, XLV (1990).

LINDBERG, L.: *The Political Dynamics of European Economic Integration*, Stanford (Stanford University Press) 1963.

LINDBERG, L. and SCHEINGOLD, S.: *Europe's Would-be Polity: Patterns of Change in the EC*, N.J. (Prentice-Hall: Englewood Cliffs) 1970.

LODGE, J.: "EC Policy-making: Institutional Considerations", in: J. LODGE (Ed.): *The EC and the Challenge of the Future*, London (Pinter) 1992.

LOUIS, J.-V.: *The Community Legal Order*, Luxembourg (Office for Official Publications for the EC) 1990.

LUDLOW, P.: "The European Commission", in: R. KEOHANE and S. HOFFMANN (Eds.): *The New European Community: Decision-Making and Institutional Change*, Boulder (Westview Press) 1991.

MAJONE, G.: "Independence vs. Accountability: Non-Majoritarian Institutions and Democratic Government in Europe", paper, EUI, 1994.

MARKS, G.: "Structural Policy in the EC", in: A. SBRAGIA (Ed.): *Europolitics: Institutions and Policy-Making in the New European Community*, Washington (Brookings Institution) 1992.

MATLARY, J.H.: *Energy Policy in the European Union*, London (Macmillan) 1997.

McGOWAN, F.: *The Struggle for Power in Europe: Competition and Regulation in the Electricity Industry*, London (RIIA) 1993.

MAYER, P., RITTBERGER, V. and ZURN, M.: *Regime Theory: State of the Art and Perspectives*, in: RITTBERGER, op.cit.

METCALFE, L.: "After 1992: Can The Commission Manage Europe?", *Australian Journal of Public Administration*, 51, No.1 (March 1992).

MONTAGNON, P. (Ed.): *European Competition Policy*, London (Pinter) 1990.

NUGENT, N.: *The Government and Politics of the European Union*, London (Macmillan) 1994.

NUGENT, N. (Ed): *At the heart of the union. Studie of the European Commission*, London (Macmillian) 1997.

PETERS, B. G.: "Bureaucratic Politics and the Institutions of the EC", in: SBRAGIA, *op.cit.*

PETERSON, J.: "Playing the Transparency: Consultation and Policy-making in the European Commission", *CEPS paper*, Brussels, March 1994.

ROSS, G.: *Jacques Delors and European Integration*, Oxford (Oxford University Press) 1994.

ROSENTHAL, G.: *The Men behind the Decisions: Cases in European Policy-making*, D.C. Massaccutes (Heath: Lexington) 1975.

SANDHOLTZ, W., ZYSMAN, J.: "1992: Recasting the European Bargain", *World Politics*, 42 (1989).

SANDHOLTZ, W.: "Institutions and Collective Action: The New Telecommunications in Western Europe", *World Politics*, January, 45, No. 2 (1993).

SANDHOLTZ, W.: *High-Tech Europe: The Politics of International Cooperation*, Berkeley (University of California Press) 1992.

SCHMITTER, P.: *Interests, Powers, and Functions: Emergent Properties and Unintended Consequences*, (unpublished paper) Stanford University 1992.

SJØSTEDT, G.: *The External Role of the European Community*, Westmead, Hampshire (Saxon House) 1977.

UNDERDAHL, A.: "Arena or Actor? The Role of IGOs in International Environmental Management", Memo, CICERO, 1992.

VAHL, R.: "The European Commission's Leading Role: The Conditions for Effectiveness", paper presented at the Inaugural Pan-European Conference in International Studies, Heidelberg, 16-20.9.1992.

WESSELS, W.: "Staat und (westeuropaische) Integration: Die Fusionsthese", in: M. KREILE (Ed.): *Politische Vierteljahrschrift*, special issue 23 (1992).

YOUNG, O.: "Political Leadership and Regime Formation: On the Development of Institutions in International Society", *International Organization*, 45 (1991).

YOUNG, O. and OSHERENKO, G.: *Polar Politics. Creating International Environmental Regimes*, Ithaca (Cornell University Press) 1993.

WIELER, J.: "The Transformation of Europe", *Yale Law Review*, 100 (1991).

Chapter 4

The EU Intergovernmental Conference 1996/97: The Moment of Constitutional Choice for a Democratic Europe?[1]

MICHAEL NENTWICH

---

1 A previous version of this paper has been presented in the workshop "The Political Theory of European Constitutional Choice" at the ECPR Joint Sessions of Workshops Oslo 29 March - 3 April 96; I am most grateful to the participants of this workshop for their valuable input. The paper is based on a book written by GERDA FALKNER and me (FALKNER/NENTWICH [1995],) and on two working papers of the Vienna 1996 IGC research group (GRILLER/NENTWICH/FALKNER/DROUTSAS/FORGÓ) dealing with the initial positions (IEF Working Paper No. 20, June 1996) and the interim results of the Dublin-II summit (IEF Working Paper No. 25, January 1997).

I. Introduction

The sixth major intergovernmental conference (IGC) of the European Union[2] started 29 March 1996. Preceding this conference, three main developments led to a vivid reform debate among experts, academics, and the EC institutions:

First, during the difficult ratification process of the Maastricht Treaty, it became obvious that the "Maastricht Union" marked a still unsatisfactory stage of the institutional development at the European level. The pertinent issue of the democratic deficit and lacking legitimacy of the Union's decision-making structure were highlighted during numerous debates at both European and national levels; also the call for more transparency in the working of the institutions, the question of subsidiarity and hence the division of competences/powers between the Union and its Member states were discussed intensively. Second, the perspective of a Union further enlarged to the East and South made it clear that the institutional mechanisms designed for a Community of only six members which had until then only been adapted mechanically, without changing the original principles, would not match up with the needs of a Union of some 28 Member states. Third, the formal agenda of the IGC as agreed upon in the Maastricht Treaty (Article N) has been widened accordingly to the two first developments. During 1995/96, these three developments converged into a genuine constitutional debate, and some thought that it might well be that the negotiations during the present IGC would lead to a qualitative leap in the development of the Union.

This paper addresses the following key issues of the IGC 1996/97: What institutional and procedural reforms are in the pipeline? And: What are the proposals for the future relationship between the Union and the Member states? Based on earlier contributions to this reform process[3] and, in particu-

---

2 1950/51: ECSC; 1956/57: EEC, Euratom; 1965: Merger Treaty; 1985/86: Single European Act; 1990/92: Maastricht Treaty; (there have been further IGCs leading to the four enlargements of the Union; with respect to Groenland, the Antilles; and with respect to certain budgetary provisions).

3 I.e. the various academic and expert contributions in the years 1993/94; the reports of the so-called reflection group which prepared the IGC agenda; of the EU institutions, in particular of the European Commission, and of the Institutional Committee of the EP; and the various contributions by the Mem-

lar, on the so-called Dublin-II paper in which the Irish Presidency tried to summarise the state of the negotiations in December 1996, I shall try to draw a multifaceted picture of this debate as it stands at half-time.

II. Democratic Issues

1. The Role of the European Parliament vis-à-vis the Council

The codecision procedure worked surprisingly well according to the accounts of all three institutions involved (Council 1995; Miller 1995; Commission 1995). However, a number of further questions are being raised with a view to future democratic reforms of the European Union's procedures. I shall group them under three major headings: first, proposals on the reform of specific details or certain stages of the codecision procedure; second, introduction of a uniform decision-making procedure for the Union; and third, establishment of a two-chamber-system.

(1) Codecision seems to be at the heart of many considerations about the future decision-making structure of the Union. Most advocate simplification and clarification of the rules as laid down in Article 189b ECT. Some also make detailed proposals for changes to the codecision rules.

The most elaborated proposals are to be found in the EP's resolution (1995, pt. 30). Central is the elimination of the possibility for the Council to act unilaterally by reconfirming its Common Position in the event of non-agreement. Thus, the major imbalance between Parliament's and Council's stand in the procedure would come to an end and Article 189b would indeed merit its label 'codecision'. Other EP proposals aim at simplifying and shortening the procedure in cases of obvious agreement between the two institutions.

At half time of the IGC, the Irish Presidency states the general will to improve this procedure and presents a new version of Article 189b ECT on the basis of the negotiations. The EP's proposals are incorporated in it to a large extent. However, perfect procedural equality between it and the Council is still not established in the Irish proposal.

---

ber states of the Union (for an in-depth analysis of these earlier inputs, see FALKNER/NENTWICH [1995]; GRILLER et al. [1996]).

(2) Ever since the original Rome Treaties entered into force, based on a comparatively simple decision-making model, the procedural rules became both more complicated and more numerous. New procedures include the complicated budget procedure; the co-operation, codecision and assent procedures; specific provisions for economic and monetary union (EMU), CSFP, as well as justice and home affairs (JHA). Including all sub-variants, there are more then twenty different procedures in use and some are admittedly hard to understand in all details, even by insiders. In addition, the implementation procedures (i.e. the famous committee procedures nick-named 'comitology') "do not operate with a particularly high degree of openness" (Commission 1995, p. 23).

According to the Commission, additional weaknesses have become obvious: the continuing divergence between legislative procedures and the budgetary procedure[4], and the lack of logic in the choice of the various procedures and the different fields of activity where they apply (1995, p. 23). It also criticises sharply that, in the institutions' day-to-day business, the proliferation of procedures harms the internal operation of the Union, because it creates conflict over legal bases.

Accordingly, many have argued in recent times that for the sake of transparency and continuing citizens' support for the integration process, a simplification was indispensable. The most far-reaching proposal is thus, evidently, the introduction of one single legislative procedure, possibly applied with different majority requirements such as in the various national political systems. However, the Commission itself is not very explicit in that regard: it advocates a "radical simplification" of legislative processes (1995, p. 14). With respect to the second and third pillar of the European Union, however, the Commission is far from openly advocating uniform procedures. It rather puts forward the argument that concerning the CFSP, the EP "plays a role similar to that of national parliaments in relation to national foreign policy" (1995, p. 14) – without mentioning the fact that national parliaments may dismiss national governments, and may *de iure* oppose government action by legislation, which is not the case for the Parliament at the EU level. By contrast, the Commission argues that in the area of JHA, "questions (...) are

4 The classic example of this divergence concerns the common agricultural policy: Parliament adopts the general budget, of which roughly half is devoted to this policy, on whose substance Parliament is, however, only 'consulted'.

likely to have a direct effect on individuals' basic rights and public freedoms", so that "they actually warrant a greater degree of parliamentary control especially where binding legal instruments are involved" (1994, pt. 14; see also 1996, pt. 17). According to the Commission, one uniform decision-making procedure could, at best, apply within the EC and the third pillar of the Union. The same has been argued by the Economic and Social Committee (ESC; see ESC 1995, pt. I.5.9 and I.5.10).

This line of reasoning is also followed by the EP, which in its Bourlanges/Martin (1995) and Dury/Meij-Weggen 1996 reports takes a pragmatic stance by not asking for codecision without exception, but only for consultation within the CFSP. Within the first pillar and JHA, however, the EP is a strong advocate for a uniform decision-making procedure in legislative matters: it wants the number of procedures to be cut to only two: codecision, and assent only in 'constitutional matters' (Dury/Meij-Weggen-Report 1996, pt. 19.6).

This view seems to be widely shared if we look at other contributions to the current reform debate. The Federal Trust for Education and Research Round Table, for instance, wants codecision to apply to virtually all Community legislation (1995, p. 19 f). The assent procedure should be kept for Treaty amendments and revenue ceiling, while consultation is again suggested for the field of the CFSP (similar: Justus Lipsius 1995, pp. 36 and 46). The Europäische Strukturkommission (1994, p. 35) elaborates a specific model whose eye-catching characteristic is indeed simplicity: initiative by the Commission; where appropriate consultation of the ESC, as well as the Committee of the Regions; then adoption (with or without amendments) by the EP, and adoption in the Council. If the latter cannot arrive at the necessary majority, a Conciliation Committee consisting of equal numbers of Council and Parliamentary representatives may search for a compromise solution to be adopted by both chambers.

The Irish report of December 1996 establishes that 'codecision' will most likely *not* be the only procedure in the future; in particular the co-operation procedure will be applicable in EMU matters, and the assent and consultation procedures will persist. The latest Commission's report on the scope of the codecision procedure (1996a) distinguishes between 'legislative' and 'executive matters'. In the first cases codecision is being advocated, in the latter only consultation. However, the Commission's and the EP's (1996) criteria to distinguish between the two are still different, and Ireland reports that there is still no consensus on this question in the IGC. As in many other institutional questions, the Dublin-II paper articulates hopes that the question might be settled in a package deal in a very late stage of the conference.

(3) Extending the field of application of Article 189b ECT to other areas of Union competence on the one hand, and amending the procedure in order to balance the respective powers of the Council and the EP, on the other, may be seen as steps towards a fully-fledged two-chamber-system within European legislation. Quite obviously, such a development is the EP's main goal of the IGC – despite the fact that the notion of a two-chamber-system is not being used. The above mentioned proposals concerning amendments to Article 189b ECT combined with the extension of the codecision procedure to a wider scope if not to virtually all fields of Union activities [except for the Common Foreign and Security Policy (CFSP)] virtually builds up to a two-chamber system. This would consist of the Council as the representation of the Member states (quasi a 'European Senate') and the EP representing the European peoples (quasi a 'European House of Representatives').

This follows the lines drawn by the Herman Report to the previous EP (1994, Article 32), under whose proposed Constitution the Parliament and the Council would have been put on an equal footing, as they would both have had to pass each legislative act, by specific majorities according to the type of law.

It is hardly surprising that the two other major EC institutions, the Council and the Commission, have been reluctant vis-à-vis this far-reaching option (thus, they do not make any explicit proposals in this regard). In the Member states' statements at the beginning of the IGC, we do not find any explicit statement in this regard (Griller et al. 1996, pp. 72 ff.). However, the German Bundesrat asked for joint decision-making powers for the EP whenever the Council decides by a majority (German Bundesrat 1995). This constitutes one specific version of the much-debated division of parliamentary control between the national and the European level: whenever the national governments can – at least theoretically – be controlled by the national parliaments, the latter should stay responsible, while the supranational EP should control in those cases where single national governments can be outvoted. The EP, by contrast, would clearly adhere to the more integrationist model, arguing that national parliaments are busy with the national agendas and have no means to fully overview European politics. Thus, the specifically elected European parliamentarians should be the responsible democratic co-actor in all European legislation.

An alternative, pro-nationally oriented model is advocated by the European Constitutional Group (1993, 2b, p. 10) who suggests a three-chamber-system, with the parliamentary side consisting of two bodies: the "Chamber of Parliamentarians" with representatives of the national parliaments, and the "Union Chamber", i.e. a smaller version of the directly elected EP. Both bodies and the Council would have to give their assent to any Union measure. The problem of double workload and split attention for the delegated national parliamentarians, however, is not taken into consideration by this Group.

Two other expert contributions, by the Europäische Strukturkommission (1994, p. 32) and Justus Lipsius (1995, pp. 36 and 49) respectively, answer the question of a two-chamber-system to the affirmative. Facing the fact that the Union has taken a number of important competences from the Member states, the same standards in terms of democracy should apply according to the Europäische Strukturkommission. This relies on the consideration that the importance of democratic legitimacy grows along with the number and weight of decisions taken at a specific level. If the indirect democratic legitimacy via national election of the governments represented in the Council of Ministers might have been sufficient in the early days of EEC integration, the Europäische Strukturkommission does not consider the increase of competences for the EP within the Maastricht reforms to be sufficient. Considering, in addition, the persisting lack of European social identity, the Europäische Strukturkommission considers that only a system of double representation could offer a satisfying base of legitimacy for the Union. A combination of European and national resources of legitimacy are accordingly suggested, crystallised in a two-chamber system. The Council and the EP should decide all essential European acts on an equal footing – thus combining both the democratic principle[5] and the principle of participation of the lower levels within the multi-tiered system. No decision should be taken without the consent of either chamber (1994, pp. 34 ff.).

At half time of the IGC, the issue seems *almost* settled: there might be equal weight for the EP and the Council (in so far as Article 189b applies) and there will be one standard procedure in most cases; to call this a two-chamber-system, however, seems still premature not least because of the distinctive role of the Council in many other areas.

5 The EP has to be decisive because effective control of the European policy process via national Parliaments is seen to be de facto impossible.

2. The Role of the Commission in Decision-Making

At the national level, the right to propose legislation is usually not restricted to one actor. Not only the governments, but also committees of parliaments or groups of MPs, and sometimes even (large) groups of citizens, have the right of initiative. In the context of the Union's decision-making procedures, by contrast, the right of initiative is in principle granted exclusively to the Commission. However, the Council and, since the Maastricht Treaty, also the EP can request a specific proposal from the Commission. The Commission is of the opinion that "[s]uch requests do not require the Commission to put forward a proposal, but, under the code of conduct recently concluded with Parliament, the Commission will take the greatest possible account of them" (1995, p. 14). The main difference to the national systems is thus that national MPs can draft a legislative proposal and bring it to a vote in their parliament, while both chambers of the European legislation can suggest a topic for legislation, but can neither force the Commission to actually take the idea on board[6], nor have any influence on how the Commission formulates a relevant proposal[7]. This speciality of the EC system has been increasingly debated with a view to the IGC. Among the central arguments are that this distribution of powers is historically outdated and, thus, the present state of power distribution may be considered illegitimate: deciding what should be tackled by a legislature is a political question from which the democratically legitimated institutions should not be excluded. Furthermore, a right of initiative of the citizens (in the form of legislative petitions) is being discussed with a view to involving the Europeans in the EU decision-making structure and to enhancing its legitimacy (see below 5.).

The Commission itself, as one might expect, argues strongly in favour of preserving the exclusivity of its right of initiative, "if the inevitable confusion and lack of overall direction which would result from multiple competing sources of initiative is to be avoided" (1995, p. 3). Furthermore, preserving the exclusive right of initiative of the Commission seemed to be one of the few points of consensus in the Reflection Group (1995, pt. 109). As a surprise, compared to previous statements, the EP's resolution of May 1995

6 Article 175 ECT on legal actions for failure to act seems to apply in principle. However, the relevant provisions (Articles 138b and 152 ECT) are probably not specific enough to create a legal obligation for the Commission.

7 Except for the fact that, theoretically, a motion of censure might be voted against the Commission by the EP.

and the Dury/Meij-Weggen report 1996 suggest maintaining the Commission's right of initiative more or less unchanged. However, the Parliament requests that Article 138b (2) ECT should be altered to require the Commission to respond to Parliament's initiatives[8].

Accordingly, the Dublin-II paper includes no hint whether this debate had been taken up in the IGC or not. Most probably, no change will be made in this respect.

3. The Role of National Parliaments

During the past years, a tendency to increase the national parliaments' attention to the single governments' European policies prevailed. Yet, there has so far been little or no debate on any direct legislative role for national parliaments at the European level. Such ideas have only recently been thrown into the debate preceding the forthcoming IGC, by mainly the French polity. In its so-called Guéna Report, the French Senate seeks to enhance democratic legitimacy of the Union almost exclusively by giving the national parliaments competences at the Euro-level. Thus, representatives of the national parliaments sitting in a 'European Senate' should play a crucial role in questions of subsidiarity and in the intergovernmental pillars (Guéna 1995, pp. 14 and 39 f). Guéna also suggests that representatives of national parliaments participate in the formation of some Council delegations, and that all interinstitutional agreements be submitted to a simplified ratification procedure in the national parliaments. To better enable national parliaments to follow European policy debates, he calls for quicker transmission of Commission proposals. Other French politicians have also promoted the idea of involving the national parliaments in EC decision-making. The British tend to stress the role of the national parliaments for the legitimacy of the EC, too:

> The EP sees itself as the future democratic focus for the Union. But this is a flawed ambition, because the European Union is an associa-

8 Before that, the proposed Constitution of the HERMAN Report had distinguished between ordinary laws on the one hand, and constitutional laws on the other. The initiative for the latter could come from either the European Parliament, Council, Commission, or any Member state, while the first group could only be proposed by the Commission (HERMAN 1994, Article 32).

> tion of States, deriving its basic democratic legitimacy through national parliaments. That should remain the case (...) It is national parliamentary democracy that confers legitimacy on the European Council (John Major 1994, p. 8).

The British government wants to see the role of the national parliaments enhanced, without, however, suggesting a direct role for national parliaments at the European level.

Many commentators and politicians have stressed that a systematic division of tasks is necessary between the national parliaments and the EP. For example, Jacques Delors argued that a second parliamentary chamber consisting of national parliamentarians would confuse European citizens with regard to the tasks of either group (1995, p. 2).

The Santer Commission, while admitting that the "difficulties experienced in ratifying the Treaty in certain countries showed how important it is to involve the national parliaments in the work of European integration", also wants to keep national parliaments active at the national level. It suggests that improvements of their traditional role be sought, "in accordance with the internal rules of each Member state, both in shaping the position of each Member state in the Council and in monitoring the implementation of Union decisions at national level" (1995, pp. 16 f).

Within the EP, the future role of national parliaments was a quite controversial matter. In the end, the general approach chosen was to advocate "an EP-national parliaments partnership" in democratic control of EU matters (EP 1995, pt. 24). Within the field of the so-called first pillar, this strategy aims at improved co-operation between equivalent parliamentary committees of the sixteen assemblies[9]. Outside the first pillar, however, the EP wants to see democratic accountability "shared between both the EP and national parliaments". This aims at abolishing 'grey areas' of the Union's powers in which neither the EP nor the national parliaments have any power of control so far, and builds on a rather realist expectation of the future of the Union's pillar structure.

Within the academic input for the IGC, it is mainly the European Constitutional Group (1993, Article VII) which has promoted the establishment of

9 Furthermore, the EP requires opportunities for specialised bodies of national parliaments to discuss major European proposals with their ministers prior to Council meetings (this latter proposal is obviously mainly directed to the Member states because it concerns an internal matter).

an additional parliamentary body. Their "Chamber of Parliamentarians" would consist of representatives of the national parliaments in numbers close to the current weighted votes for qualified majority votes in the Council [then ranging from 13 to 3]. The members should be chosen every fifth year by the Parliament of that Member state from amongst its members. This chamber would have to give its assent to any (association) treaty. Before voting on any bill, the chamber would review whether the former falls within the powers delegated to the Union; whether there is any need for Community action and for regulation; and check costs and benefits. Most expert contributions, however, explicitly take a stance against direct and specific involvement of national parliamentarians at the level of European legislature (Federal Trust Round Table 1995, pp. 11 ff.; Ludlow/Ersbøll 1995, p. 50; Justus Lipsius 1995, pp. 36 f). The main arguments are:

A third chamber would further complicate the decision-making process: it would be either superfluous but expensive, or effective but potentially stultifying. The main 'European' function of national MPs is ensuring proper accountability of their own ministers in the Council. The second task of national MPs would be co-operation with MEPs in order to feed relevant concerns into the EP's legislative work. Therefore joint standing committees of MPs and MEPs are advocated to deal with matters such as fraud, the CFSP and JHA, where responsibilities are shared between the Union and the Member states. Some oppose also the recently much-debated widespread application of the 'Danish system' (now also 'Austrian system') of strict parliamentary control over national ministers which could, in the end, undermine the principle enshrined in Article 146 which insists that any member of the Council must be in a position to commit his or her country. Some 'softer' forms of participation for national MPs are suggested: the Commission should systematically request the opinion of national parliaments prior to adopting an important legislative initiative, for example via 'green books'. Governments should systematically organise consultation of their national Parliament before their representatives vote in the Council on legislative proposals. More frequent contacts should be organised between members of national parliaments and MEPs.

Even COSAC, the conference of EC bodies of national parliaments and the EP, rejected at its February 1995 meeting proposals to set up a new chamber consisting of representatives of the national parliaments (see Commission 1995, p. 16). Also the representatives of the Member states are against the creation of new institutions in this respect and consider that "the national parliament's role in relation to EU decision-making lies in the monitoring and control that each parliament exercises over its government's action in the Council. The procedures for exercising these powers are not a matter for the Union but are for each State to organise" (Reflection Group 1995, pt. 91 ff.).

At half time, it is quite clear that national parliaments will not be involved in EU decision-making in a direct manner, i.e. through new institutions. By contrast, the Irish proposed a new Protocol to be annexed to the Treaty which would clarify the consultative role of COSAC outside the Union framework and establish an information procedure allowing early discussion of issues on the agenda of the Council by the respective committees in the national parliaments.

4. The Transparency Issue

One of the main arguments in the debate on the democratic deficit of the Union has for a long time been the fact that the European legislature acts in secrecy: Until very recently, no Council meetings were open to the public, neither were the results of Council votes. The situation changed slightly after the debate on transparency was boosted in the aftermath of the ratification problems with the Maastricht Treaty. The Danish government, after having been confronted with a referendum opting against the Treaty revision, launched proposals to open meetings and publicise results of legislative votes, as well as the minutes of Council meetings. However, due to the reluctance of all other governments except the Dutch, reforms have not, so far, met expectations. According to the Council's new Rules of Procedure 1995, the meetings of the Council remain non-public in general; however, after a specific decision by unanimous vote, it is now possible that individual meetings be broadcast. The Council's statistics show that there were only 21 such public debates from January 1994 until March 1995, held on topics of general political perspectives or on important legislative proposals (Council 1995, Annex III a). Since a request by the British newspaper Financial Times to be informed of the existing number of qualified majority votes created considerable turmoil during summer 1994, the Secretariat of the Council also keeps a register of votes on legislation. But still, the Council is an institution which prefers to keep politics behind closed doors. This is prominently shown in the fact that there is no general access to the minutes of the meetings of the major legislative actor at the European level. Due to the political positions of the Member states which they contain, the minutes are deemed to be confidential documents. The respective Decision of 20 December 1993 concerning the public's access to Council documents has been amended by a Decision of 2 October 1995 (not published!)[10] agreeing on a code of conduct that "establishes much greater access to Council minutes (when the Council is acting as legislator) and minutes statements" (Reflection Group 1995, pt. 107). In this respect, the EP criticises the still existing possibility of an exemption of the general rule, and the non-binding character of the code of conduct.

Also within the debates preceding the IGC 1996, many commentators have stressed the need for a change in attitude by the Council. For instance, the Commission urges the Council to become more open in its legislative function and furthermore considers the abolition of the provision allowing for a Council decision against making voting outcomes public (1995, pp. 32 and 35). The EP goes even further and asks for an explicit statement of the 'principle of openness' in the Treaty: "where the Council is acting in its legislative capacity, its proceedings should be public and its agenda binding" and "[a]ll meetings on proposed legal acts are to be held in public unless a specific and duly justified exception is decided by a two-thirds majority" (1995, pt. 22.i; see also Dury/Meij-Weggen-Report 1996, pt. 18.4). This is also the proposal of the Federal Trust Round Table, which acknowledges that decisive discussions might, if formal proceedings are public, take place elsewhere. Still it argues that "public formal sessions, at which ministers should present their grounds for supporting or opposing the law in question, would nevertheless provide a sounder basis for their accountability, and would be seen by the citizens to do so" (1995, p. 11).

A "new right of all EU citizens to information on EU matters" figures among the proposals of the EP (1995, pt. 7). The Commission, although acknowledging that the measures taken by it and the Council concerning access to documents "are still in their infancy", argues that "it is clear that the principle of access to information is now undisputed. The basic instruments are in place, and a review of the code [providing for access to EU documents] is planned after two years' experience" (1995, p. 89).

The Dublin-II document includes several proposals for respective amendments of the Treaties. In particular, a basic right of access to the institutions' documents is being proposed, and the Council would have to adopt new rules

10 See summary in BullEU 10-1995, 1.9.1.

of procedure granting access to the results of votes and explanations of vote as well as statements in the minutes, when acting in its legislative capacity. What the latter notion encompasses would be open for definition by the Council itself.

5. European Citizens and the Union's Decision-Making Processes

While the old EEC treated the people as subjects to the Common Market and holders of some economic rights (such as the right to move freely within the Community), the TEU introduced European citizenship which acknowledged the special role of the citizens in the European polity, at least in principle. The European citizens have been granted some specific political rights, such as the right to vote and stand for local elections. However, the discussions following the adoption of the Maastricht Treaty revealed that the demands of the citizens are much higher than anticipated by the European political elite. Nevertheless, a few commentators actually discuss an increased direct involvement of European citizens in the policy-making process. At least the EP wants to develop "'political citizenship', inter alia through measures that facilitate participation in political life in a Member state of Union citizens residing in that State" (1995, pt. 7). Furthermore, it proposed in 1995[11] a Union-wide referendum in order to ratify the outcome of the next IGC and calls for application and development of Article 138a ECT on European political parties "in order to develop the means of expression for citizens at European level" (1995, pt. 8). The European Parliament furthermore calls for "greater substance" of the concept of EU citizenship through development of special rights linked to it (1995, pt. 7). Some of them are being mentioned in other chapters (fundamental rights catalogue; secrecy in the Council; transparency). The ESC calls for "grass-roots involvement in the integration process", for "opportunities and machinery for involvement in and supervision of the application of decisions" by the citizens, and for "a developing democratic and participatory society" (1995, pt. I.2, I.3.1 and I.3.2). It nevertheless sticks to mediated involvement when requesting mainly improvements for the ESC's participation in the decision-making. By contrast, the European Constitutional Group provides for the possibility of direct involvement of the citizens, however only with a view to selective issues: "the

11 This is not to be found in the Dury/Meij-Weggen report 1996 any more.

group considered the need to have a means within the constitution for changing the fiscal limits. Here, an element of direct democracy for the tax payers is introduced in the constitution as additional tax payer protection" (1995, 2b, p. 17).

Direct political involvement of the citizens (via popular initiatives) has been advocated in an Italian-Austrian proposal to the IGC on Union citizenship[12], but was not taken up so far.

6. The Protection of Fundamental Rights

One important aspect within the drafting of a European constitution would certainly be the question of how to deal with the protection of fundamental rights – something directly linked to the very notion of democracy itself. This is a long-standing debate which led to considerable tension between some national constitutional courts and their European counterpart over the question whether there is an appropriate protection of basic rights by the ECJ. This is a matter which is closely related to the doctrine of supremacy of EC law even over constitutional law of Member states. The ECJ's position, which has increasingly been accepted by national courts, is based on the acknowledgement that fundamental rights be an unwritten part of the Community's primary law. The Court of Justice protects them as part of the general principles of Community law against violation by secondary Community legislation. The ECJ draws upon the Convention on the Protection of Human Rights and Fundamental Freedoms of the Council of Europe and on relevant national provisions. Article F (2) TEU took this established practice on board. Without going into the details of this complex area, one can conclude that although the Community in practice respects the fundamental rights, their protection in the Union context might nevertheless be improved.

Therefore, innovations are in discussion. Apart from the Federal Trust Round Table's proposal to simply insert in the Treaty a provision explicitly charging the Court with the task of ensuring that the institutions respect the fundamental rights (1995, p. 26 f), there are two major alternatives. First, the Union (or the European Community) could join the European Convention. The recent opinion by the ECJ[13] whether this is even legally possible for the Community stated that this could only be done after via a Treaty amendment

12 CONF/3941/96 from 3 October 1996.

13 Opinion 2/94 from 28 March 1996.

and not based on Article 235 ECT only. Among others the EP (Dury/Meij-Weggen 1996, pt. 4.2) and the British Federal Trust Round Table (1995, p. 6) favour this alternative. The other option would be to draw up a catalogue of fundamental rights as part of the primary law of the Union, as a part of the TEU or a formal European Constitution. E.g. the Europäische Strukturkommission states that with regard to giving the judicial system the necessary amount of authority, democratic basis and acceptance, any democratic community ought to have basic rights enshrined in a treaty by directly legitimised institutions[14].

In one of the most detailed proposals concerning the content of such a catalogue, the Europäische Strukturkommission suggests a limitation to the 'essential basic and human rights', including dignity, the equality principle, the respect for one's physical integrity, and freedom of the individual, as well as derogated rights such as the right to property and professional freedom. While the inclusion of specific social rights is left open for political negotiation within the Member states, the Strukturkommission considers at least basic social rights to be indispensable within the Internal Market (1994, p. 42). The Constitution proposed by the Herman Report includes a list of 24 items, ranging from the right to life, the freedom of thought, including the right to conscientious objection, the protection of the family, to some social rights – such as the right to work – and collective social rights, including the freedom to strike. The ECJ would be responsible for actions by individuals claiming violation of these human rights by the Union (see also EP 1995, pt. 7).

A specific provision on xenophobia and racism seems one matter where consensus on the appropriateness to act at the European level might be a realistic perspective (Commission 1996, pt. 9; Dury/Meij-Weggen-Report 1996, pt. 4.5; Reflection Group 1995, pt. 39). The intergovernmental negotiations are also eased by the fact that xenophobia and racism are not yet a very common issue in existing national constitutions. This is quite different when compared to many other fields of prospective European fundamental rights, where clashes of culture and values might hinder easy compromise at the IGC. Despite all the political and legal obstacles, it is hard to see how the

14 1994, 42: for the Union they seem to suggest that the appropriate institutions be both the EP and the national parliaments; similar Committee of the Regions 1995, 8.

question of fundamental human and social rights can be left out in any constitutional text that aims at serving as a reference point for human identities.

The interim report from December 1996 of the Irish Presidency includes a new Article 3c ECT taking over the jurisdiction of the ECJ into the EC Treaty, but refers also to the still ongoing debate in the IGC whether to accede to the European Human Rights Convention. It also proposes a new Article 6a ECT giving competence to the Community's institutions to take "appropriate action to prohibit discrimination based on sex, racial, ethnic or social origin, religious belief, disability, age, or sexual orientation".

III. Federal Issues

1. Subsidiarity and the Overall Division of Competences

So far, delimitation of the respective spheres of activity between the Union legislature and the Member states, as laid down in the Treaties, is rather an allocation of functions than a concrete and unambiguous division of competences. Although European lawyers used to call it a system of 'single authorisations' (Einzelermächtigungen), meaning that, in principle, the supranational level can only act if there is a specific authorisation to be found in the Treaties, it is also acknowledged that some of these authorisations are quite comprehensive and allow for a very broad range of activities 'to attain, in the course of the common market, one of the objectives of the Community'[15]. In the past, the Union legislator tended to make frequent use of these subsidiarity competences. The so-called principle of subsidiarity in Articles A TEU and 3b ECT was introduced at the last IGC in order to counter-balance the tendency towards centralisation. Article A affirms that 'decisions are taken as closely as possible to the people'; Article 3b makes the principle somewhat more operational, although by no means unambiguous. It requires that the Community acts only where the objectives

> cannot be sufficiently achieved by the Member states and can therefore, by reason of the scale or effects of the proposed action, be better achieved by the Community. (EC Treaty)

15 Article 235 ECT; see also Article 100a ECT.

This compromise formula obviously falls short of a clear-cut legal solution to the problem of division of competences in a quasi-federal setting such as the EU. Therefore the issue is on the agenda of the present IGC, and was discussed in the preceding reform debate.

The Europäische Strukturkommission for instance argues that the subsidiarity principle as formulated in Article 3b ECT cannot satisfy the demands because it does not provide clear enough criteria for the division of competences, but leaves the decision to actors such as the Commission and the governments which cannot be expected to always apply it systematically or in a restrictive manner (1994, p. 17). By contrast, a detailed catalogue of competences ('Kompetenzkatalog') should, according to this group, describe a given division of competences as transparently as possible, and provide principles for further transfers as well as for the exercise of competences. Thus, the Europäische Strukturkommission wants to stop the traditional trend towards ever more supranational policies. Therefore, its detailed catalogue of competences attributes in the case of all major policy areas primary and partial competences to either the Union or the Member states. In general, primary competences of one level should allow only for interventions by the other level if an explicit enumerative partial competency has been provided. In the absence of subsidiary competence provisions like Article 235 ECT, any further transfer of additional competences would only work with ratification by the Member states.

The proposal of the Europäische Strukturkommission has been welcomed by some commentators (e.g. the German Christian Democrats). While agreeing with the idea of a 'Kompetenzkatalog' as proposed by the Europäische Strukturkommission in principle, Ludlow and Ersbøll argue that it should not be accompanied by a total elimination of Article 235 ECT[16]. Most of the other contributions also want to retain Article 235 ECT, some see the drafting of a catalogue of competences as a too difficult task for the upcoming IGC (EP 1995, pt. 12.ii; ESC 1995, pt. I.9; Justus Lipsius 1995, p. 41; Federal Trust 1995, p. 28).

16 "[I]n any healthy polity there must be room for the interplay of political forces to redefine the frontiers between the different levels of government as an[d] when circumstances change. Something like Article 235, remodelled perhaps to allow a stronger role for the European Parliament through the introduction of codecision procedures, would therefore seem to be indispensable." (1995, p. 16)

Another relevant matter of debate is the further elaboration of the principle of subsidiarity, either in combination with the drafting of the Kompetenzkatalog, or without it. The European Constitutional Group sets comparatively narrow limits upon the powers of the Union, without specific conditions for Union action being fulfilled, its bodies should not have any explicit powers (1993, 3a. p. 71). Among the existing competences of the Union, a number would have to be cancelled, for example in the fields of environmental protection and social policy. In cases where amendments to Union measures would, in the view of a qualified minority of a 'Chamber of [national] Parliamentarians', pertain to the distribution of powers between the Member states and the Union, the final decision would lay with this Chamber which is expected to protect national autonomy.

But the European Constitutional Group wants to go even further in the direction of re-nationalisation: if any of the judgements by the ECJ pertained to the distribution of powers, a Member state or a qualified majority of the Chamber of Parliamentarians might call for review for adjudication by the Union Court of Review, consisting of representatives of national judiciaries (1993, 2c, p. 9). Members of national judiciaries making up this additional Court shall therefore see that Union competences are not exceeded, and that directly applicable Union law and the jurisdiction of the ECJ be very limited.

It seems that already the Reflection Group reached agreement in this regard, and opted against "incorporating a catalogue of the Union's powers in the Treaty", while suggesting "to maintain the present system" (1995, pt. 125). The latest Commission's and EP's reports do not address this question at all so that it seems probable that no departure from the status quo will happen at least in the medium run. However, some proposals for new Union competences are on the agenda[17]. This is also reflected in the Dublin-II paper where these far-reaching proposals are not mentioned at all. Only a new Protocol on the Application of the Subsidiarity Principle should be included which follows strictly the lines of the already existing guidelines, however improving their legal status.

17 See declaration No. 1 annexed to the Maastricht Treaty: e.g. energy, tourism; see also DURY/MEIJ-WEGGEN (1996), pt. 13 f.

2. Reform of Voting in the Council of Ministers

Two issues with respect to voting in the Council of Ministers have been brought up by almost all contributions to the reform debate: the abolition of unanimity (1) and the reform of qualified majority voting (2).

(1) The requirement of unanimity for Council votes, although very important in the early stages of the European integration process, has been on constant retreat since then. The adoption of the Single European Act marked the turning point, as the so-called co-operation procedure (with qualified majority voting) was introduced in order to facilitate the Single Market legislation. The Maastricht Treaty followed the same direction in general, but introduced unanimity with respect to some new activities. Although unanimous decision-making happens within the supranational context of the wider European policy-making, it is deemed to be a safeguard for national sovereignty, especially for smaller states. However, the unanimity requirement is one of the major obstacles to efficiency in the Union's legislative process. Its democratic legitimacy is very doubtful as a single Member state may block all others, even when it comes to adapting existing legislation to a change of circumstances. With a view to future enlargements to the East and South, the argument becomes even more pertinent since the Council might have as many as 28 members.

Therefore, the abolition of unanimity is even more widely debated now than ever. Some proposals are radical, some are very careful with respect to which areas should be opened to majority voting. The Commission, for instance, does not suggest a radical abolition, but points at the lack of a consistent underlying principle in the choice of procedure. However, the Commission has so far not pointed at specific provisions to be changed (1995, p. 24).

The EP is more explicit and radical in that respect: it suggests further extension of qualified majority voting, and wants to see unanimity restricted to the "areas of particular sensitivity": Treaty amendment, Article 235 ECT, and other "constitutional decisions" being enlargement, own resources, and uniform electoral system[18]. Charlemagne expects that the unanimity principle will persist for constitutional questions[19], for the CFSP and certain as-

18 1995, pt. 22.iii.; see also: "The IGC should concentrate on identifying a very limited number of well-defined exceptions where unanimity should still be required." (Dury/Meij-Weggen-Report 1996, pt. 19.1)

19 With the exception of some nominations such as the one of the Commission's President.

pects of JHA (1994, p. 60). The Guéna Report suggests the requirement of a double majority within qualified majority voting in order to politically ease the abolishment of unanimity requirements by lifting the political handicap of a disproportionate weight of the smaller states[20].

Some want to replace unanimity by a stronger but majority criterion in order to make the proposal less radical (e.g. Federal Trust 1995, p. 8). A very strong qualified majority (VSM) could for example mean four-fifths of the Member states and four-fifths of the total population, or even 90 % of each (Justus Lipsius 1995, p. 39). Lipsius suggests this VSM be applied in all cases where Commission proposals are changed by the Council (Article 149 ECT), concerning nominations and modification to the Treaties, and in most cases where the codecision procedure now applies. The European Constitutional Group suggests that "for some constitutional decisions, such as accession, unanimity should be interpreted as 'quasi unanimity' (i.e. the assent of mini-states with a population of 3m or less would not be needed for other Members to go ahead)" (1993, 2c, p. 5).

Because of the still heavily differing positions on this subject among the Member states as reported by the Dublin-II paper, we may already conclude at half time that there will be no general abolishment of unanimity voting in the Council. There is, however, consensus to enlarge the scope of qualified majority voting. How to identify the new areas of majority voting though seems still a matter of considerable disagreement among the delegations. Ireland reports two different approaches: the case-by-case approach or the agreement on more general criteria to be applied in a more systematic way. The idea of VSM is not in the half time report but seems still to be a viable option when we consider the openness of the debate on the second aspect on the agenda:

(2) Majority voting is another big issue in the IGC: it was put on the agenda by the Council after considerable problems with the adaptation of the traditional system to the last enlargement. The European Council adopted a compromise concerning the lifting of the blocking minority. The so-called 'Ioannina Compromise'[21] did solve the immediate problem of getting the

20 Furthermore, GUÉNA refers to the 'Luxembourg Compromise' which could still be invoked in cases of 'emergency' (1995, p. 18).

21 Before the 1995 enlargement the blocking minority in the Council of Ministers was set at 23 votes; it is now at 26 votes. The Ioannina compromise suggests that in the event of a minority between 23 and 25 votes, it is under-

necessary ratification of the adhesion treaties of two Member states, namely Great Britain and Spain, but left open the wider question of how to tackle the in-built problems of the weighting of the votes in the Council.

Justus Lipsius was first to point at the fact that, with successive enlargements, the relative weight of Member states having a more numerous population, under-rated from the beginning, has been decreasing, "contrary to democratic principles. The threshold of the populations which can be minoritised has increased from 30 % to 40 % (...)" (1995, p. 38). The EU is not confronted with the fact that all prospective new Member states would be relatively small. Charlemagne discusses the continuation of the present weighting of votes in this case. Based on two tables, he argues that mechanic extrapolation of the present system to a Union of 28 members would lead to consequences which to him seem unacceptable in terms of democracy: first, a minority of 47 % of the European population could in principle constitute a qualified majority; and second, the smaller states of Eastern and Central Europe could form a blocking minority (1994, pp. 62 ff.).

There are two proposals to tackle the problem: double majority and/or re-weighting.

(i.) A system of double majority: to adopt a decision, it would be necessary to attain not only a majority of votes, but also a majority of the population (Bourlanges/Lamers proposal). The idea has found widespread support (e.g. Federal Trust 1995, p. 9; Ludlow/Ersbøll 1995, p, 41; Justus Lipsius 1995, p. 38). Already in 1994, the Herman Report proposed the principle of double majority of states and population, without weighting of votes, as a general rule (1994, Article 20). Clearly, this gives the smaller states much more weight than at present. By contrast, the European Parliament opposes the principle of 'double majority' of States and population in Council voting in its latest report, while acknowledging the need for adjusting the system of voting within the Council: It "is in the Parliament that population is represented", whereas the "Council represents States". In fact, Parliament goes even further in the opposite direction when it argues that the threshold for obtaining qualified majority should be lowered "from the very high level of 71 % that it is at present" (1995, pt. 22.iii).

(ii.) The introduction of a 'double majority' of votes and population would overcome only the first paradox (a minority of the European popula-

stood that negotiations should continue in order to reach agreement in due time.

tion could constitute a qualified majority), but not the second one (a group of smaller states, e.g. of Eastern and Central Europe, could form a blocking minority). The only possible solution therefore seems to be a re-weighting of the votes which could reduce the present disproportion which favours the small countries. Charlemagne suggest that the re-weighting observe three guiding principles: (1) abolishing the anomaly that a minority could impose itself on the majority; (2) the accumulated weight of the new Member states should not be able to hinder progress of the Union; and (3) the relations of the respective weights of the bigger states should not be put indirectly into question (Charlemagne 1994, p. 65).

Some authors, however, argue in support of the smaller states. E.g. Ludlow/Ersbøll conclude that "[t]he bias in favour of small states in a Union of national states is in other words desirable in itself and should be enshrined in 'normal' procedures." (1995, p. 41) The EP opposes the voting power to reflect strictly the proportion of the population, too (1995, pt. 22.iii.).

Analysing the Dublin-II paper we may conclude that this very important question has not been decided yet. The Irish Presidency only reiterates the well-known approaches while acknowledging that there is no consensus at the present time. However, there seems to be some optimism to come to an overall agreement in the last stage of the negotiations.[22]

IV. The Moment of Constitutional Choice for a Democratic Europe?

The objective of this paper was to provide an overview of the central issues and arguments put forward with a view to possible constitutional and democratic reforms in the present IGC.

---

22 There are two more federal issues debated in the IGC regarding membership in the European Parliament and the European Commission: (1) the fixing of a maxium size of the EP: there seems to be consensus that 700 MEPs should be the maximum; however, the IGC did not yet tackle the problem of how to fix the size of each national delegation in the event of enlargement; (2) the size of the Commission: here only different models are being debated so far, without any compromise arising on the horizon. See FALKNER/NENTWICH (1995), pp. 70 ff and 79 ff.

We may conclude that, at least from the perspective of most experts, the moment of constitutional choice for a democratic Europe has definitely arrived. However, the political debates, and in particular the Irish half time account of the negotiations leave us with doubts whether the negotiators will be able to stand up to these challenges.

The latest opinions of the Commission and the EP's Institutional Committee show at least some convergence (e.g. regarding transparency; codecision). The reports of the Reflection Group and the Irish Presidency, however, reveal still considerable differences in many aspects between the Member states, although the Dublin-II paper concludes that "the negotiations to date have shown that on some institutional issues there is already a good deal of common ground". Only a few points of overall consensus[23] among the national representatives could be identified in the field of institutional and democratic reform – and even there, consensus was reached only at a very general level, without any specific details: the number of decision-making procedures should be reduced; the unanimity requirement for Treaty amendments should be kept; the codecision procedure should be improved and simplified; the exclusive right of initiative of the Commission should be uphold; the size of the EP should be limited; and to enhance transparency in the Union is indispensable. It is noteworthy that this list could not be amended after nine months of negotiations: it is still the same as extracted from the Reflections Group's report some months before the actual start of the IGC.

On the one hand, there is still some hope for a substantial democratic reform of the Union during the negotiations in the last stages of the IGC despite these rather meagre preliminary results: First, empirical evidence suggests a growing awareness not only at the EU level (Commission, EP), but also among the national representatives that that the European citizenry is expecting considerable improvements with respect to the democratic dimension of the European constitutional order. Second, the Irish Presidency expressed in a very open manner its hopes that most of the issues could be re-

23 It should be stressed that even a broad majority of Member states agreeing to a specific Treaty amendment is not sufficient for an amendment to be adopted at the IGC: all governments (and later all parliaments and, eventually, the voters) have to agree. Therefore, only a reported 'consensus' in the Dublin-II paper is a reliable indicator for a change of the status quo during the conference. However, essential features of political bargaining at the highest level (such as package-dealing and log-rolling) will only come into play at the IGC itself, see below.

solved at a late stage of the IGC when the negotiations will be raised to the highest political level where package deals and political trade-offs will be more easily possible. Third, the negotiators still uphold that important issues are at stake:

> There is general agreement at the Conference on the central importance of this issue. The institutions must function efficiently and effectively now and in the future; the balance between institutions must be respected; and they must operate as democratically and as openly as possible so that their representative nature is clearly seen and their legitimacy in the eyes of the public is maintained and reinforced. (Dublin-II paper, 91)

On the other hand, we cannot overlook that negotiations over a period of one and a half years (including the Reflection group) have not brought about considerable consensus on the constitutional future of Europe so far. It will come as a surprise when fundamental improvements could be agreed on under the pressure of an eventual closing date of the IGC. Furthermore, package deals always include the danger of incoherence which is of crucial importance when it comes to far-reaching structural decisions.

However, this IGC has to be successful. In the event of the contrary, dangers to the integration process are inevitable, both in the short and in the long run: A "Maastricht destiny" might wait for the new Treaty amendments, i.e. rejection in some national ratification referendums. But, even without such a crisis scenario, a continuation of the present unsatisfactory constitutional situation might well endanger the stability of the EU model during the early years of the third millennium.

References

CDU/CSU-FACTION IN THE GERMAN BUNDESTAG: *Überlegungen zur europäischen Politik*, Bonn 1 September 1994, release no. 10793.

CHARLEMAGNE: "L'Équilibre entre les États membres", in: *Volume in Honour of Niels Ersbøll*, Bruxelles 1994.

COMMISSION OF THE EUROPEAN COMMUNITIES: *Report on the Operation of the Treaty on European Union*, SEC(95) 731, 10 May 1995.

COMMISSION OF THE EUROPEAN COMMUNITIES: *Opinion: Reinforcing Political Union and Preparing for Enlargement*, http://europa.eu.int/en/agenda/igc-home/eu-doc/commissn/ avis-en.html, 28 February 1996.

COMMISSION OF THE EUROPEAN COMMUNITIES: *Report according to Article 189b (8) of the Treaty on the scope of codecision*, SEC(96) 1225 fin, 3 July 1996a.

COMMITTEE OF THE REGIONS: *Opinion on the Revision of the Treaty on European Union (Pujol Report)*, Brussels, CdR 136/95 (SP) HB/M/CW/R/ms, 21 April 1995.

COUNCIL OF MINISTERS: *Projet de Rapport sur le Fonctionnement du Traité sur l'Union Européenne*, Brussels, SN 1821/95, 14 March 1995.

DELORS, J.: *Speech before the European Parliament's committee on Institutional Affairs*, cited from Agence Europe, 25 Februray 1995, 2.

DUBLIN-II PAPER: *The European Union Today and Tomorrow – Adapting the European Union for the Benefits of its Peoples and Preparing it for the Future – A General Outline for a Draft Revision of the Treaties*, CONF 2500/96 CAB, 5 December 1996.

DURY, R. and H. MEIJ-WEGGEN: *Report of the Institutional Committee of the European Parliament: Avis du Parlément européen sur la convocation de la Conférence intergouvernmentale et Évaluation des traveaux du Groupe de Réflexion et précision des priorités politiques du Parlement européen en vue de la Conférence intergouvernmentale*, 5 March 1996, PE 216.237/fin.

ECONOMIC AND SOCIAL COMMITTEE: *The 1996 Intergovernmental Conference: The Role of the Economic and Social Committee*, ESC Bureau Report, Brussels, 26 April 1995, CES 273/95 fin, 4 May 1995.

EUROPÄISCHEN STRUKTURKOMMISSION, in: W. WEIDENFELD (Ed.): Europa '96. *Reformprogramm für die Europäische Union. Strategien und Optionen für Europa* (Verlag Bertelsmann Stiftung) 1994.

EUROPEAN CONSTITUTIONAL GROUP (ECG): *A Proposal for a European Constitution – A Report*, December 1993.

EUROPEAN COURT OF JUSTICE (ECJ): *Report Concerning Certain Aspects of the Application of the Treaty on European Union*, Luxembourg, May 1995.

EUROPEAN PARLIAMENT: *Resolution on the Functioning of the Treaty on European Union with a View to the 1996 Intergovernmental Conference – Implementation and Development of the Union*, PE 190.441, 17 May 1995.

EUROPEAN PARLIAMENT: *Resolution on the Report of the Commission accroding to Article 189b (8) of the EC-Treaty on the Scope of the Codecision (SEK(96) 1225)*, A4-0361/96, 14 November 1996.

FALKNER, G. and NENTWICH, M.: *European Union: Democratic Perspectives After 1996*, Vienna (Service Fachverlag) 1995.

FEDERAL TRUST FOR EDUCATION AND RESEARCH ROUND TABLE: "Building the Union: Reform of the Union. The Intergovernmental Conference of the European Union 1996", *Federal Trust Papers* 3 (1995).

GERMAN BUNDESRAT: as cited by *Agence Europe*, 1 April 1995, 3.

GRILLER, S., DROUTSAS, D., FALKNER, G., FORGÓ, K., KLATZER, E., MAYER, G., and NENTWICH, M.: *Regierungskonferenz 1996 – Ausgangspositionen*, IEF Working Paper No. 20 (Research Institute for European Affairs, Vienna), July 1996.

GRILLER, S., DROUTSAS, D., FALKNER, G., FORGÓ, K., and NENTWICH, M.: *Regierungskonferenz 1996 – Der Vertragsentwurf der irischen Präsidentschaft*, IEF Working Paper No. 25 (Research Institute for European Affairs, Vienna), January 1997.

GUÉNA, Y. (rapporteur): *Rapport d'information n° 224*, deuxième session extraordinaire 1994-1995 du Sénat, sur la réforme de 1996 des institutions de l'Union européenne.

HÄNSCH, K.: *On Relations Between the EP and National Parliaments*, speech delivered in Brussels at the European Policy Forum on 23 January 1995, Europe Documents 1920/27 January 1995.

HERMAN, F.: *Second Report of the Committee of Institutional Affairs on the Constitution of the European Union*, PE 203.601/endg.2 - A3-0064/94, 9 February 1994.

LUDLOW, P. and ERSBOLL, N.: *Preparing for 1996 and a Larger European Union: Principles and Priorities*, CEPS Special Report, No 6 Brussels (1995).

JUSTUS LIPSIUS: "The 1996 IGC", (1995) 20 ELR 235; see also (1995) 23 RTDE 51.

MAJOR, J.: *Europe: A Future That Works*, manuscript of a speech delivered at University of Leiden, 7 September 1994.

MILLER, G.: *Post-Maastricht Legislative Procedures: Is the Council "Institutionally Challenged"?*, paper presented to the 4th Biennial International Conference of ECSA, Charleston, South Carolina, 11-14 May 1995.

REFLECTION GROUP ON THE IGC 1996: *Final Report*, SN 520/95 (REFLEX 21), Brussels, 5 December 1995.

Chapter 5

Double Asymmetry as Normative Challenge

SVERKER GUSTAVSSON

I. What Is the Problem?

The third stage of Karl Polanyi's Great Transformation — in which markets become embedded in a democratic system (Polanyi 1957, pp. 237 ff.) — is no longer thought irreversible. During the first quarter of a century following the Second World War, it had seemed that this stage was here to stay. Then the oil crisis came, and the breakdown of the Bretton Woods system with it (Scharpf 1996 c, pp. 214 ff.). The current economic and political scene presents a sharp contrast to the institutions of the first postwar decades, for it exhibits strong tendencies towards disembedding markets (Cerny 1994, pp. 334 ff.), non-simultaneous de-nationalisation (Zürn 1992, pp. 490 ff., Zürn 1995, pp. 150 ff.) and neo-voluntarism (Streeck 1996, 64 ff.). Furthermore, the need for an unaccountable European central bank has been met with normative acceptance (Arndt 1996, pp. 208 ff.).

The changing nature of markets and of borders, then, has had consequences for democratic accountability. The recent demise of totalitarianism in Eastern and Central Europe has contributed, moreover, to a more pragmatic view of democracy. Paradoxical as it may seem, democracy is *less* taken for granted today than it was during the 1950s and 1960s. Not since before 1914 have we heard a discussion of the kind we hear today — in which it is considered an open question as to whether or not the political system should exhibit the fundamental democratic traits of congruence, identity, reversibility and accountability (Zürn 1996, 36 ff.). No longer are these notions useful weapons in the ideological contest with fascism, nazism and communism. They have lost their utility in the anti-totalitarian struggle; now they must be defended in their own right.

Double asymmetry (Scharpf 1996 a, pp. 109 ff; Scharpf 1996 b, pp. 15 ff.) — i.e., the set of inter-related and mutually reinforcing imbalances between positive and negative integration on the one hand, and between suprastatism and democratic accountability on the other — confronts us with a challenge which is not only *descriptive* (Kohler-Koch 1996, pp. 185 ff.; Risse-Kappen 1996, pp. 53 ff.) and *explanatory* (Caporaso 1996, pp. 29 ff.) but *normative* as well. I do not propose in this paper, to inquire into the nature of this asymmetry, or to explore the historical causes behind its appearance. My purpose, rather, is to ask how it should be evaluated and what we should do about it. What are the options? Which of these is best ?

When searching for a tenable basis upon which to evaluate and recommend different options, we face a critical choice: should 'is' or 'ought' be our decisive criterion ? Should we reject normative democratic theory as 'unrealistic' in the light of disembedding markets, uneven de-nationalisation, neo-voluntarism and the demise of totalitarianism ? Or is it rather double asymmetry that we should see off, in order that the rise of a benevolent, post-modern technocracy might be averted ?

II. What Are the Options?

In one previous book chapter I tried to clarify the concept of the 'democratic deficit' (Gustavsson 1996 a); in another, I sought to elucidate the concept of 'double asymmetry based on provisional suprastatism' (Gustavsson 1997). I introduced the second of these notions in an effort to explain how the German Constitutional Court argued when, in October 1993, it found the Maastricht Treaty to be in accordance with the demand for democratic accountability enshrined in the German Basic Law.

Thanks to these attempts at clarification, three options clearly stand out. Two of these are fundamental, i.e., they follow from the distinction between abolishing and preserving the democratic deficit. The abolitionist option then divides into two sub-options, for the deficit may be abolished either by abandoning suprastatism or by democratising it.

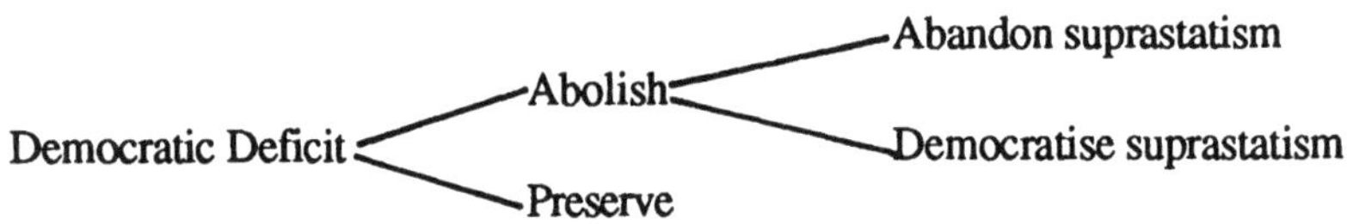

Figure 1. *Three Recommendations Concerning the Democratic Deficit*

The two abolitionist options both aim at setting the asymmetry at nought — either through the abandonment of suprastatism (the confederal option) or through the introduction of democratic accountability at the European level (the federal solution). The preservationist option, on the other hand, is oriented towards preserving the double asymmetry, i.e., the imbalance between positive and negative integration, on the one hand, and that between power and accountability at the European level, on the other.

In practise, confederalists and federalists are very far apart. In theory, however, their abolitionist policies are rooted in the same notion. States (and organisations comprised of states) should not just be based on civil rights and universal suffrage. They must also be founded on the notions of congruence, identity, reversibility and accountability (Zürn 1996, pp. 36 ff.). The categories of subjects and of citizens should be congruent. Citizens must identify with the regime to such an extent that they accept majority voting. Public policies have to be reversible. Legislatures and executives must be accountable, i.e., citizens must be able to re-elect their representatives or to turn them out of office.

Both confederalists and federalists view the established asymmetries of the European Union against the background of the developmental schema: city-state, nation-state, federal state. In the city-state, leaders can be held accountable directly. In a nation-state organised on a representative basis, this is done indirectly. To a confederalist, member states must retain sovereignty in order to remain democratic. International organisations are a matter of negotiation and agreement between governments. For a federalist, on the other hand, the federal state meets the criteria of congruence, identity and accountability through a compromise between the one-state-one-vote and one-person-one-vote principles, in combination with the so-called either/or criterion for democratic accountability (Dahl 1983, pp. 100 ff.).

According to the either/or criterion, the federal state meets reasonable democratic requirements, provided that its governing agenda is possible to master at the level either of the union or of its constituent states, and provided that the constitution is common to all the states of the union. The European Union could only meet such requirements by transforming the character of its legislative body. For notwithstanding its name, the European Parliament is essentially an assembly, not a parliament. In a federal Europe, the European parliament would have the same status at the European level as the member state parliaments have at the national level.

Federalists and confederalists disagree as to whether suprastatism should be democratised or abandoned, but all abolitionists agree on the need to get rid of the democratic deficit. Both sub-options, consequently, accord with the established version of normative democratic theory. According to that established version, it is not enough that there be a free society, i.e., that the constitution grant freedom of association and expression, or the right to strike. It does not suffice that citizens have the right to form parties, to engage in debate, or to exert political pressure. In addition, all adults must have the right to vote. Furthermore, the government of the day must be accountable — both in principle and in practise — to the electorate (which would mean, in the case of the EU, a *European* electorate). Since the governing institutions of the EU do not, either in theory or in practise, fulfill this last criterion, abolitionists urge that the double asymmetry be abolished, i.e., that suprastatism be either democratised or abandoned.

The confederalist and federalist options are both textbook-friendly. Already as elementary-school students we become acquainted with — and probably sympathetic to — normative democratic theory, and abolitionist recommendations fit this theory nicely. In order better to clarify the practical options facing us, therefore, I propose to undertake the more demanding task of arguing that the asymmetry characterising the European Union today should be *preserved*. This position may not be textbook-friendly, yet it is the most frequently taken position in the debate on the future of the European Union. How can it best be formulated, attacked and, thus, corroborated ?

As far as constitutional discourse is concerned, no better defence of the democratic deficit has been devised than that set forth in the 1993 verdict (*BVerfGE*, 17, pp. 155-213) of the German Constitutional Court. The question facing the Court was whether the Law of Accession to the European Union — which the Bundestag had passed by a large majority in December 1992 — could be reconciled with the demands for democratic accountability enshrined in the German Basic Law. Not until the Court had answered that question in the affirmative could the Maastricht Treaty be ratified.

The argument of the German Constitutional Court ran as follows: the suprastatism established in the first pillar of the Union Treaty, the Court argued, is *provisional*. Sovereignties are *delegated* rather than *surrendered*. Such a delegation of sovereignties is acceptable as long as the criteria of the German Basic Law are upheld. According to these criteria, the common use of competences must be *marginal* in relation to the functioning of German democracy as a whole, and the uses to which these competences are put at the European level must be *predictable*. The delegation of German sovereignty must also be *revocable;* that is, if the criteria of marginality and predictability are not met, the German authorities must retain the prerogative to re-assume the powers delegated. The Court deemed these three criteria to have been met, and so concluded that the ratification of the Treaty was consistent with the demands for democratic accountability laid down in the Basic Law.

A critical observation is in order here, however: the provisional character of suprastatism has never been demonstrated in practise. Besides its lack of realism, moreover, the argument presented by the Court is inconsistent. For the Court defends the democratic deficit in terms of marginality, predictability and revocability, leading one to expect that the Court would be disinclined to view the EMU as democratically acceptable. Yet the converse actually obtains. In adducing the position of the Bundesbank, the Court makes a European virtue out of a German exception from the general rule of popular sovereignty and democratic accountability.

Notwithstanding its vulnerability to such criticisms, however, the preservationist position is in fact widely embraced. It can be examined in one of its most interesting formulations, moreover, in the work of Fritz Scharpf. He calls for an arrangement which is compatible *both* with the demands for autonomy put by the member states *and* with the advantages associated with collective action that arise from the principle of provisional suprastatism (Scharpf 1994). He argues that we should attempt, on the basis of the established multi-level system of government, to achieve as much democracy as possible. "Democratic policy in Europe" (Scharpf 1996 d, p. 136) presupposes a realistic picture of "the political options facing us in view of the completed internal market" (Scharpf 1996 a, p. 109) based on a notion of the difference between "negative and positive integration in the political economy of the European welfare states" (Scharpf 1996 b, p. 15). Otherwise, we will be stuck with less democracy than is in fact achievable under present historical circumstances.

Scharpf presents the reader with a democratic dilemma:

> ... On the one hand, the capacity of member states to shape the collective fate of their citizens by means of their own policies has been reduced. Aside from the factual constraints and limits to action generated by integration into the world economy and the globalization of capital markets, the formal policy-making capacities of the western European states have been significantly limited by the guarantee of the four basic freedoms of movement within in the internal market — of goods, persons, services and capital. Thus western European nation states have less authority today to resolve economic or economically generated problems than they had twenty years ago.
>
> On the other hand, the policy-making capacities of the Union have not been strengthened nearly as much as the capabilities at the level of member states have declined. In spite of the Commission's monopoly on policy initiatives and the return to qualified majority voting in the Council of Ministers, the important decisions of the Community continue to come out of multilateral negotiations between national governments. They are cumbersome and time-consuming, and they are easily blocked by conflicts of interests between member states (Scharpf 1994, pp. 219 f.).

Yet, Scharpf points out, "national governments, which also control the development of the treaties, resist any reduction of their powers". From an empirical standpoint, of course, this is hardly astonishing. As long, however, as

> the Community lacks its own democratic legitimation, normative reasons also speak against the rapid dimunition of the powers of these governments. In the absence of European media, European political parties, and genuinely European processes of public-opinion formation, constitutional reforms could not, by themselves, overcome the present democratic deficit at the European level ... In the short term, at any rate, expanding the legislative and budgetary powers of the European Parliament could render European decision processes, already too complicated and time-consuming, even more cumbersome (Scharpf 1994, p. 220.).

The critical problem is that the Europeans do not consider the EU sufficiently legitimate, democratically speaking, for it to be possible to achieve, in the area of positive integration, a degree of suprastatism comparable to that already established in the area of negative integration. As a contrary case, Scharpf adduces the example of the United States during the New Deal in the 1930s. Previous to 1937, the American system had been one of dual federalism, i.e., the Supreme Court had recognised a sphere of 'police power' reserved to the states, which the federal government was not permitted (even in the exercise of its own 'commerce power') to invade.

Conversely, the American states were prevented from encroaching on the federal prerogative to regulate interstate commerce. Dual federalism ultimately broke down when the expansion and growing interdependence of governmental activity at both levels frustrated the search for clear lines of demarcation between federal and state areas of responsibility. "Since federal programmes appeared to be indispensable in the economic crisis of the 1930s, dual federalism was jettisoned and, as far as the Supreme Court is concerned, the federal government now has a blank cheque whenever it chooses to employ the commerce power *vis-à-vis* the individual states" (Scharpf 1994, p. 224.).

What explains this contrast between the demise of dual federalism in the United States sixty years ago and the assumed impossibility of achieving a corresponding positive integration by suprastatist methods in today's Europe? I would suggest, along the lines of Scharpf's general argument, that we consider the democratic legitimacy of Franklin Roosevelt's administration. The European Commission and the European Council of Ministers are not able to make suprastatist programmes "appear to be indispensable" in the convincing manner that the American president did in the 1930s. Roosevelt had been elected by the American people. Let us imagine, as an intellectual experiment, that Franklin Roosevelt had instead been elected by the state governors of the United States. In that case he would *not* have possessed, obviously, the legitimacy needed to overthrow the established system of dual federalism. The 'need' for a New Deal, and for a federal policy to relieve the massive unemployment then afflicting American society, would not have sufficed in themselves.

Confederalists respond to double asymmetry in the converse fashion. They call for the renationalisation of policy responsibilities. Scharpf rejects this version of abolitionism (Scharpf 1994, p. 220.). He remains silent, however, about the second variant of that doctrine, i.e., the federalist option.

By implication from his overall attitude, however, it would seem quite clear that he considers the democratisation of suprastatism a utopian project. Whence would the democratic legitimacy come — in a system which is intergovernmental in its constitutional structure at the outset — for transferring competences to the European Parliament which would place it above the parliaments of the member states ?

To a researcher like Fritz Scharpf, the notion of 'piecemeal social engineering' (Popper 1945, ch. 9) is essential. The challenge for 'utopians' in the Popperian sense lies in assessing how much suffering may be accepted for the sake of realising a desirable program in the future. For reformists, the problem is deciding how much suffering they are prepared to accept as the price for not daring a leap into the unknown. It is not enough, in other words, to compare one's blueprint for a better political order with the textbook version of normative democratic theory. One must also calculate, as best one can, the *actual* consequences of different courses of action.

That one wishes neither to surrender nor to democratise suprastatism is no alibi, however, for an *unreflective* preservationism. The adoption of piecemeal constitutional engineering does not entitle one to seek comfort in a narrow-minded defence of the status quo. It is quite obvious, according to Scharpf, that national governments cannot

> continue to enlarge the competencies of the European Union, while comforting themselves with the thought that they would still be able to control actual decisions in the Council of Ministers. The problem-solving capacities of member states and the integrity of their democratic processes are impaired even by agreed European decisions (and even more so by European deadlocks). There is no longer any question that European democracies discredit themselves when, for an ever-growing number of urgent problems, national political leaders admit their importance by calling for 'European solutions', while in Brussels interminable negotiations will, at best, lead to compromises that are declared unsatisfactory by all concerned, and for which nobody is willing to assume political responsibility (Scharpf 1994, p. 220.).

Against this background, Scharpf recommends the adoption of autonomy compatible co-ordination. In this version of the preservationist option, the multi-level European political system as a whole is to be rendered compatible *both* with the demands for autonomy put by the member states *and* with the practical advantages — in terms of enhanced policy effectiveness — arising from provisional suprastatism. In his own words:

> On the one hand, the limited policy-making capacities of the EU ought to be used sparingly, and only for issues that need to be settled on the European level. On the other hand, an effort should be made to restrict as much as possible the negative repercussions of European integration on the problem-solving capacities of national politics. In this regard, the interlocking federalism of Germany, where the states have practically lost all legislative powers, would be a most suitable model indeed. The question is whether, structural similarities notwithstanding, the practice of European policy-making can avoid the course taken in German federalism (Scharpf 1994, pp. 222 f.).

The "course taken in German federalism" refers to the risks of being caught in the 'joint decision trap' *(Politikverflechtungs-Falle)*. Scharpf described this trap in a prominent article in 1985. When decision-makers are caught inside the trap, he argued in that article, political problems cannot be solved. This is because those responsible are locked into a joint structure of multi-level decision-making which is unable to reform itself — either by extending the scope of suprastatism or by restricting it.

There are two ways, in principle, of avoiding the joint decision trap. One is to keep negotiating. This means the avoidance of voting, i.e., influence is divided according to the strength of the governments and interests negotiating. Unanimous decision-making runs the risk, however, of producing excessively diluted results. The other method is to limit joint decision-making (and thus negotiation) to issues that *really* have to be settled at the suprastatal level. Fritz Scharpf's proposal amounts basically to a recommendation that we adopt the latter method. This position meets with wide favour, moreover, both in Brussels and in the national capitals, which makes examining it more closely a matter of still greater interest.

European suprastatism is provisional, in the view of the German Constitutional Court. It has no democratic legitimacy of its own, as for instance Franklin Roosevelt had when he attacked the dualistic distribution of powers prevailing in the United States before 1937. Since then, the Supreme Court has denied the possibility of substantively defined areas of state jurisdiction beyond the reach of the federal commerce powers. In much the same way, Scharpf argues that "there must be no fields of national or subnational competence which cannot be touched by European measures safeguarding the four basic freedoms or regulating transnational problems. In an increasingly interdependent world, the goal can no longer be the clear separation of spheres of responsibility in accordance with the model of dual federalism" (Scharpf 1994, p. 226.).

Since the European suprastatal level lacks a democratic legitimacy of its own, however, getting the European and the national competences to work in the same direction is a far more demanding task than that faced by Franklin Roosevelt in the United States of the 1930s. Accepting this fundamental difficulty as an established historical fact, Fritz Scharpf argues for a multi-level structure of policy-making in the European Union, in which "central authority, instead of weakening or displacing the authority of member states, accepts and strengthens it — and in which member states, for their part, will respect and take advantage of the existence of central competencies in devising their own policies" (Scharpf 1994, p. 227.).

According to an older verdict of the German Constitutional Court from 1969, federal comity *(Bundestreue)* is a principle which "sets limits to the egoism of federal and state governments in as far as their constitutional authority would otherwise have given them the freedom and opportunity to 'ruthlessly' realize their own conceptions and exclusively pursue their own interests" (as quoted in Scharpf 1994, p. 225.). This requires more than just a balance between competing jurisdictional claims; a self-imposed restriction on the manner in which powers are exercised is necessary as well. "The criterion is *mutual compatibility,* and the characteristic outcome is not the displacement of one jurisdiction by the other, but the obligation of both to choose mutually acceptable means when performing the proper functions of government at each level" (Scharpf 1994, p. 225.).

These formulations — "mutual compatibility", "mutually acceptable means when performing the proper functions of government at each level" — leave a great deal more to be said. What we should ask ourselves, of course, is how this idea of combining respect for the autonomy of member states with a sense of the need for European-level regulation can be *institutionalised.* This double objective is supposed to be achieved, clearly, through political discourse and a Europe-wide will-formation, and without any further changes in the treaty between the member states. We must, Scharpf avers, ideologise *neither* the demise *nor* the persistance of the system of sovereign nation-states. What is primary for Scharpf is democracy's survival. If democracy is to survive, democracies must be able to act *either* at the European *or* at the national level. If democracy is our decisive value, we must redistribute responsibilities between the two levels. What cannot be achieved collectively in terms of positive integration should be done in each member state singly.

Public faith in democracy will be undermined severely if we look forward to measures of positive integration — in such areas as industrial relations and social policy — which do not take place in practise (since there is not enough consensus between the governments of the member states). Only by admitting that positive integration is impossible within the context of provisional suprastatism, Scharpf argues, can we avoid losing our confidence in the idea of democratic accountability (Scharpf 1996d, p. 150.).

Or, to translate Scharpf's point into a more straightforward Popperian language: our political commitments should be restructured in a business-like, pragmatic and down-to-earth fashion. It is pointless to argue over the end-result of the process for an 'end' there can never be of either history or ideology.

III. What Should Be the Decisive Criterion?

When it comes to suggesting constitutional improvements, Michael Zürn is a 'piecemeal engineer' and reformer of much the same stripe as Fritz Scharpf. Rather than searching for the 'ideal' format for the multi-level European system of decision-making, he argues for small improvements in order to make the established structure 'less bad'. Before turning to his practical recommendations, however, I would like to introduce his four basic criteria for European constitutional choice (Zürn 1996, pp. 38 ff.).

To my mind, Michael Zürn's suggestion of a fourfold checklist has brought the discussion of double asymmetry as normative challenge a large step forward. At the top of his list comes *congruence*. In principle, those who are affected by decisions (as objects) should also be those responsible for them (as mandators). If the degree of congruence is too small, the persons affected will consider the system of governance to be alien *(fremdbestimmt)*, in the same way that the law was alien under feudalism. There is a lack of fit, under such conditions, between the range over which democratically legitimated decisions apply, on the one hand, and the range of relevant social and economic relations, on the other. This lack of fit creates a new form of alienation and non-decision-making (Zürn 1996, p. 39.).

The second criterion with which Zürn presents us is *identity*. Of course, a 'demos' need not be an 'ethnos' as well. However, the members of a demos must be 'identical' in the sense of recognising each other as members of the 'same' political community. In practise, this means a preparedness to accept the use of the majority principle. Joseph Weiler and his co-authors (Weiler, Haltern and Mayer 1995, p. 13 f.) provide a good example. They suggest, as an intellectual experiment, the entry of the Kingdom of Denmark — with its four million citizens — into the Federal Republic of Germany as a seventeenth *Land*. How would the Danes then be different from the four million Germans who vote for the Greens (and who form something of a permanent minority within the political system of Germany as a whole) ? Accepting the majority principle presupposes, in other words, the existence of a community of communication, of memory, and of experience. The countries of Western Europe do not, taken as a whole, constitute a community of communication. Nor do they form a community of memory, and only to a very limited extent are they a community of experience (Kielmannsegg 1996, p. 57.).

The third criterion in Zürn's fourfold scheme is *reversibility*. Democratic theory rests on the epistemological notion that decisions are not eternal truths. They should be seen, rather, as resulting from an interplay between interests and convictions. We must therefore accept that future decisions on any given issue may differ from past ones, i.e., new decisions may proceed in a different and even contrary direction. This is an important, if largely implicit, reason for accepting majority rule in a democracy (Zürn 1996, p. 41.). Under modern circumstances, it is true, reversibility is hard to achieve for two reasons. One has to do with the empirical character of technologies like nuclear power, which are difficult to decide about by simple majority rule because they have irreversible consequences as to their substance. The second reason derives from the phenomenon here discussed, i.e., a system of double asymmetry in which prevailing procedure tends to make decisions irreversible. For neither in the public discourse nor (all the less) in an election campaign is the actual majority on any specific question confronted, in such a system, with a potential majority for an alternative policy.

Michael Zürn's fourth criterion is *accountability*. Democracy is not preferable to other forms of governance just because the majority is entitled to rule. A still more critical reason is that democracy makes it possible to dismiss bad or incompetent rulers. Not only decisions but the holding of political office as well should be reversible. For an electorate *vis-à-vis* its parliament, and for a parliament *vis-à-vis* its government, this is an imperative demand. Its effective execution requires, moreover, a minimum of accurate information and a general grasp of the achievements of the political system as a whole (Zürn 1996, p. 41 f.).

This fourth criterion, in my view, could stand some improvement. Zürn's description here is too vague. The concept of accountability must entail — if it is to be substantial and real — the right of voters to force office-holders to part with their positions. Democracy should be taken to mean, I would argue, that upon the completion of a term of office, the electorate evaluates the performance of the legislature, and the legislature evaluates the performance of the government. General elections must translate votes into parliamentary seats, and parliamentary seats into government posts. Both legislature and government must find their tenure insecure, and not just for legal but also for political reasons. For neither legislature nor government can otherwise be judged accountable in parliamentarian democracies.

I bid the reader recall, moreover, the either/or-criterion (Dahl 1983, pp. 100 ff.). According to that notion, the federal state meets reasonable democratic requirements, provided that its governing agenda is possible to master at the level either of the union or of its constituent states. This should not be regarded, in my view, as a fifth criterion in its own right, but rather as a very important specifiction (which Michael Zürn does not mention) of the special form accountability must take in a *multi*-level system of government.

We can use Zürn's four criteria, with these slight modifications introduced, as a normative guide in deciding whether to abandon suprastatism, to democratise it, or to preserve it in its present form. The abandonment of suprastatism entails the establishment of a confederation. In an association of states of this sort, all four criteria are satisfied. Citizens decide for themselves, and they have no difficulty in accepting the majority principle within their own state. As far as the element of multi-level decision-making is concerned, policies can be easily reversed. And the power of citizens to force governments and legislative majorities from office for political reasons is in no way threatened, for decisions in a confederal system are taken in each member state singly. Common decisions in a confederation are not binding until they are ratified by each and every member state in accordance with its own constitutional provisions.

Democratising suprastatism means founding a federation. If the EU were transformed into a multi-level state of that kind, the European parliament would be made the ultimate repository of the legislative and — indirectly — the executive suprastatal powers. A federation would work in the same way as such member countries as Austria, Belgium and Germany, all of which are federal in character. The criterion of accountability would then be satisfied. The same could be said of the criteria of congruence and identity. The matter is trickier in the case of the reversibility criterion, which is difficult to satisfy (because of the 'joint decision trap') in *any* federation. Reversibility is satisfied far better, however, in an outright federation than in the present system of double asymmetry and provisional suprastatism. If the EU were a federation, central political issues would be the stuff of a Europe-wide discourse and will-formation, and the composition of the European Parliament would be the decisive factor in resolving conflicts between the member states and the suprastate.

Provisional suprastatism represents the maintenance of the status quo, which is preferable, it may be argued, to the other options available. Double asymmetry based on provisional suprastatism maybe can be said — at a stretch — to fulfil the criteria of congruence and identity, but it certainly cannot be deemed satisfactory in the case of reversibility and accountability. Avoiding majority decisions and making as few decisions as possible at the suprastatal level is a pragmatic way to avoid violating the criteria of identity and congruence more than is absolutely 'necessary' to defend the four freedoms. However, a multi-level decision system which is not federal — in the sense that governance at its suprastatal level is not founded in direct and general elections — cannot be accepted from the standpoint of reversibility and accountability. As long as elections to the European Parliament do not carry any political weight, policy alternatives and policy openings are kept secret in accordance with the rules and customs of international diplomacy. The result is that important policies are non-accountable and irreversible (Zürn 1996, p. 47.).

Enough for now of the three main options — abandoning suprastatism, democratising it, and preserving it in its present form — in the light of congruence, identity, reversibility and accountability. I turn now to Michael Zürn's practical recommendations, which are aimed at satisfying his checklist more fully than do the options of federalism (and confederalism too, I take it) and autonomy compatible co-ordination.

Zürn makes three practical recommendations. Europe-wide referenda *(Europaweite Referenda)* could be used, he suggests, for issues of a "majoritarian" kind, i.e., issues which are neither constitutional nor redistributive in character. Most suitable for EU-wide referenda, and in satisfaction of all four criteria, are issues in which both costs and benefits are diffuse (in the sense of being spread out all over the continent and all over the population). This means, in practise, security and (large-scale) environmental issues. Unlike referenda on constitutional questions and redistributive issues (agricultural subsidies, for example), referenda on "majoritarian" issues could generate identity. The use of referenda for constitutional and redistributive issues, by contrast, would be counter-productive, because it would undermine already established common identities. This is because, where such issues are concerned, costs and benefits are unevenly spread between the member states and among the population at large. Both the citizens of small member states and farmers, for example, would consider themselves to run the risk (as in fact they would) of becoming permanent minorities, were referenda introduced for resolving such questions (Zürn 1996, p. 49 f.).

Direct elections *(Demokratisierung der territorialen Vertretung)* could also be used to choose each member state's representatives in the European Council of Ministers. Much the same reform was introduced in the United States in 1913, when the senators representing the constituent states were elected in direct elections for the first time. Such a reform would clarify lines of accountability. As long as the Council of Ministers is comprised of the very people who wield executive and legislative power in the member states, Zürn argues, the present tendencies towards scapegoating and false credit-claiming cannot be avoided (Zürn 1996, p. 50 f.). It must be said that this is a suggestion of considerable interest. It would no doubt also fulfil all four criteria. I would argue, however, that the parallel with the United States should be taken one step further. It bears recalling that the American Senate is constituted according to the principle of two senators per state, irrespective of size of population. This is no small difference as compared to the present European formula, in which the larger member states cast more votes than the smaller ones. Michael Zürn does not indicate whether, in his would-be system of direct elections to the European Council of Ministers, the twenty or so "European" ministers from each member state would be elected according to the principle of equal representation for each member state. That would clearly mean a revolution, especially if ten more countries were to become members. It would also mean, in practise, that France and Germany would carry no more weight in the European Council of Ministers than the big states in the U.S., like Texas and California, carry in the American Senate.

Zürn also recommends the use of transparent, non-governmental decision networks. These refer to regulatory regimes which are 'epistemic' in nature. They involve, in practise, the regulation of environmental and analogous issues in which scientific discourse plays a prominent part, and in relation to which the public interest is highly generalised. Questions of this sort involve 'arguing' more than 'bargaining'. As an empirical matter, moreover, sectoral public spheres *(sektorale Öffentlichkeiten)* of this kind are good at counterbalancing interests which are "too well" represented. When it comes to congruence and identity, Zürn argues, "balance" can be achieved more easily at the "correct" level. Networks of this kind cannot function, however, unless they derive their legitimacy from a scientific or analogous discourse. Whenever such networks need, moreover, to make binding decisions (and not just to inform or advise), they encounter trouble. The same is true when 'networking' involves costs for those taking part; when the participants have to tax each other, for example, the network must be organised in accordance with the criteria of identity, congruence and accountability (Zürn 1996, p. 51.).

These practical recommendations — all three of them — deserve to be taken seriously as suggestions for how to improve the *social* legitimacy of the preservationist alternative. None of them, however, is satisfactory from the standpoint of furnishing a *principled* "yes" or "no" to the question of preserving or abolishing the democratic deficit. Zürn is well aware of this objection, as is evident from the general disclaimer with which he introduces the last part of his paper:

> Quite consciously when formulating these practical recommendations, I will not let my own reasoning be hampered by problems of constitutional theory and low probabilities of being able to implement *(verfassungsrechtliche Schwierigkeiten und Fragen der Durchsetzungschansen)* ... Our discussion needs institutional imagination and should not be limited by a parallel discourse on feasibility *(Durchsetzbarkeitserwägungen)*. Therefore, first of all we should concentrate on the aspect of democratic quality. In this paper, political implications are considered important only when they have implications for the pre-conditions and characteristics of the democratic process as normative standard, i.e., not as to the difficulties to bring them about (Zürn 1996, p. 48.).

The overall import of this disclaimer is to set political feasibility aside in favour of "democratic quality" — which is *entirely* founded, be it noted, on the checklist. Having introduced the reader to this provocative notion of a "pure" democratic quality, I propose now to take up the question of which criterion should be judged decisive. Is there any such thing as a "pure" democratic qualityn ? Or should normatively oriented researchers consider political feasibility as well ? In brief: according to what *meta*-criterion should one particular criterion be granted precedence over the others ?

According to a Popperian view of democracy,

> politicians must be alert to the unintended consequences of their policies and programs and should be prepared to modify or abandon a course of action if events falsify their expectations. Policy should be directed not toward maximizing happiness, a notoriously difficult objective, but toward minimizing avoidable suffering. Policy should be formed in small, clearly stated stages so that the 'falsifiable' premises of policy can be tested (Mattausch 1995, p. 979.).

Michael Zürn's concept of a 'pure' democratic quality seems expressive of what Karl Popper described as *"utopian engineering,* as opposed to another kind of social engineering which alone I consider as rational , and which may be described by the name of *piecemeal engineering".* According to a utopian approach,

> we must determine our ultimate political aim, or the Ideal state, before taking any practical action. Only when this ultimate aim is determined, or a rough outline at least, only when we are in possession of something like a blueprint of the society at which we aim, only then can we begin to consider the best ways and means for its realization, and to draw up a plan for practical action (Popper 1945, p. 138.).

According to the piecemeal approach, by contrast, we should

> be aware that perfection, if at all attainable, is far distant, and that every generation of men, and therefore also the living, have a claim; perhaps not so much a claim to be made happy, for there are no institutional means of making a man happy, but a claim not be made unhappy, where it can be avoided. The piecemeal engineer will, accordingly, adopt the method of searching for, and fighting against, the greatest and most urgent evils of society, rather than searching for, and fighting for, its greatest ultimate good (Popper 1945, p. 139.).

Viewed from a utopian standpoint, double asymmetry based on provisional suprastatism is no good solution. In piecemeal practise, however, it *might* be preferable to its abolitionist alternatives. Fritz Scharpf implicitly argues in such terms, when presenting the preservationist position. Economic interdependence is nowadays so far-reaching that it would be irresponsible to adopt a strategy of abandonment. The re-introduction of member state self-determination into the negatively integrated single market — the confederal solution — would not just violate the treaty. "[E]scalating national protectionisms would not just mean the end of the Union, it would also plunge the European economy into catastrophic straits" (Scharpf 1996 d, p. 149.). Nor, Scharpf avers, should the suprastatal order be democratised. The legitimacy of the suprastate is admittedly weak. In practise, however, a strategy of democratising suprastatism — in accordance with the federal solution — would lead to unacceptable results. For it would mean that, during a transitional period of uncertain length, the more legitimate law would be superseded by the less — all in order to achieve a better state of affairs in a distant future. This would mean, in practise, that member state democracies would decline without a corresponding growth in the democratic legitimacy of the suprastate.

> Much is therefore at stake if politics at European level cannot act while politics at national level has lost its effectiveness. The only means of avoiding this horror scenario is to employ the limited possibilities of action at both levels, national and European, in such a way that the existing but limited opportunities for effective policy at both levels are exploited and predictable frustrations sidestepped. This has important implications for the relationship between European and national policy (Scharpf 1996 d, p. 150).

Comparing different options in terms of piecemeal constitutional engineering, that is the thrust of my argument in this chapter, means that we must identify, specify and try to falsify our premises. A piecemeal approach should not be thought, however, to imply a defence of the status quo, i.e., in this context a preservationist position. The point is that the premises underlying each and every step in the development of our policy should be rendered clear and falsifiable. Premises supporting the status quo are quite as important to clarify and to corroborate as premises underlying policies of change.

Virtually all of us have, at the very root of our thinking on double asymmetry, a psychological tendency to let ourselves be inspired (consciously or not) by a well-known three-stage metaphor. I have in mind the threefold tale of Paradise, Fall and Resurrection. From the Medieval Paradise the Renaissance and Reformation were sprung, and the system of sovereign states replaced the indivisible Universal Community in sacred union with the Holy Church. Yet the modern system of sovereign states in Europe has never lost its *telos*, according to this implicit and idealistic creed. Through its *re*-unification, Europe shall be resurrected from the consequences of the Fall of Man. At present, it is true, divisions, splits and schisms prevail. In the future, however, Europe shall return to its true self, as once it existed under Pope and Emperor.

According to the principle of piecemeal engineering, however, policies should be formulated in small, clearly stated stages so that their premises can be tested. If, furthermore, we refuse to accept *telos* as an argument, it becomes urgent to criticise what is often said in the current political debate on the process of European integration. For criticism in fact is called for, and should be delivered along two different lines.

My first point — and an elementary one it is indeed — is that there *is* no immanent goal called "united Europe". Events and developments in the area of European integration are not the servants of some underlying purpose or cunning of history. Only individuals exist — individual people who actively prefer that certain steps be taken or not taken. The surrender of congruence, identity, reversibility and accountability cannot be justified by reference to 'integration' as an historical 'process' aimed at bringing Europe back to its 'true self'. Double asymmetry cannot be defended on the grounds that is a 'necessary' element whereby the 'natural' development of things is accelerated. Double asymmetry can only be discussed, and should only be discussed, in terms of *falsifiable* propositions relating to the intended and unintended consequences that it brings — in terms of employment, economic growth, social improvement, the loss of democracy, the risk of war, etc.

Second, more 'integration' should not be considered, *by definition,* to be 'better' than less. The preferable outcome as regards congruence, identity, reversibility and accountability must be argued for in terms of falsifiable propositions concerning the anticipated consequences of accepting double asymmetry vs. not accepting it. The question is which option is preferable to the available alternatives at any particular time. What is considered better must be allowed, moreover, to change over time and in accordance with experiences gained. A step in the direction of more integration is not *a priori* better; it should not be equated automatically with progress. Such a step may indeed take the member states one step higher, in terms of the oft-used staircase metaphor for European integration. Higher, however, is not the same thing as better.

One can of course always say, as Bela Balassa did when presenting his staircase metaphor in 1961, that the various steps "represent varying degrees" of integration:

> In a free trade area, tariffs (and quantitative restrictions) between the participating countries are abolished, but each country retains its own tariffs against non-members. The establishment of a custums union involves, besides the suppression of discrimination in the field of commodity movements within the union, the creation of a common tariff wall against non-member countries. A higher form of economic integration is attained in a common market, where not only trade restrictions but also restrictions on factor movements are abolished. An economic union, as distinct from a common market, combines the removal of restrictions on commodity and factor movements with a degree of harmonisation of economic, monetary, fiscal, social and countercyclical policies. (Balassa 1961, p. 5 f.).

A political union, finally — or what Belassa calls "total economic integration" — involves "the unification of economic, fiscal etc. policies and requires the setting up of a supranational authority whose decisions are binding for the member-states" (Balassa 1961, p. 5 f.).

A terminology for describing varying degrees of integration is not the same, however, as a theory of European integration as a pre-determined process of an ever closer union. As an acceptable scientific theory, such a notion would have something falsifiable to say in three respects. First, is it an accurate *description* that the various steps in the staircase are being reached in accordance with an inherent logic ? Second, is it a plausible *explanation* that the process of integration is determined by its immanent purpose ? Third, is it a reasonable *prescription* to recommend that these steps be ascended one after the other, in accordance with some functional, neo-functional or federal logic?

Eight years have passed since 1989. It is about time we realise that the period between the Second World War and the fall of the Berlin Wall represents something of a parenthesis in the intellectual history of Western Europe, as well as in the adjacent American research on "what should be done" about the Westphalian system of sovereign states. During those forty-five years, the notion of a "necessary" integration was closely associated with the idea that the survival of democracy and a market economy on the European continent was greatly to be desired. Historicist thinking on European integration has to be understood as a part of this all-out concentration of powers — politically successful but, on this particular theme, intellectually problematic — to meet the military, economic and cultural threat from Soviet totalitarianism.

In post-communist Europe, the fundamental political problems are of another sort than those emphasised during the Cold War. As we approach the 21st century, it seems a reasonable guess that large-scale structural unemployment, wavering welfare states, and competitive difficulties on the world market will be the predominant political problems of the coming years. Nor did democratic stability come overnight to Northern, Southern, Western, Eastern or Central Europe as soon as the Cold War ended. In a sense this is not to be wondered at, since for the first time since 1933 democratic leaders cannot mobilise support by pointing to a totalitarian threat.

It may be of some interest to consider this problem in a somewhat broader historical perspective, by recalling the discussion conducted among British political scientists (Wilson 1996, pp. 39 ff.) and their opposite numbers in the continental resistance movements (Lipgens 1986, pp. 60-188) during the Second World War. These scholars were writing *during* the war about what ought to be done *after* the war. My point here is that, *before* the Cold War broke out, these early theorists were discussing the problems that we now face. They did not, in those years, take anything for granted about the future of Europe. Indeed, authors like David Mitrany and E.H. Carr emphasised again and again the illusions that had played such a disastrous role in the evolution of the 'twenty years crisis' between 1919 and 1939 (Mitrany 1943; Carr 1942, 236 ff., 1945, passim).

Paradoxical as it may seem, the New Europe debate during the Second World War was conducted to a great extent in 'piecemeal' terms. Down-to-earth, non-metaphysical arguments were marshalled for and against different steps that could and should be taken. It was not until the 1950s and 1960s (Frei 1985, pp. 113 ff.; Navari 1996, pp. 63 ff.; Rich 1996, pp. 183 ff.) that the idea of an inherent developmental logic towards an immanent *telos* became dominant. This is why, in my view, the idea of double asymmetry as a *normative* challenge (as distinct from a descriptive or explanatory one) was thought preposterous for so long a time in both neo-functionalist and federalist quarters.

References

ARNDT, HUBERTUS: "Zur Frage der Legitimität der Europäischen Zentralbank-autonomie", in: A. MAURER and B. THIELE (Eds.): *Legitimationsprobleme und Demokratisierung der Europäischen Union*, Marburg (Schüren) 1996, pp. 208-228.

BALASSA, BELA: "Towards a Theory of Economic Integration", *Kyklos*, 14 (1961), pp. 1-17.

BVerfGE [Entscheidungen des Bundesverfassungsgerichts], 89, 17, 155-213. (In addition, the complete text of the Maastricht verdict is available in English, German and French in Winkelmann 1994, pp. 697-799.).

CAPORASO, JAMES: "The European Union and Forms of State: Westphalian, Regulatory or Post-Modern?", *Journal of Common Market Studies*, 34 (1996), pp. 29-52.

CARR, E. H.: *Conditions of Peace*, London (Macmillan) 1942.

CARR, E. H.: *Nationalism and After*, London (Macmillan) 1945.

CERNY, PHILIP C.: "The Dynamics of Financial Globalization: Technology, Market Structure, and Policy Response", *Policy Sciences*, 27 (1994), pp. 319-342.

DAHL, ROBERT A.: "Federalism and the Democratic Process", *Nomos*, 25 (1983), pp. 95-108.

FREI, DANIEL: "Integrationsprozesse. Theoretische Erkenntnisse und praktische Folgerungen", in: W. WEIDENFELD (Ed.): *Die Identität Europas*, München (Carl Hanser) 1985, pp. 113-131.

GUSTAVSSON, SVERKER: "Preserve or Abolish the Democratic Deficit?," in: E. SMITH (Ed.): *National Parliaments as Cornerstones of European Integration*, London (Kluwer Law International) 1996, pp. 100-123.

GUSTAVSSON, SVERKER: "Defending the Democratic Deficit", in: A. WEALE and N. NENTWICH (Eds.): *The Political Theory of European Constitutional Choice*, London (Routledge) 1997, forthcoming.

KIELMANSEGG, PETER GRAF: "Integration und Demokratie", in: M. JACHTENFUCHS and B. KOHLER-KOCH (Eds.): *Europäische Integration*, Opladen (Leske + Budrich), pp. 47-71.

KOHLER-KOCH, BEATE: "The Strength of Weakness: The Transformation of Governance in the EU", in: S. GUSTAVSSON and L. LEWIN (Eds.): *The Future of the Nation-State*, Stockholm (Nerenius & Santérus) 1996, pp. 169-210.

LIPGENS, WALTER: *45 Jahre Ringen um die Europäische Verfassung*, Bonn (Europa Union Verlag) 1986.

MATTAUSCH, JOHN: "Karl Popper", in: S. M. LIPSET (Ed.): *The Encyclopedia of Democracy*, London (Routledge), 1995, pp. 978-979.

MITRANY, DAVID: *A Working Peace System*, London (Royal Institute of International Affairs) 1943.
NAVARI, CORNELIA: "Functionalism Versus Federalism: Alternative Visions of European Unity", in: P. MURRAY and P. RICH (Eds.): *Visions of European Unity*, Oxford (Westview Press) 1996, pp. 63-91.
POLANYI, KARL: *The Great Transformation*, Boston, Mass. (Beacon Press) 1957. Original 1944.
POPPER, KARL R.: *The Open Society and Its Enemies*, London (Routledge) 1945.
RICH, PAUL: "The Transformation of the European Ideal Since World War II", in P. MURRAY and P. RICH (Eds.): *Visions of European Unity*, Oxford (Westview Press) 1996, pp. 183-199.
RISSE-KAPPEN, THOMAS: "Exploring the Nature of the Beast: International Relations Theory and Comparative Policy Analysis Meet the European Union", *Journal of Common Market Studies*, 34 (1996), pp. 53-80.
SCHARPF, FRITZ W.: "Die Politikverflechtungs-Falle: Europäische Integration und deutscher Föderalismus im Vergleich", *Politische Vierteljahresschrift*, 26 (1985), pp. 323-356. In English in: *Public Administration*, 66 (1988), pp. 239-278.
SCHARPF, FRITZ W.: "Community and Autonomy: Multi-level Policy-making in the European Union", *Journal of European Public Policy*, 1 (1994), pp. 219-242.
SCHARPF, FRITZ W. (1996a): "Politische Optionen im vollendeten Binnenmarkt", in: M. JACHTENFUCHS and B. KOHLER-KOCH (Eds.): *Europäische Integration*. Opladen (Leske + Budrich) 1996, pp. 109-140.
SCHARPF, FRITZ W. (1996b): "Negative and Positive Integration in the Political Economy of European Welfare States", in: G. MARKS, F. W. SCHARPF, P. C. SCHMITTER and W. STREECK, *Governance in the European Union*, London (Sage) 1996, pp. 15-39.
SCHARPF, FRITZ W. (1996c): "Föderalismus und Demokratie in der transnationalen Ökonomie", in: K. von BEYME and C. OFFE (Eds.): *Politische Theorien in der Ära der Transformation*, Opladen (Westdeutscher Verlag) 1996, pp. 211-235 (= *Politische Vierteljahresschrift*, Sonderheft 26/1995.).
SCHARPF, FRITZ W. (1996d): "Democratic Policy in Europe", *European Law Journal*, 2 (1996), pp. 136-155.
STREECK, WOLFGANG: "Neo-Voluntarism: A New European Social Policy Regime?", in: G. MARKS, F. W. SCHARPF, P. C. SCHMITTER and W. STREECK: *Governance in the European Union*, London (Sage) 1996, pp. 64-94.
WEILER, JOSEPH H. H., ULRICH R. HALTERN and FRANZ C. MAYER: "European Democracy and its Critique", in: J. HAYWARD (Ed.): *The Crisis of Representation in Europe*, London (Frank Cass), pp. 4-39.

WILSON, PETER: "The New Europe Debate in Wartime Britain", in: P. MURRAY and P. RICH (Eds.): *Visions of European Unity*, Oxford (Westview Press) 1996, pp. 39-62.

WINKELMANN, INGO (Ed.): *Das Maastricht-Urteil des Bundesverfassungsgerichts vom 12. Oktober 1993. Dokumentation des Verfahrens mit Einführung*, Berlin (Duncker & Humblot) 1994.

ZÜRN, MICHAEL: "Jenseits der Staatlichkeit: über die Folgen der ungleichzeitigen Denationalisierung", *Leviathan*, 20 (1992), pp. 480-513.

ZÜRN, MICHAEL: "The Challenge of Globalization and Individualization: A View from Europe", in: H-H. HOLM and G. SØRENSEN (Eds.): *Whose World Order?*, Boulder, Colo. (Westview Press), pp. 137-163.

ZÜRN, MICHAEL: "Über den Staat und die Demokratie im europäischen Mehrebenensystem", *Politische Vierteljahresschrift*, 37 (1996), pp. 27-55.

Part B

Historical and Comparative Perspectives

Chapter 6

Democracy in Multicultural Societies and Multinational Settings*

RUSSELL L. HANSON

I. Introduction

For centuries the nation state has been the primary unit of political organization, but it seems to be the wrong size for today's world. In a global economy, nation states are often too small to make a difference. Governments no longer control their economies because many economic decisions are now made outside their borders, in the capitals of other countries, the home of international organizations (e.g. the World Bank or the International Monetary Fund), or the headquarters of multinational corporations. The loss of control is less obvious in large nation states, but even they will loose their economic sovereignty if the integration of finance and commerce proceeds on an international scale. The only way for policy makers to recover a measure of influence is to form alliances with other nations, creating multi-

* I received many helpful suggestions from participants in a seminar at ARENA, and I particularly want to thank Johan Olsen, Andreas Føllesdal, and Janne Haaland Matláry.

national organizations capable of operating over an entire continent or hemisphere.

Although the nation state is too small for economic purposes, it seems too big for many political purposes. Big states are now deemed inflexible and inefficient; in the popular language of the day they are too bureaucratic. Big states are said to be unresponsive to the demands of their citizens, who want greater control over their lives. In developed nations, these complaints have led to the devolution of power and the emergence of federalism (in practice, if not theory). In other places, the process of decentralization has gone even further. Big states are being dissolved, sometimes by relatively peaceful methods (as in the Velvet Revolution or the disintegration of the U.S.S.R), but more often through insurrection and violence (as in the case of what was once called Yugoslavia). The result is a proliferation of states enjoying political sovereignty over a small area. The new states are jealous of their independence, but their diminutive size makes them vulnerable to invasion and minimizes their economic leverage. Evidently, the only solution is to join confederations that promise collective security and commercial growth — objectives that are also shared by larger, more developed, nations.[1]

Thus, economic integration and political decentralization point to the same conclusion, even though they exert opposing pressures on the nation state.[2] The nation state is being eclipsed by multinational organizations of one sort or another. Naturally, the form of these new organizations is a matter of intense concern among policy makers and citizens alike. It will not be easy to design institutions that win political acceptance from people of different nations. Misunderstanding, distrust, and rivalry will prevent them from embracing supranational organizations unless nations believe their interests are adequately protected by the new institutions. For this belief to flourish, multinational organizations must be thoroughly democratic. Democracy is the ultimate source of legitimacy in contemporary politics because it promises a fair hearing of all interests in a political community. This is true at the local level, it is true at the national level, and I submit that the legitimacy of higher levels of government depends on democracy, too.

Hence, it is important to ask how a multinational federation can be constructed along democratic lines. I explore this question in the following pages, drawing on a particular understanding of democracy and its require-

1 See D. ELAZAR, et al.: *Federal Systems of the Word*, London (Longman) 1994.

2 B. BARBER: *Jihad vs. McWorld*, New York (Times Books) 1995.

ments. My analysis is grounded in liberal democratic theory, partly because that is what I know best, and partly because it has the greatest relevance for international affairs. The other candidates, social democratic theory and the theory of consociational democracy, are less useful in this regard. A strong consensus on values is the bedrock of social democratic politics, but consensus is rarely found in nations, and is rarer still in multistate regions.[3] Consequently, the image of a social democratic federation is not very helpful in thinking about organizations that must harmonize different national values and interests.

Theories of consociational democracy hold greater promise, insofar as they build on dissensus. However, this does not insure the relevance of consociational democracy to multinational regimes. Consociational democracy addresses domestic conflicts that are clearly defined, sharply felt, and long-lived. The differences between nations in a federation are rather different. Often, they are not defined very clearly. It may be hard to map the lines of cleavage in a federation, especially since the cleavages shift with the passage of time. Moreover, divisions between nations are not felt as sharply as those between religious or racial communities living on the same soil, contending for the same goods.[4] Consequently, it may be impossible to identify "pillars" that might support a consociational federation in the way that pillars uphold a consociational nation.

Liberal democratic theory does not suffer from this shortcomings, since it is concerned with conflict between interests that are fluid, and whose intensity varies. Yet it may seem an unpromising site for development because of liberal democrats' well-known preoccupation with individual rights and their antipathy toward groups and collective entities. With few exceptions the antipathy extends to nation states, which are usually portrayed as a threat to liberty. Even liberal democrats who admit the positive contributions of the state harbor suspicions about governments' tendency to abuse their powers. Indeed, that is one reason liberal democrats are democrats: popular control of-

3 Scandinavia may be an exception to this rule, although it is hard to imagine Norwegians, Swedes and Finns agreeing on all aspects of social policy. The level of consensus across nations is bound to be lower than it is within each nation, and that renders problematic any notion of a social democratic federation even in the most likely place of all.

4 National differences can lead to war, of course, but I am here concerned with multinational organizations that function in peaceful times.

fers some protection from persistent abuses of power.[5] According to this line of thinking, supranational organizations pose an even greater threat to individual liberty, making liberal democratic theory an unlikely source of inspiration for designing multinational federations.

Not all versions of liberal democratic theory are preoccupied exclusively with individual rights, however. In *Multicultural Citizenship* Will Kymlicka argues that group rights are compatible with liberal democracy, and may even be required for the protection of certain minorities in multicultural societies.[6] The members of a cultural minority should be able to pursue their objectives as freely as members of the majority or dominant culture in a democratic nation, he avers. Group rights insure this possibility by limiting the cultural power of the majority, which might otherwise overwhelm minority ways of life (even when that is not the objective of a majority). In this way group rights complement individual rights in multicultural societies.

Kymlicka focuses on democracy within nations, but his argument can be extended to multinational arrangements. In the following pages, I suggest how this might be done and what we might learn from the exercise. One set of lessons concerns the rights of nations within the federation, where the people of any nation are a group entitled to protection from other nations that form a majority in the federation. At issue here are procedures that allow the majority to rule without imposing unacceptable decisions on any single nation, or small number of nations. The European Union's desire to eradicate "mad cow disease" in the United Kingdom is one example of what I have in mind, although a better one is the decision to compel British employers to abide by EU regulations concerning the maximum number of hours that employees may be forced to work. Both controversies illustrate a well-known problem in liberal democratic theory, that of balancing minority rights and majority interests. There are solutions to the problem within nations, and some of them are also appropriate in multinational federations, or so I argue.

Another set of lessons concerns the role of a multinational federation in securing the rights of cultural minorities within a member state whose government is insensitive to the needs of people who are not part of the major-

5 J.S. Mill falls into this category, according to C.B. MACPHERSON: *The Life and Times of Liberal Democracy*, New York (Oxford University Press) 1977. In contrast J.J. Rousseau embraces the state without reservation, although some may question his credentials as a liberal democrat.

6 W. KYMLICKA: *Multicultural Citizenship*, Oxford (Oxford University Press) 1995.

ity culture. If Kymlicka is right, some cultural minorities are entitled to group rights. Democratic federations should promote these rights, not only when a member discriminates against a cultural minority, but also when it fails to extend group rights to cultural minorities who have a genuine claim to them. The offending governments are likely to regard the issue as a domestic matter, but I believe federations should, indeed must, intervene on behalf of cultural minorities under certain circumstances. Thus, in this essay I suggest what federations ought to do, and how far they ought to go, in upholding individual and group rights against governments which are themselves members of the federation.

A third set of lessons concerns the relation between the first two. In my view, the case for group rights within nations is based on the very same principles that nations use to justify their rights in a multinational federation. Hence nations that seek protection from federation majorities are obliged to recognize the rights of cultural minorities within their own borders — just as nations that refuse to acknowledge the rights of cultural minorities cannot claim group rights for themselves in a multinational federation. They must submit to the authority of the federation in matters of group rights, or withdraw from it; they cannot have it both ways.

Since my analysis builds on Kymlicka's account of democracy in a multicultural society, I begin with his defense of group rights for some minorities. Then I consider how democracy might be achieved in three different types of federation: a federation of monocultural nations, a federation of multicultural nations, and a federation comprised of some monocultural and some multicultural nations. By construction, each type of federation raises distinct questions about the rights of member states and the sort of rules that ought to govern collective decision making in democratic bodies. Together these cases shed light on the problems of forming federations in the real world, although I resist the temptation to comment extensively on specific instances, e.g. the European Union.

II. Democracy in a Multicultural Society

I start with Kymlicka's description of a single, multicultural society governed by a nation-state. The cultures comprising this hypothetical society are geographically concentrated, and each was self-governing at one time. In fact, this is what distinguishes a multicultural society from a polyethnic society in Kymlicka's eyes. A polyethnic society is a the result of demographic forces, e.g. immigration. Since ethnic groups often settle in the same areas of the new homeland, their population may be geographically concentrated. However, these ethnic enclaves are not, and never were, independent. The situation is quite different when previously sovereign people living in close proximity become united. That is a genuine multicultural society, and it is the result of a political process of incorporation.

The incorporation may be voluntary, as in the case of the American colonies or Canadian provinces after they obtained independence. More often, incorporation is achieved by conquest. In neither case do the members of the cultures comprising a multicultural society give up their cultures in favor of a national system of values. Instead, the members of each culture strive to maintain their way of life within the union. After all, self-governing peoples would never abandon independence unless incorporation offered better prospects for survival in a rapidly changing world. They would fight to the death in order to preserve their culture outside the union, if being in the union meant extinction for their way of life. Hence the more or less peaceful coexistence of different cultures in the same nation suggests that members of each culture believe their way of life is well-served in a political union.[7]

In a multicultural society some cultures are bound to be more powerful than others. There will be a dominant culture or cultures, and there will be subordinate or minority cultures. If the multicultural society is democratic, this does not matter as far as individual rights are concerned. All members of the polity will have the same rights, regardless of their cultural background. This includes individuals who are members of minority cultures. Like members of the majority culture, they will have basic freedoms, e.g. freedom of conscience, freedom of expression, and freedom of association. Members of minority cultures will also enjoy certain guarantees under civil and criminal law, including equal protection and due process. Finally, as individuals the members of minority cultures will be entitled to participate in making laws by petitioning government, forming political parties, and electing representatives.

7 This is not an empirical claim, but an analytical proposition. Those who value a way of life want to maintain it, and if incorporation offers the best chance of survival, compared to all available options, then unification is the most reasonable course of action.

Should the members of minority cultures have other privileges, apart from basic rights enjoyed by every individual in the polity? Kymlicka believes they must have additional protection. Even if the society is democratic and extends basic rights to all citizens, the survival of minority cultures requires group rights. Majorities often expect members of a minority culture to assimilate, and they may exert pressure toward that end. Overt pressure is not always necessary, however. Some minority cultures never achieve the "critical mass" that is needed to resist being washed away in the mainstream. Small minorities, or those who cultural bonds are weak or easily penetrated, may be unable to maintain their way of life. They will be overwhelmed by images of the good life drawn from the majority's art, commerce, politics, and religion. Inexorably, the values of the majority will become their own unless the sheer power of numbers can be curtailed, or its effects counteracted in some way. That is the function of group rights, which make it easier to resist absorption by the dominant culture.

By definition, group rights are not established on an individual basis. Neither are they universal; only the members of a cultural minority may claim these rights. The rights themselves fall into three categories. Some group rights authorize a substantial amount of self-determination at the local or regional level, limiting the power of majorities over geographically concentrated minorities. Other group rights involve government support for practices essential to the preservation of a culture, including the use of native languages in official proceedings and bilingual education. Then there are rights of representation, guaranteeing minority cultures a place in national government, and hence some influence over policies that affect minorities (and majorities, too). These three types of group rights, which are restricted to minority cultures in multicultural societies, complete Kymlicka's vision of liberal democracy.[8]

Group rights can be justified in many ways. They may originate in agreements that were made at the time of incorporation, i.e. when people of different cultures became politically unified. Hunting and fishing rights of indigenous peoples are an example of group rights that are recognized on historical grounds by dominant culture. Alternatively, group rights can be justified in the name of diversity. Diversity may serve all cultures, including the

8 According to Kymlicka, minorities in polyethnic societies are not entitled to group rights, except perhaps when migration to the society in question was forced, as in the case of slaves. I will return to the issue of group rights for ethnic and political minorities at the end of my essay.

dominant one, by fostering debates about values that keep cultures alive, as J.S. Mill noted long ago. To this defense may be added arguments about the intrinsic value of diversity and the importance of acknowledging group differences as a matter of fairness.[9]

Kymlicka points to another, even stronger, rationale for group rights. Liberal democrats promote personal autonomy, on the assumption that individuals must decide how to conduct themselves throughout the course of their lives. To be meaningful, these decisions must be free, in the sense of being uncoerced. Consequently, the exercise of freedom depends on rights, for rights allow individuals to make choices without interference from others. But which choices should an individual make? For that matter, which choices should even be considered by individuals who want to live a life that is worth living?

For answers to these questions individuals depend on culture, which supplies them with meaningful images of the good life and corresponding patterns of right conduct. The relevant culture is the one into which a person is born, which in the case of minorities is manifestly different from the culture of the majority. To be sure, an individual from a minority culture may eventually decide to abandon traditional ways in favor the dominant mode of life, and this possibility must be allowed in a multicultural democracy. However, for most minorities the costs of cultural conversion are so high that it would be grossly unfair to require it. For these people, the opportunity to act in traditional ways must be preserved, and this can only be achieved through group rights, or so Kymlicka argues.[10]

In short, liberal democracy in a multicultural society requires basic rights for all, and special rights for cultural minorities, if justice is to be served. However, minority cultures may not abuse the power than comes from group rights. The right to local control or self-determination does not justify policies that violate the rights of individuals living within minority communities. The political leaders of a minority may not enforce cultural practices that are inconsistent with the idea of individual autonomy. Neither can they penalize individuals who deviate from cultural norms, even if those norms are

9 See, for example, C. TAYLOR: "The Politics of Recognition", in: A. GUTTMAN (Ed.): *Multiculturalism: Examining the Politics of Recognition*, Princeton (Princeton University Press) 1994, pp.25-73.

10 These identities are not codes, they are scripts that allow for creativity. At some point, though, creativity becomes unrecognizable by those who are familiar with the script, i.e. other members of a culture.

essential to a cultural way of life. Individuals must be free to accept a way of life, and they must be free to reject it without fear of government sanctions.[11] Hence group rights apply exclusively to relations with other cultures in the polity, not to the internal affairs of a cultural minority.

III. Democracy in a Federation of Monocultural Nations

Much more could be said about group rights in general, and Kymlicka's defense of them in particular. I have merely repeated his claims without explaining them in detail, and without subjecting them to the critical scrutiny they deserve.[12] That is because I want to move from the philosophical question of whether group rights are valid to the practical question of how group rights might be protected effectively. Hence I shall proceed as if the case for group rights in a multicultural society has been settled, so that I may concentrate on the role of multinational federations in enforcing both individual and group rights.

As it happens, the composition of the federation affects the role it plays in furthering democracy by protecting rights. Consider first a multinational federation comprised entirely of single culture polities. This hypothetical federation is analogous to the multicultural society discussed by Kymlicka, insofar as it combines culturally distinct and politically independent entities.[13] For purposes of this discussion, I assume that each member of a multinational federation is committed to the preservation of its national iden-

---

11 Social sanctions are another matter; from a liberal democratic point of view "the problem arises when a group seeks to use *governmental* power, or the distribution of public benefits, to restrict the liberty of members." See W. KYMLICKA: "The Good, the Bad, and the Intolerable", *Dissent* (Summer 1996), pp. 22-30.

12 See, for example, A. FØLLESDAL: "Minority Rights: A Liberal Contractualist Case", in: Juha Raikka (Ed.): *Do we need minority rights? Conceptual issues*, The Hague (Kluwer Law International) 1997, pp. 59-84.

13 The parallel is exact. Kymlicka's prescriptions for a multicultural society are consciously based on the idea of compacts between nations. In this essay I am reversing the argument, projecting Kymlicka's description of a multicultural society onto a multinational federation.

tity, and that democracy is a part of each member's identity. Democracy is not the whole of any nation's identity, but for the federation I have in mind it must be a characteristic feature of each state's conception of itself. The fact that democracy means different things, and may be institutionalized in different ways, loosens the restrictiveness of this assumption.

In my fictive federation of monocultural nations, citizens in each nation enjoy democratic rights. Individuals have basic freedoms, equal protection under the law, and rights of political participation. The list of rights may be long in some nations and short in others, but there is an overlapping consensus on the essential rights of individuals.[14] Special rights for cultural minorities are not an issue in this case. Since each nation encompasses a single culture, group rights are not required (and in fact are not warranted). Individual rights of the sort I mentioned are all that is needed for internal democracy to exist.

There are collective rights in this example, but they are enjoyed by nations in the federation. The rights include self-determination in a wide range of matters not under the control of the federation. Naturally, the extent of self-determination will vary from federation to federation. Some federations have broad mandates covering many aspects of social life; the European Union is good example and will become an even better one if a single currency is widely implemented. Other federations have a narrow mandate; defensive alliances fit this description. Of course, the breadth of a mandate may change with the passage of time, as members expand or contract the functions of a federation. However, in all true federations the sovereignty of each member remains more or less intact and is the basis for participation in collective decision making.[15]

Thus, each member in my imaginary multinational federation enjoys a group right to substantial self-determination, just as cultural minorities in a multicultural society are entitled to a large measure of local control. The analogy holds for measures designed to protect or promote institutions that are central to a group's identity or way of life, too. The federation formally recognizes the authority of each members' political institutions, and the right of each government to represent the interests of its people. This is an enduring commitment, but it might also happen that a member or members of a

14 J. RAWLS: *Political Liberalism*, New York (Columbia University Press) 1993.

15 When nations withdraw from federations they are demonstrating the fact that sovereignty has not been ceded, but is ultimately reserved to themselves.

federation require political, economic, or military support from others. The support is restricted to members whose national survival is in danger, or whose position within the federation will suffer great harm unless aid is rendered. In extraordinary instances, the support may become permanent, although in most cases support will cease when the danger passes or a member can stand on its own within the federation.

Rights of representation in government are the third type of group right advocated by Kymlicka. Extending his argument from a multicultural society to a multinational federation is straightforward. If each nation is a distinctive group, then every nation, no matter how small, must be represented in policy making bodies at the federal level. Since the legislature is be the most powerful body in a truly democratic federation, each nation must have voting rights in the parliament, although these rights need not be equal.[16] In fact, a unit rule would be unfair to populous nations; larger nations should have more votes than smaller countries, so that each *citizen* in the federation is more or less equally represented.

However, it also seems unfair to leave control of the federation in the hands of a simple majority, especially if that majority is based on the votes of a few large countries. The national interests of smaller or less influential members of the federation might be ignored by a simple majority. Worse, they might be harmed arbitrarily by majorities who want to shift the impact or cost of federation decisions onto someone else's shoulders. This problem of "tyrannical majorities" is well-known in multicultural societies, and the usual solution is to delay action unless or until an extraordinary majority forms.[17] In a multinational federation this translates into a requirement that legislation can only be adopted by a large majority, a provision that affords some protection to minorities, since majority coalitions can only expand by offering concessions to minorities outside the coalition.

The degree of protection depends on rules that govern the federation, any number of which might qualify as democratic. For example, the rules might require a majority of three-fifths, or two-thirds, or three-fourths for approval of policy. The exact location of the threshold will have an enormous impact on the federation's capacity to enact legislation, especially if it applies to all

16 The legislature has, and should have, the most power in a democracy because it is the most representative organ of government. Its popular mandate is broader than any other institution's, or so I presume.

17 E. SPITZ: *Majority Rule*, Chatham, NJ (Chatham House Publishers) 1984, provides a helpful review of the problem of majority rule and its solutions.

actions, and not just important decisions. Just as obviously, the location of the threshold will determine the level of protection enjoyed by minorities; lower thresholds afford less protection, higher thresholds more. Still, it is impossible to say in advance that one threshold is intrinsically more democratic than another. That depends on circumstances, and for that matter, on the collective judgment of those who form a democratic federation and fashion its rules.

Instead of requiring approval by an extraordinary majority in the federation, parliamentary action may be contingent on the approval of concurrent majorities. If there are distinct voting blocs in the legislature, and a majority in each bloc favors the same action, the action has the support of concurrent majorities. The arrangement offers a high level of security for those who constitute a majority within a bloc, even though they might be outnumbered in the legislature as a whole. Of course, a rule requiring support from concurrent majorities is only practical if there are obvious blocs in the federation. For example, the blocs may consist of founding members of the federation, on the one hand, and newcomers, on the other. They might consist of large and small nations, or perhaps regional combinations within the federation (north-south, east-west, etc.). Any enduring line of demarcation can define the blocs, and if there really are enduring divisions, rule by concurrent majorities may help maintain the federation by restricting its action to policies endorsed by a dispersed majority. (Of course, this kind of federation is likely to be a sluggish body; that is the key to its longevity).

A rule of unanimity is the extreme version of concurrent majoritarianism; each nation constitutes a bloc of one, and if the agreement of all blocs is required, any nation can veto federal actions it opposes.[18] Thus, national vetoes provide the highest degree of protection for individual members, and the greatest challenge to majority rule, especially if the veto is absolute. However, a veto that cannot be over-ridden places enormous power in the hands of a single nation, power that may be used to frustrate the will of majorities that may be massive in size. Precisely for this reason, vetoes threaten the survival of a federation and should be avoided since there is an alternative for nations that feel threatened by policies preferred by a majority of the federation.

18 I do not see any democratic grounds for giving a veto to some nations and not others, especially if every nation is entitled to group rights, as I am arguing here.

Nations enter a federation to insure their survival as distinct societies, I have said. The federation is instrumental in this regard; otherwise there is no reason to join. Similarly, if the federation proves indifferent to a member's interests, or worse, if the federation pursues policies that undermine a member's fundamental interests, that nation should withdraw from the federation. There is no longer any reason to remain within the organization, except to cause mischief. Using its veto a nation may immobilize a federation, whereas if it leaves the federation it may find itself at the mercy of majority preferences. As John Major knows, Britain with a veto is more effective inside the EU than it could be outside of it. Take away the veto, or better yet, never confer it in the first place, and the possibilities for disruption are limited.

That does not mean the majority will always get its way. If secession is an option, national vetoes should not be necessary in a democratic federation. When members are free to leave a federation whenever it suits them, their preferences must be respected by nations that want to preserve the federation as a way of sustaining their own national identities. In some cases this will require forbearance on the part of majorities. Suppose an extraordinary majority has the right to make policy under the existing rules of voting, but its preferred course of action faces strong objections from a minority of members. If the objections are coupled with a threat of withdrawal, and the withdrawal could weaken the federation, the majority can only win a Pyrrhic victory by imposing its will. In that situation members of the majority must decide where their own interests lie: Are their nations' best served by pursuing policies that cause other members to leave the federation, reducing its future utility? Or will the members of the majority fare better if they forego action in order to maintain the federation at full strength? The decision will depend on the issue in question and the value of the federation in other policy areas, but the majority is constrained by the need to assess the consequences of divisive action.[19]

Not all of the rules are tilted toward minorities in the federation I have constructed, however. The federation must be able to sanction or even expel recalcitrant members. A nation can place extraordinary burdens on others by obstructing federal actions that promote the national interests of those who favor it. Moreover, nations in a federation are autonomous in policy areas

19 Thus, national vetoes and majority decision-making under the threat of secession can lead to the same outcome, but in the latter case the decision belongs to the majority. This is a crucial difference, for democrats.

outside of the federation's mandate. By exercising its powers of self-governance without regard for other nations' interests, a nation may inflict substantial damage on its brethren in the federation. This is unavoidable when national interests collide, but the effect of such actions clearly damages the federation and lessens its value to other members. In such cases the rogue member ought to face disciplinary action by the federation.

A federation may impose sanctions whenever a member refuses to comply with its policy, assuming the requisite majority believes sanctions are warranted. If sanctions do not produce compliance, the offending nation should be expelled from the federation. Voting under the rules of the federation, the legislature majority may revoke a nation's membership and cancel any benefits that would otherwise accrue to the ousted member. No further punitive sanctions are warranted, however. Nations expelled from the federation should be treated like any other nonmember country. Of course, any subsequent application to rejoin the federation may be viewed with skepticism, since past relations with the federation are a relevant consideration whenever applications for membership are weighed.

There is one other instance in which the federation may sanction a member. Since all members admit the existence of basic rights for individuals, a nation cannot abridge the rights of its citizens without violating the terms of federation membership. Hence the federation is not only authorized, but is positively obliged to defend the rights of citizens against member governments who abuse them. The obligation extends to rights formally guaranteed by the federation in its charter, if there is one, or in its traditions, where there is no charter.

The role of the federation in protecting rights is not restricted to rights that are part of an overlapping consensus in the federation. The federation is also the ultimate guarantor of rights that are recognized in the constitution of the offending government, even if those rights are not recognized anywhere else in the federation. To be sure, the primary defense of these rights must come from agencies within the nation, but those agencies may be assisted by the federation. The reason? Such rights are part of the democratic identity of the nation, which the federation is pledged to protect. Thus, it may be necessary to confront the government of a member nation in order to preserve democratic rights in that country.[20]

20 An example from the United States illustrates what I have in mind. Education is not a fundamental right under the U.S. Constitution, but it is in some state

IV. Democracy in a Federation of Multicultural Nations

A federation of nations may exert pressure on members that violate individual rights, but does it have the authority to safeguard the rights of minority cultures in member states? This question does not arise in federations of monocultural nations. However, it is an important issue in federations with members that have minority cultures. Such federations may be composed entirely of multicultural nations, or they may be mixed, including some multicultural nations, and some monocultural nations. I defer discussion of the mixed federation until the next section. Here I consider another hypothetical federation in which every member is a multicultural society in the sense described by Kymlicka.

Because every member of the federation is a multicultural society, each includes at least one cultural minority that is entitled to group rights. The group rights in question consist of one or more of the following: the right to self-governance on a local or regional basis, the right to national support for practices that are crucial to the preservation of a minority culture, and guaranteed representation in the law-making body of the nation. The rights are not self-enforcing, however; even democratic governments sometimes fail to respect the acknowledged rights of minorities. In such cases, is there any basis for outside intervention on behalf of cultural minorities?

Certainly there is if the offending nation is a member of a democratic federation.[21] The logic of federation suggests why intervention is justified. As I stipulated in the previous section, nations join federations in order to advance their interests and preserve their identities. But if a nation's identity is multicultural, in Kymlicka's sense of that term, the federation is bound to protect each of the cultures that comprise a nation's identity. It cannot ignore minority cultures; to the contrary it must support minorities against any government that fails to respect group rights. In so doing, the federation is

---

constitutions. In these states courts are often asked to remove barriers to equal education. When they fail to do so, the U.S. Supreme Court may intervene, because the Fourteenth Amendment guarantees equal protection under state laws, whatever those laws may be (and they are not the same in all states).

21 The answer may be yes in any case, but I think the case for intervention is particularly compelling when a nation is part of a federation.

merely doing what a nation asked when it entered the federation: maintaining the (multicultural) identity of the nation in question.

Intervention by a federation in the domestic politics of a member nation is bound to be controversial, but the justification seems clear enough, at least in this imaginary example. Perhaps that is because the example involves a government that does not respect group rights that have already been acknowledged as such. Complications arise when group rights have not been formally extended to cultural minorities by their government, even though some or all of these minorities are entitled to special protection under the terms of Kymlicka's argument. In this case, the question is whether the federation ought to intervene with the intention of establishing group rights, not merely upholding previously recognized rights.

In my view, intervention is justified in this case. It makes little sense to say that a cultural minority is entitled to group rights, but those rights need not be recognized (and hence need not be enforced) by their government. Otherwise, why would any government recognize the claims of cultural minorities, except by mistake or out of a misplaced conviction that recognition does not entail enforcement? Far better to say that when a minority claims special protection, it may ask the federation to evaluate its claims, and if the evaluation is positive, to insure their recognition by the appropriate national government. (Once recognized, the rights must be enforced, as I have already shown.)

Several restrictions apply to federal intervention of the sort I am discussing. The federation may not support movements trying to break away or secede from a member state. That would be inconsistent with the federation's purpose, which is the preservation of each member's national identity. This commitment is in fact the basis for minority appeals to the federation, and it precludes any action that might destroy or undermine an existing, multicultural identity. The most a federation can do is press for group rights within the existing polity, i.e. some measure of local control, a degree of protection for vital cultural practices, and assurances of representation in national policy making councils.

Although a federation may insist that a member state establish meaningful group rights for a cultural minority, it cannot specify which rights ought to be established. Each member must decide for itself how minorities will be protected in the nation; particular institutions and practices cannot be imposed by the federation without contradicting the basic purpose of federation, which is the preservation of an existing identity. Part of that identity is a commitment to specific institutions and practices of democracy, so the negotiation of group rights will require consultation with all cultures comprising the nation. These negotiations, and the specifics of the situation, will determine which measures are needed to preserve minority cultures, and hence what sort of concessions must be made by the dominant or majority culture in the way of group rights.

Importantly, the federation may only insist on group rights for cultural minorities that existed prior to the formation of a multicultural nation. As I mentioned previously, some of these groups entered the nation voluntarily in order to extend their cultural heritage, while others were integrated by conquest or enslavement. Regardless of how incorporation was accomplished, no minority culture ever abandoned its right to self-determination. It is this inherent right which justifies special protections for cultural minorities, and only cultural minorities, in Kymlicka's view.

Therefore, cultural groups that emerge as the result of individual or familial migration do not qualify for group rights. Migrants choose a destination knowing it does not recognize their group as a distinctive minority at the time of relocation. Having made this choice, they cannot claim group rights after resettling. Migrants must be content with what they find, which may include many important individual rights, even if there are no group rights for them.[22] Alternatively, they must move again; they cannot assert a right to self-determination equivalent to peoples whose homelands were absorbed by the union with other peoples.

Another exclusion applies to marginalized or oppressed groups in a diverse nation: women, homosexuals, the disabled, etc. The members of each group have many experiences in common, but they do not share a way of life as cultural minorities do, according to Kymlicka. Marginalized groups are not an "intergenerational community, more or less institutionally complete, occupying a given territory or homeland, sharing a distinct language and history" (Kymlicka 1995, p. 18). Hence they are not entitled to group rights, and in fact group rights may not be appropriate insofar as marginalized groups do not seek a separate existence. Typically, marginalized groups seek inclusion in the mainstream, albeit on their own terms, not those of the ma-

22 M. WALZER: "Comment on The Politics of Recognition", in A. GUTTMAN (Ed.): *Multiculturism: Examining the Politics of Recognition*, Princeton (Princeton University Press),1994, pp. 99-103.

jority. For this purpose, measures like affirmative action may be justified, but affirmative action is a policy, not a right in the usual sense of that term.

The most important limitation on federal intervention on behalf of minority cultures in a member state derives from the composition of the federation itself. Since the members of the federation under consideration here are all multicultural nations, every member of the federation will be reluctant to intervene in the affairs of another country. This is not out of any sympathy for the target of intervention, but out of a desire to avoid setting a precedent that might later be invoked against themselves. To minimize that possibility, members of the federation will only support intervention when cultural minorities present a convincing case, i.e. unless their claim to self-determination is credible on historical and political grounds.

The decision on intervention will be tempered by one other consideration. A multicultural nation that finds itself at odds with a federation of other multicultural nations may decide to withdraw from the federation instead of complying with a directive to extend group rights to a cultural minority. On democratic grounds this withdrawal must be allowed, and indeed it cannot be prevented. If that happens, the federation has lost much of its influence over the recalcitrant government (or perhaps I should say the recalcitrant majority, since it is unlikely that in a democracy a government would be recalcitrant without support from the majority). On the other hand, the federation may continue its support for cultural minorities and even expand it, since the stricture against encouraging independence movements does not apply to nonmember nations. That consideration may make cooperation with the federation more attractive than withdrawal for a nation confronted with demands for group rights.[23]

23 Would a democratic federation side with a cultural minority, driving a government from its fold, and then supporting war against it? An idealist hopes so, but the realist says no. In truth, everything depends on the political skill of federation members in fostering recognition without forcing a showdown.

V. Democracy in a Federation of Mono- and Multicultural Nations

My last hypothetical case involves a mixed federation, i.e. a federation including some multicultural nations and some monocultural nations. This is a more realistic construction, and it is more complex. It is more complex because the mixed membership affects the role of the federation vis-á-vis cultural minorities in multicultural nations that belong to the federation. Since the membership includes distinct blocs of nations, a rule of concurrent majoritarianism is appropriate. Thus, in my version of a mixed federation cultural minorities may seek relief from an oppressive national government, but the federation cannot demand group rights for the minority without the agreement of a majority of monocultural AND multicultural nations in the federation.

Of course, this consideration applies only to group rights. With respect to individual rights, the mixed federation has the same responsibility as a federation of multicultural nations or a federation of monocultural nations. The mixed federation must uphold democratic rights that form the core of each member's national identity; since the federation exists to preserve members' identity it is obliged to correct violations of rights that are committed by member governments against their own citizens.

The protected rights include any guarantees mentioned in the charter of federation, plus other rights guaranteed in the constitution of the nation in question. At a minimum, individuals' freedom of conscience, expression and association must be assured. Individuals must be treated equally under the law, and they must receive due process in all legal proceedings. (What counts as due process may vary from nation to nation.) Also, individuals must be allowed to participate in politics: suffrage must be universal, citizens must be able to petition their government, etc. Any other political, social or economic rights mentioned in a nation's constitution, or which are part of its constitutional tradition, should also be upheld by the federation since they form part of the identity of the nation and the preservation of that identity is the purpose of federation.

Group rights are an issue in a mixed federation, since some members of the federation are multicultural nations. For reasons I set out in the preceding section, a mixed federation may require a member state to acknowledge and enforce group rights for cultural minorities with a legitimate claim to self-determination ("intergenerational communities that are more or less institutionally complete, occupying a homeland and sharing language and history"). This includes geographic minorities who once governed themselves and are now part of a multicultural nation, whether by choice or conquest. The federation may not specify which group rights must be established, however; this is a matter to be decided by cultures comprising the nation in question.

Intervention by the mixed federation follows a successful appeal for relief by a cultural minority. In a federation of multicultural nations the likelihood of success is tempered by members' sympathy for each other's political predicament: when every member of the federation is a multicultural nation, members will not endorse intervention lightly because each of them is potentially a target of investigation. That presumption does not hold in the present case, since some of the members of a mixed federation are monocultural nations. They may be more willing to support intervention because they will never suffer it themselves. Monocultural nations are also likely to be are more sympathetic to arguments about cultural preservation. After all, cultural preservation is a vital component of every monocultural nation's identity; none of them has any reason to doubt the value of group rights, as multicultural nations do. To the contrary, governments in nations with a singular identity often pursue policies intended to preserve a national way of life, especially if the nation is small.[24]

Monocultural nations' favorable disposition toward cultural minorities is valuable to the federation. Multicultural nations will probably be too reluctant to intervene in another member's internal affairs. They may reject appeals for relief even when cultural minorities have genuine grievances, so as to avoid setting a precedent that might expose themselves to intervention in the future. Monocultural nations have no such inhibitions. They will be more inclined to accept appeals from cultural minorities. If so, this will encourage cultural minorities to use the federation as a forum for airing grievances that have been ignored by their own governments.

---

24 Most monocultural nations are small, and this may increase their sympathy for cultural minorities in multicultural societies: they, too, have felt the weight of the offending majority in federation affairs. On the important differences between small, homogeneous states and large, diverse nations see J. OLSEN: *Europeanization and Nation-State Dynamics*, Oslo (ARENA Working Paper No. 9) 1995.

Of course, multicultural nations will claim with some justification that monocultural nations do not understand the complexities of governance in multicultural nations. Indeed, multicultural nations may argue that monocultural nations ought to be excluded from the decision-making process because they lack relevant experience in such matters. They may insist that appeals from cultural minorities be heard only by multicultural members of the hypothetical federation I have constructed. While this may seem self-serving, there is a pragmatic justification for it: the restriction could make any decision to intervene more acceptable to the affected nation. According to this line of argument, intervention will be tolerated if it is backed by nations that have their own minorities and are familiar with the political difficulties of multicultural governance. Or at least a multicultural nation is more likely to respond constructively to intervention that has been authorized and shaped by its peers, i.e. other multicultural nations.

The practice of restricted voting may be defended on pragmatic grounds, but it is hard to justify in democratic terms, especially if the restriction applies only to questions involving group rights. That is because restricted voting is either unjustified in all cases, or it is appropriate for any issue where expertise or relevant experience is indispensable. The issue of group rights is not the only area in which expertise or experience are crucially relevant; surely the same argument applies in defense matters, where some nations have unusual security concerns, or economic affairs, where the nature of industry or the relative importance of farming or fishing vary from country to country. Many more examples could be listed, but the point is obvious: if expertise or experience is important in deciding appeals from cultural minorities, then it must be important in other policy discussions, too, and these discussions ought to be settled by restricted voting too.

The conclusion is unworkable. Nations' expertise and experience vary from policy to policy, and so will the list of nations entitled to control each policy discussion. The ensuing proliferation of restricted voting arrangements will make the make the operation of the federation too complex; indeed, it would convert the federation from a single, multipurpose organization into several single purpose organizations with different memberships. Neither outcome is acceptable, so the premise that leads to them must be rejected: decision making in a democratic federation should not be confined to experts. By implication, in the mixed federation appeals from cultural minorities should not be controlled only by multicultural nations.

A better solution to the problem is a rule requiring the approval of concurrent majorities.[25] That is, federal intervention in behalf of a cultural minority is warranted only when a majority of monocultural nations approves AND a majority of multicultural nations concurs. This arrangement permits each type of nation to make a distinctive contribution to the decision. Because of their openness to minority appeals, monocultural nations supply the impetus for action. Multicultural nations inject caution into the proceedings, based on their own experience with group politics. If concurrent majorities form, the basis for federal intervention will be unassailable.

The arrangement leaves multicultural nations with a veto on action, it is true. If a majority of multicultural nations rejects an appeal from a cultural minority, no intervention can occur. Given what I have said about multicultural nations reluctance to intervene, minorities cannot expert much relief under concurrent majoritarianism. However, a minority's chances are better in the mixed federation than they are in a federation composed entirely of multicultural nations. If the appeal finds favor with a majority of monocultural nations, multicultural nations will be under political pressure to endorse intervention. The costs of saying no will rise, and this may offset the reluctance of multicultural nations to act against one of their own kind.

Of course, a multicultural nation that is a member of the federation may decide to withdraw from the organization instead of complying with a directive to extend group rights to a cultural minority within its borders. The escape must be allowed, but all benefits of membership cease upon exiting the federation. Also, the federation is no longer proscribed from endorsing a cultural minority's call for independent status. The federation is not bound to respect the multicultural identity of an ex-member; it may prefer the dismemberment of a departed nation. It may even promise membership to cultural minorities if they succeed in obtaining their independence, and if they are committed to democracy.

Considering the costs of secession, offending nations may decide to comply with federal directives to extend group rights to cultural minorities. In so doing offenders will avoid the disopprobrium of other democratic nations, na-

---

25 M. NENTWICH and G. FALKNER: "Intergovernmental Conference 1996: Which Constitution for the Union?", *European Law Journal*, 2,1 (1996), pp. 83-102, discuss some of the controversies over voting rules in a diverse federation. See also their paper "The IGC 1996: The Moment of Constitutional Choice for a Democratic Europe?", presented to a workshop on "The Political Theory of European Constitutional Choice", Oslo, 29 March-3 April, 1996.

tions with whom they have identified in the past. (They were part of a federation of democratic nations, after all). The extension of group rights may also stabilize the domestic political situation of a multicultural nation. Indeed, group rights may be the only way of preserving a multicultural identity in combustible political situations.

VI. Other Considerations

When nations become federated, collective decision making must respect each nation's right to self-determination. A people's right to selfdetermination is based on historical claims and political realities that simply cannot be ignored in multinational federations. This may be inconvenient, in the sense that the desire to preserve national sovereignty may prevent federations from functioning smoothly. On the other hand, that same desire generates motives for joining federations and remaining within them. Governments may conclude that their nation's distinctive identity is better preserved within a federation than outside (or against) it. To foster that conclusion, federations ought to be constructed in such a way that the sovereignty of every member is respected.

To these pragmatic considerations I have added a moral one. In the three hypothetical examples I discuss, every member of the federation is a democracy. That is to say, the exercise of sovereignty somehow reflects the will of a nation's people. Consequently, it is popular sovereignty that is being preserved when national sovereignty is respected in a federation. It is important to keep this in mind, because it confers on the federation a responsibility for maintaining democracy in member states. Precisely because national sovereignty and democracy are linked, the federation must insure that nations themselves function democratically. Toward that end the federation must secure the rights of individuals in each of its member states, and it must support group rights for cultural minorities in members that are multicultural. In so doing the federation fulfills the primary purposes of collective organization, the preservation of its members' national identity.

The enforcement of group rights for cultural minorities is based on the same principles that underlie participation in a federation of democratic nations. The people of each nation are a collectivity with a history of self-determination, and on this basis they claim group rights in the federation. These rights include substantial powers of self-determination, special rights in the federation, and guaranteed or assured representation in the federal parliament. The same logic applies to cultural minorities in member states. Consequently, a multicultural nation cannot deny group rights without undermining its own position in a federation of democratic nations.

The logic applies only to cultural minorities, as defined by Kymlicka. Other minorities and disadvantaged groups are not entitled to group rights; they cannot demand self-government at the local or regional level, linguistic rights, or assured representation in government. Those rights are reserved for cultural minorities, and marginalized or disadvantaged groups have no basis for seeking them, at home or through federation channels. Ethnic minorities and other disadvantaged groups can only claim individual rights that are available to every citizen in their nation, and they can demand federal action in support of these rights.

Admittedly, this conclusion is not completely satisfying. It restricts group rights to those who were able to achieve independence at some point in history, whether by luck or pluck. Less successful groups are denied access to group rights, even though their ways of life may be seriously threatened by the dominant culture. The disparity in treatment raises a troubling question for democratic federations: Shouldn't marginalized or disadvantaged groups be protected, too, since they are in the same situation as cultural minorities?

It may be that marginalized groups deserve protection, but not in the same way the cultural minorities are secured. Upon closer inspection, it seems the two types of groups are not in the same situation after all. Cultural minorities want to preserve their distance from the dominant culture, but marginalized groups generally want to overcome that distance. They have been excluded from the mainstream, and they seek inclusion on fair terms. To achieve inclusion, protective measures that are temporary may be justified. For example, affirmative action may be the only or best way of overcoming the effects of past discrimination. If so, affirmative action is a defensible policy for realizing a more inclusive society, even though it treats groups differently.

However, affirmative action is not a right, in the strict sense of the term. It is a means toward an end, a society in which race, gender, or physical disabilities have no bearing on individuals' status in the polity. That end is not in question, but the proper means toward that end are open to dispute. Like other disputes, it must be resolved in politics -- and in democracies, political disputes are decided by the majority. Consequently, affirmative action may be warranted, but it must be justified to the majority, which ultimately decides policy questions in a democracy. The majority may accept affirmative action, or it may not; the policy is discretionary in a way that group rights, or for that matter any other rights, are not.

Concessions by the majority may not satisfy the demands of marginalized groups, but the marginalized are not without resources. Members of these groups have individual rights, which are ultimately guaranteed by a federation of democratic nations. Individuals may exercise these rights defensively, to resist discrimination against members of oppressed groups. The rights can also be exercised aggressively by individuals who want to promote collective identities and advance the political interests of their groups. This is normal politics, and it is open to everyone in a multicultural society.

Of course, politics are normally dominated by the majority and there is no assurance that the members of marginalized groups will obtain their goals, even if they exercise their individual rights with great energy and skill. There cannot be any guarantee of victory, however. Individuals' success in exercising their rights can only be determined in a political competition that is democratically conducted. Liberal democrats cannot make any assurances about the outcome of this competition without undermining political equality and the rightful authority of political majorities. The same applies to federations constructed along liberal democratic lines.

Chapter 7

How to Create Supra-National Institutions Democratically*

Some Reflections on the European Union's 'Democratic Deficit'

THOMAS W. POGGE

There are two distinct democratic deficits in the emerging European Union. On the one hand, ordinary citizens of the EU have very little meaningful influence on the political decisions made in their name by the centralized organs and agencies, such as the European Commission, the Council of Ministers, and the European Parliament. Having produced some public expressions of discontent and alienation (Euro-fatigue), this problem has been discussed quite extensively, and various proposals have been made by politicians, Eurocrats, and academics for how EU institutions can be made more user-friendly. This elite debate highlights the second problem: Ordinary citizens of the EU have had very little meaningful influence on the designing of

---

* Many thanks to Dagfinn Føllesdal for the kind invitation to join him at the Centre for Advanced Study in Oslo, where this essay was written, to Sverker Gustavsson for essential materials, and to Robert Goodin for valuable comments.

the emerging European institutions, which have been shaped and modified by a small politico-bureaucratic elite. And this elite is now likely to decide, quite undemocratically, what sorts of democratizing modifications they are going to implement in order to reduce public hostility to their intransparent and undemocratic rule. The present essay addresses only this second democratic deficit in institutional designing.[1]

Some terminology may help clarify the issue. By a *political* decision, I mean any legislative, executive, judicial, or administrative decision that is authoritative for (or within) some comprehensive social system (such as a city, province, state, association of states, etc.). We can then define a sequence of *types* of political decisions.[2] By *everyday* or *first-order* political decisions, I mean any political decisions that are *not* about political decision-making, i.e. not about where, how, when, and by whom political decisions are to be made.[3] By *second-order* political decisions, I mean any political decisions that are about first-order political decision-making, i.e. about

1 CASTIGLIONE (1995), pp. 61-63, distinguishes three democratic deficits. The first is a democratic deficit in the narrow sense: "strictly speaking, 'democratic deficit' denotes the lack of input which directly representative institutions, namely the European Parliament, have in the legislative activity of the Union." The second is the 'federal deficit': "on the one hand, many of the institutions of the Union ... have an intrinsic federal nature ...., while on the other the main political actors, the national governments, tend to maintain the political process in a state of ambiguity so that they can play the system according to their own contingent interests." The third is a 'constitutional deficit,' which "refers to the way in which the political-administrative élite of the Union has systematically underplayed the constitution-making processes which have progressively transformed the European Community into a de-facto polity, and to the general lack of awareness and debate on constitution-making as a process intrinsic to the formation of a political community." My topic corresponds to Castiglione's constitutional deficit, though my effort will be in a more normative and constructive vein.

2 I use the word "type" in allusion to Bertrand Russell's theory of types, though my use of the term can surely be grasped without an understanding of this theory.

3 I do not pretend that this distinction is entirely clear-cut. One can quibble over whether the decision about a dress code, or a new air conditioning system, for parliament is or is not ***about*** political decision-making in the relevant sense. I will proceed on the assumption that the distinction is clear enough for our purposes.

where, how, when, and by whom everyday political decisions are to be made. *Third-order* political decisions are then decisions about second-order political decision-making, and so on up. The two democratic deficits I have introduced at the beginning can now be clarified as follows: The first democratic deficit concerns the lack of democratic participation in first-order political decision-making for the EU. Here one is looking for appropriate second-order political decisions that would make the political institutions of the EU more democratic. The second democratic deficit concerns the lack of democratic participation in second-order political decision-making for the EU. The present essay focuses on this second democratic deficit, seeking appropriate third-order political decisions that would make the ongoing *shaping* of the EU's political institutions more democratic.[4]

I. The Maastricht Verdict of the German Constitutional Court

To help clarify the issues involved, let us briefly examine the German Maastricht Verdict, which is the most elaborate official attempt to-date to show the compatibility of European integration with the principle of democracy. The German Constitutional Court was asked to judge the constitutionality of Germany's ratification of the Maastricht Treaty[5] and of various related amendments to Germany's Basic Law[6]. Of the various constitutional

---

4 Some rudimentary proposals have been made in this direction by others. Weale, for example, has proposed that a European federal constitution should receive a "democratic baptism" through a European constituent assembly. WEALE (1995), pp. 90-94.

5 The Maastricht Treaty was adopted on February 7, 1992. The Bundestag voted for ratification (with 543 of 568 valid votes) on December 2, 1992; the Bundesrat (unanimously) on December 18, 1992. German ratification became effective on December 31, 1992. The German Bundestag is the lower house of parliament, whose members are chosen in nationwide elections. The Bundesrat is the upper house, whose members are appointed by the governments of the German provinces ("Länder").

6 These amendments entered into force on December 25, 1992, after the Maastricht votes of Bundestag and Bundesrat. The Basic Law ("Grundgesetz") functions as the German constitution.

challenges, raised by two separate complainants, only one need interest us here[7]. This challenge invokes the democracy requirements of Articles 20 and 38 of the Basic Law, whose relevant passages read as follows:

> All state authority emanates from the people. It is exercised by the people in elections and referenda and through special legislative, executive, and judicial organs.[8]
>
> The deputies to the German Bundestag are elected in universal, direct, free, equal, and secret elections. They are representatives of the whole people, not bound by orders and instructions, and subject only to their conscience.[9]

The challenge is that these requirements[10] rule out the kind of transfers of sovereign powers from organs of the Federal Republic to organs of the European Union that are specifically envisioned in the Maastricht Treaty and specifically authorized through the new amendments[11] of the Basic Law.

The German Constitutional Court found this challenge admissible only insofar as it appeals to Article 38 and only insofar as it challenges the ratification of the Maastricht Treaty (171).[12] These findings are strange and convenient. The first finding is strange, because Article 38 alone (detached from

7 The remaining challenges were ruled inadmissible by the Court.

8 Article 20(2): "Alle Staatsgewalt geht vom Volke aus. Sie wird vom Volke in Wahlen und Abstimmungen und durch besondere Organe der Gesetzgebung, der vollziehenden Gewalt und der Rechtsprechung ausgeübt." All translations from the German are my own.

9 Article 38(1): "Die Abgeordneten des Deutschen Bundestages werden in allgemeiner, unmittelbarer, freier, gleicher und geheimer Wahl gewählt. Sie sind Vertreter des ganzen Volkes, an Aufträge und Weisungen nicht gebunden und nur ihrem Gewissen unterworfen."

10 Which the Court obfuscatingly conflates into "the democracy principle" (cf. note 16 below).

11 Most important is the addition of Article 23(1), whose second sentence reads: "The Federal Republic may for this purpose [the realization of a united Europe] transfer sovereign powers by law with the consent of the Bundesrat." ("Der Bund kann hierzu [zur Verwirklichung eines vereinten Europas] durch Gesetz mit Zustimmung des Bundesrates Hoheitsrechte übertragen.")

12 All simple page references in the present section refer to the official text of the Court's verdict in *Entscheidungen des Bundesverfassungsgerichts*, volume 89, 155-213.

Article 20) would seem to have no relevance to the case at all, while Article 20 (even without Article 38) would seem to be highly pertinent.[13] The first finding is convenient, because Article 20 belongs to the immutable core of the Basic Law which must not even be touched ("berührt") through changes in the Basic Law, let alone be altered or revoked.[14] The second finding is convenient, because, having found the challenge to the constitutional changes inadmissible, the Court could then liberally appeal to the new constitutional provisions in defense of the constitutionality of ratification of the Maastricht Treaty (e.g., 182, 208, 211f).

The Court responded elaborately (181-212) to the narrow challenge it found admissible. It laid down that, to be constitutional, transfers of tasks and powers from the Bundestag must not empty out citizens' capacity through elections to legitimate and to influence the exercise of state authority (181-87; cf. also 155, 171f). The Court clarified this condition by drawing out some of its implications — among them the following four:

1. The German Bundestag must retain tasks and powers of substantial weight (186).

2. The Federal Republic must retain the power to renounce membership in the European Union and to reject further steps toward integration (190; cf. 203f).

3. As the tasks and powers of the European Union expand, there is a growing necessity ("wächst die Notwendigkeit") that citizens be able to legitimate and influence the exercise of sovereign powers not merely through their national parliaments but also through a European parliament (184).[15]

4. So long as it is mainly by electing the German Bundestag that German voters are exercising their right to participate in the democratic legitimation of the institutions and organs that exercise sovereign powers, any powers transferred elsewhere must be sufficiently determinate ("hinreichend bestimmbar") to make clear what tasks and powers have been transferred (187f).

13 The Court itself recognizes this (181, 182; cp. 187) by construing the narrow challenge it deems admissible as implicitly invoking Article 20.

14 Article 79(3). Article 38 does not belong to this core, and the legislature could thus defeat successful legal challenges based on this Article simply by amending or revising it.

15 A growing necessity is, of course, an oxymoron. Presumably, the Court meant to say that, at some point in the integration process, the European Parliament would have to be given real powers without having to say anything further about when this point would be reached.

The Court then concluded that the European Union constructed by the Maastricht Treaty does, for now, satisfy its condition as specified.

One can find fault with this reasoning in two ways. On the one hand, one may claim that the European Union does not — by design or as a matter of practical politics — satisfy the Court's condition. In this vein, Gustavsson argues persuasively that it would be very difficult in practice for the German Bundestag to renounce membership in the European Union and that the European Central Bank will not be subject to any national or European democratic control.[16] On the other hand, one may criticize as too weak the condition laid down by the Court, on the ground that it permits German citi-

---

16 GUSTAVSSON (1997). Gustavsson nicely stresses how the Court itself felt compelled to acknowledge that the European Central Bank involves a "modification" of the democracy principle: "This limitation of the democratic legitimation emanating from the voters in the member states touches the democracy principle, but, as a modification of this principle authorized in the second sentence of Article 88 of the Basic Law, it is nevertheless consistent with Article 79(3) of the Basic Law" (208). ("Diese Einschränkung der von den Wählern in den Mitgliedstaaten ausgehenden demokratischen Legitimation berührt das Demokratieprinzip, ist jedoch als eine in Art. 88 Satz 2 GG vorgesehene Modifikation dieses Prinzips mit Art. 79 Abs. 3 GG vereinbar.") One needs many years of conditioning through legal training to be able to see this as anything but a flagrant breach of the Basic Law: Article 79(3) expressly declares inadmissible any legal changes that touch the requirement that "all state power emanates from the people." The German Constitutional Court admits that it is sanctioning a limitation of the people's power which touches and modifies the democracy principle. But it sees no inconsistency with Article 79(3). Why not? Because the second sentence of Article 88 authorizes the modification. But wait a minute! This sentence was newly added at the time of the ratification of the Maastricht Treaty and was itself under challenge in this very case. More importantly, this sentence cannot possibly make a difference to whether or not a modification is consistent with Article 79(3). For modifications of the democracy principle that do not violate Article 20 are consistent with Article 79(3) even without any help from Article 88. And with regard to modifications that do violate Article 20, the fact that they are authorized by Article 88 — far from showing the constitutionality of the modification — shows the unconstitutionality of the authorization! Insofar as an article of the Basic Law authorizes measures that violate the immutable core of the Basic Law, it can have no legal force at all.

zens to become, to a substantial extent, subject to governmental organs and agencies over which they can exercise no meaningful democratic control.

As discussed thus far, the Maastricht Verdict is concerned with (what I have called) the first democratic deficit: with the undemocratic character of the emerging European Union. Let us now look at the Court's response to the second democratic deficit: the undemocratic nature of Germany's accession to the European Union. The Court rejected this challenge as inadmissible on the basis of an exceedingly brief half-page argument (180) that lacks even a rudimentary understanding of the challenge. This is surprising, because the Court does a rather better job in summarizing this challenge (169f) as follows: The Maastricht Treaty ought not to have been ratified without legitimation by the German people (170). By expanding the tasks and competencies of the European Union, the (German) legislature is arrogating to itself powers that belong solely to the people as the subject of constitutive power (169). What is being challenged here is evidently not the constitutionality of what the Maastricht Treaty will bring about. For the result of this treaty is that the German legislature will have *reduced* powers — hardly a case of "arrogating powers to itself." What is being challenged, rather, is the German legislature's arrogating to itself the power (or "meta-power") of transferring some of the powers vested in it by the German people to other agencies of its choice. This challenge appeals to the immutable principle of Article 20(2): Since all state authority emanates from the people, its elected representatives are not entitled to institute deep changes in how the people exercise their power without securing the people's consent.

To see the force of this challenge, imagine for a moment a slightly different scenario. Imagine that the Bundestag (with consent by the Bundesrat) had altered the Basic Law so as to convert Germany into a British-style parliamentary system with winner-takes-all electoral districts and a hereditary monarch. The German Constitutional Court could probably comfortably defend the revised Basic Law (the *result* of the alteration) as consistent with its immutable core. But could it defend *the alteration itself* as effected by a legislature that leaves the people — from whom all state authority supposedly emanates — no legal way of blocking it? That such a dramatic change would be unconstitutional is particularly probable in light of the fact that Article 20(2) specifically provides for democratic participation by the people to be exercised not merely through elections, which (directly or indirectly) determine the composition of the legislative, executive, and judicial organs, but also through referenda.[17]

The German Constitutional Court wholly missed the point and construed the objection as arguing that the immutable core of the Basic Law can be changed only through a referendum. To this absurd objection the Court responded, predictably, that this core cannot be changed at all and that the absence of a referendum is therefore irrelevant: The amendments and German membership in the Maastricht Union are either consistent with the immutable core (and then beyond the need for a referendum) or inconsistent with it (and then beyond rescue through a referendum). True enough. But this does not answer the challenge to the constitutionality of the *adoption* of the amendments and the *accession* to the Maastricht Union, both of which were effected by elected politicians alone, without the people's consent.[18]

I conclude that, through its Maastricht Verdict, the German Constitutional Court has colluded with the German legislature in undermining the democratic powers that the immutable core of the Basic Law has reserved to the German people. This undermining has two aspects. First, important sovereign powers are, and will be, exercised over the German people by organs of the EU which lack democratic accountability. The undemocratic exercise of such sovereign powers — the first democratic deficit — plainly touches, and indeed violates, the requirement that all state power emanate from the people. Second, important changes in how the German people are governed have been effected without the consent of the German people. Such

17 Oddly, the word "Abstimmungen" here is often translated as "voting." But this is a mistake. To be sure, any *Abstimmung* is an instance of voting. But the word "Abstimmung" does not cover the kind of voting that takes place in regular elections ("Wahlen"). The reference to *Abstimmungen* thus clearly envisions voting activities other than elections — namely referenda ("Volksabstimmungen").

18 Note that the Court is quite alert to potential conflicts between the interests of the people and those of their elected representatives — when doing so serves the Court's argumentative objectives. Thus the Court justifies the planned European Central Bank by pointing out that "the autonomous vesting of most tasks of monetary policy in an independent central bank detaches the exercise of sovereign powers of the state from direct national or supranational parliamentary responsibility, in order to withdraw monetary matters from the reach of interest groups and holders of political office concerned about re-election" (208).

undemocratic transformations — the second democratic deficit — also touch, and indeed violate, the requirement that all state power emanate from the people.

One might think that the end of European unification is grand enough to justify the means: violating the plain meaning of the immutable democracy requirement of Article 20(2). I believe, however, that these means were not necessary to achieve that noble goal. The first democratic deficit was avoidable in that democratic accountability of the relevant organs of the EU to the German people could have been assured by giving real oversight powers to a European Parliament. This possibility is quite evident. It is much harder to show that the second democratic deficit was also avoidable. Of course, prospective member states could have held national referenda, and some of them did, about whether or not to join up. But such referenda give the people only a simple binary choice. Is it possible to do better — to afford the people a meaningful role in designing European institutions? The remainder of this essay seeks to make a start in this direction.

II. Why the People Allegedly Cannot Play a Role in Shaping Political Institutions

It is a favorite view among politicians and experts that a democratic shaping of political institutions is impossible, and that they themselves are therefore called upon to do the job. Three main arguments are offered for this alleged impossibility. The first claims that the creating of new political institutions is unlikely to be accomplished, if the people are allowed to debate and decide about competing proposals. In this vein it is said that the United States would never have come into being, if the small elite group gathered at the Philadelphia Constitutional Convention of 1787 had not decisively exercised a self-proclaimed authority to set aside the Articles of Confederation. James Madison, under the pseudonym of Publius, defended this decision as follows: "since it is impossible for the people spontaneously and universally to move in concert towards their object .. it is therefore essential that such changes be instituted by some *informal and unauthorized propositions*, made by some patriotic and respectable citizens."[19] I will argue that, if the integration of Europe were indeed the people's object, they could move toward this object — though perhaps not "spontaneously." I also believe that a better European Union would have emerged, and more quickly, if the people had been allowed a greater role. We will be better able to evaluate these claims after I will have laid out some proposals for the democratic designing of (democratic) political institutions.

The second argument affirms that there is, for societies under given historical conditions, only one best — fully just and optimally efficient — scheme of political institutions. It matters that this scheme be approximated as closely as possible; and experts will be much better able to accomplish this task than ordinary people (whose views on everyday political issues may of course be sought, once fully just political institutions are in place). This claim seems rather implausible in view of the large variety of democratic political institutions that have evolved in this world to-date. To be sure, all of these democratic orders have flaws and many have great faults indeed. Still, correcting such faults and flaws will hardly lead to convergence on one best option, or even a few, for a given set of historical conditions. It is rather implausible, for example, that there is one best form and degree of political decentralization for the states of contemporary Europe — so that the political systems of Switzerland, Germany, Britain, and France, say, all ought to be reformed toward this correct point in the multi-dimensional (de-)centralization space. It is even more implausible that there should be but one correct composition and structure for a European Union. Justice and efficiency do constrain the structure of democratic institutions, of course, but they also leave important parameters undetermined. And these, at least, should be settled democratically, or so I will argue.

The third argument asserts that the very idea of a democratic shaping of political institutions is deeply incoherent. Designing political institutions democratically presupposes that we already have democratic political institutions governing the design process. But this leads either into a vicious circle (the design is to be produced by the very procedures it is yet to design) or to an infinite regress (political procedures$_1$ are to be designed pursuant to demo-

19 ROSSITER (1961), p. 253. This passage is from The Federalist No. 40, written by JAMES MADISON. The surrounding text and Nos. 39 and 43 (likewise by Madison) are also pertinent. See also ACKERMAN (1991), Chapter 7.

cratic procedures$_2$ which are to be designed pursuant to democratic procedures$_3$ which are to be designed.... *ad infinitum*).

In response, I propose to halt the regress on the third level. It is current practice that national politicians and experts shape the EU's political institutions (which may then allow the citizens of the EU a certain measure of participation). My proposal provides that national politicians and experts should instead design a procedure that allows EU citizens a certain measure of participation in designing the political institutions of the EU. That is to say, the contribution of politicians and experts to the designing of Europe's political institutions should be confined mainly to third-order political decisions. I say "mainly" for two reasons. Experts and politicians are also citizens, and thus entitled to participate with the rest of us in second-order political decision-making. Moreover, by designing the process of second-order political decision-making, such politicians and experts will invariably frame our options and set our agenda in certain ways that are bound to affect the outcome. The key remedy to this problem would seem to be transparency: In contrast to the current second-order decision-making elite negotiating behind closed doors, I propose a third-order decision-making elite whose deliberations and decisions are fully public.

I claim two main advantages for my proposal in comparison to current practice: It gives ordinary citizens an important role in shaping the political institutions of the emerging European Union, while current practice gives them essentially no role at all.[20] This advantage is evident. And third-order decisions, being at two removes from everyday politics, are more likely than second-order decisions to elicit principled reflections and arguments from the politicians and experts charged with making them (especially if their deliberations and decisions are required to be fully public). This advantage is not obvious, and I will therefore try to show how we can begin to think about third-order decisions in a principled way.

This project requires me to switch gears. So far, I have proposed that the role of politicians and experts be confined mainly to third-order political decisions. Now I will imaginatively assume this role of a third-order political decision-maker in order to show how genuinely democratic second-order deci-

20 Citizens can vote for this or that political party in national or European Parliament elections. But the effects of such choices on the shaping of European political institutions — if any — are too remote to be foreseeable. Moreover, citizens cannot reasonably be expected in national elections to choose a party on the basis of its stance on just this one set of issues.

sion-making can be made possible. I will address this question not in a political way — asking how we might now make the best of an unhappy status quo — but philosophically: asking how EU institutions could have been shaped democratically from the beginning. This question is important not only for philosophy, but also for other regional or global integration projects that might look at the EU as a model. The consequences of my ideas for where the EU should go from here are, in any case, relatively straightforward, and I will say something about this topic toward the end.

III. The Constitutive Features of the Union

The constitutive features of a union such as the EU may be grouped under three headings: domain, scope, and procedures. The *domain* of the EU is the spatio-temporal extension of its jurisdiction, which may be defined in terms of its member states, in terms of its territory, and/or in terms of its citizens. The *scope* of the EU is the extent of its decision-making powers, which may be defined in terms of the kinds of issues over which it has jurisdiction. The *procedures* of the EU are the ways in which it exercises its powers, its ground rules, which define its various legislative, executive, judicial, and administrative organs, agencies, and offices, including how these are to be staffed and what powers and duties are going to be attached to them.

Our task is to show how a democratic specification of these features is possible. This task runs into the theoretical difficulty presented by the third argument above: It must somehow be settled *who* is going to participate in this democratic specification and also *how* this democratic specification is going to take place — that is to say, we must find a way of settling the analogues of *domain* and *procedures* on the next higher level. Moreover, we must also structure the democratic specification in such a way that the participants — the potential citizens of the EU — face a manageable menu of choices. This task is made considerably more difficult by the fact that persons' preferences concerning the three topics are likely to be interdependent. There is interdependence within each topic: You may believe that Poland should be a member only if Hungary is (domain), or you may approve of a democratically constituted European parliament only if it is checked by a strong European executive (procedure). There is also interdependence across topics: Whether you believe that the populations of smaller countries should have extra weight in democratic procedures may depend on the domain and/or the scope of the EU. Whether you believe that the EU should have an integrated military may depend on the EU's composition and/or on what procedures would govern its common defense policy. Whether you believe that the Eastern European countries should be members of the EU may depend on the EU's scope and procedures. These interdependencies count against the idea of scheduling democratic decisions about the various features one by one, because the outcome of such a sequence of decisions would be likely to depend quite heavily on the order in which the decisions were presented. Yet, it is also impossible to present the decisions together, because the number of meaningfully distinct options would be quite unmanageable: Theoretically, there are several billion ways of determining just the composition of the EU, even if we arbitrarily limit the set of possible members to states that occupy some soil on the European continent. (With 35 such states, the number of possible EU compositions is close to 2^{35} or about 34,000,000,000.) This number must be multiplied with possible settlements for the scope features and the resulting product multiplied again with possible settlements for the procedures features. It may well seem that such enormous complexities require extended face-to-face negotiation among a few political principals supported by their bureaucratic and academic experts — that any hope for a democratic shaping of a European Union is entirely unrealistic.

Still, there are ways of coping with the difficulties and complexities. My proposal is to structure the second-level democratic decision-making into three stages. In Stage One, the citizens of potential member states participate in determining the most basic features of the EU — in particular, its scope. In Stage Two, the citizens of potential member states vote on the composition (domain) of the European Union. In Stage Three, the citizens of the EU participate in determining the remaining features of the EU — its procedures, mainly, and also the remaining questions of scope.

1. Stage One: The Democratic Determination of Basic Scope

The scope of the EU, simply put, answers the question what first-order political decisions the EU will be in charge of. To render this question manageable for democratic decision-making, we may try to employ three simplifications. The first simplification divides the universe of everyday political decisions into fields or kinds. The second simplification selects those kinds of everyday political decisions which, insofar as they are to be made at the EU level at all, should be made there in a way that is binding on all member countries. The third simplification endorses a principle of subsidiarity which provides that kinds of everyday political decisions are allocated to the EU level only insofar as they have a significant impact on persons in more than one member state.[21]

The second simplification calls for some comment. The key idea is that there are fields of political decision-making in which some or all member states can decide to cooperate without thereby affecting the basic structure of the EU. Education policy may be one example. In order to construct a functioning EU, we need not decide beforehand whether there will be an integrated educational policy. The following excursus will explain the point in some detail, using educational policy as the example.

Excursus: Fields of Discretionary Centralization

To fix ideas, suppose that the composition of the EU is already fixed and that the citizens of the EU at large favor a centralized European education system while the French prefer to retain exclusive control over educational institutions on French soil. Which democratic preference should prevail? In this case, it seems reasonably clear that the preference of the French should prevail. It is instructive to examine the grounds for this result. The structure of educational institutions has a very significant influence on the development of culture within their reach. And it is among the deepest interests of persons to be able to live in a cultural context in whose evolution they can participate and in which they can feel at home. Unwelcome interference with the

21 On the meaning of "subsidiarity" as enshrined in Article 3b of the Treaty on European Union, see, for example, BLICHNER and SANGOLT (1994). The intuitive idea is quite general and thus holds equally well for subnational levels of decision-making: The point of democratic procedures is to enable persons to participate in shaping the social context that shapes their lives. Insofar as this value is better promoted if we all have rather more influence upon the social context in our own locale than if we all had rather little influence equally spread more broadly, political decision-making should be decentralized — in the limiting case all the way down to the individual.

French education system through Europe-wide regulations would therefore impose very considerable costs upon the French.[22]

On the other side of the ledger, the possible second-order decision by the French to run their own national education system would impose some burden on the rest of the Union, as it would be somewhat harder for non-French EU citizens to gain the requisite qualifications for working and studying in France. But this fact would not give the French an unfair competitive advantage, because French citizens would be similarly handicapped in their efforts to study or work in one of the other EU countries. In fact, the cost to the French might be greater, if other EU countries decided to integrate their education systems even without the French. Non-French EU citizens could then easily move to study or work in most other EU countries, while French citizens could not easily move to any.

The subject matter of education has given us a model decision on the third level (where the allocation of powers to make everyday decisions is settled). Let us call this the *discretionary model* (or *DM*). *DM* provides that the citizens of each nation decide whether everyday decisions about matters of kind X should be made exclusively by themselves for their own country alone or on a higher level by and for a larger electorate.

Some special features of *DM* call for further comment. One is that *DM* allows for asymmetry, as some EU members may choose to participate in a larger integrated education system while others do not. Such asymmetries are, I believe, perfectly feasible and have worked well elsewhere. The Canadian province of Quebec, for example, has opted out of a variety of Canadian federal programs (e.g. the Canadian pension scheme).[23] The United Nations system contains a consider-

22 One might well point out that the (partial) loss of a distinctive French culture would impose a significant loss on all Europeans. This loss may here be left aside, however, because it is one that Europeans would be free to take into account, if they were assigned the power to determine educational policy for Europe at large.

23 For more on Canada and asymmetry, see KYMLICKA (1995), esp. section 4. I take no stance here, of course, on Kymlicka's view that the Quebecois are especially entitled to asymmetrical accommodation because they constitute a national minority.

able number of major semi-independent "specialized agencies" participation in which is optional for UN member states.[24]

DM might follow these real-world examples in allowing the basic features of a possible integrated education system to be determined at the Center. The EU would decide to offer its members the option of joining the EU education scheme (EUES), perhaps requiring some supermajority for entry and/or exit in order to avoid the cost of frequent switching. Member states could then decide whether to join this and similar schemes through a single national referendum.[25]

When membership has been settled, everyday decisions within the EUES should then be made democratically by the citizens of EUES member states. The citizens of EU countries that have declined to join the EUES are not entitled to participate. They might nevertheless be granted some non-voting representation in the interest of keeping all educational decision-makers well informed about educational policies within the entire EU.

More complex asymmetries might arise, if several groups of EU countries wanted to build different integrated education systems. (Imagine a North-Eastern one, including Austria, Denmark, Finland, Germany, the Netherlands, and Sweden; and a South-Western one, including Belgium, France, Italy, Luxembourg, Portugal, and Spain). *DM* should allow for this possibility, I believe, just as it allows for the possibility of less than two countries deciding to join the EUES. In fact, the two possibilities are quite similar. When there are two major supranational education systems within the EU's domain, then neither of them can lay claim to being *the* European system (or EUES). The similarity is then that in both cases the emergence of the EUES

24 Among these are the FAO, ILO, IMF, IMO, UNESCO, WHO, and the World Bank. UNESCO, for example, has been quit by several UN-members, including Singapore, Great Britain, and the US, and has been joined by several non-UN-members, including Switzerland.

25 This proposal raises various fascinating disaster possibilities in that the preference of one national electorate may depend on the decision of another. If there are strong reasons for believing this, national referenda might be held in the appropriate order. But what if there are cyclical preference dependencies? What if Portugal wants to join if and only if Ireland does and Ireland wants to join if and only if Portugal does not? I doubt these are realistic scenarios and, in any case, I cannot deal with them here.

is prevented by the overall outcome of the democratic second-order decisions reached within each of the member states.

The subsidiarity principle limits the potential scope of the EU by shielding from its jurisdiction any issues that can be handled better, or as well, at the national level. The discretionary model further limits the potential scope of the EU by leaving under the jurisdiction of its member states various issues on which any subset of them can opt to coordinate or cooperate without unfair harm to the rest. The primary task of Stage One is then to identify and allocate the basic fields of everyday political decision-making that *neither* are shielded by the subsidiarity principle *nor* fit the discretionary model. Let me propose, in a preliminary way, that these fields are the following eight:

(A) Basic Rights: Should the EU be in charge of formulating and enforcing a single catalogue of basic rights for all citizens of the EU?

(B) Economic Justice: Should there be an EU-wide system of taxes and subsidies designed to eradicate poverty (and perhaps also roughly to equalize standards of living within the EU)?

(C) Intra-EU Migration: Should there be one single EU-wide regime governing EU citizens' options for residing, working, studying, and vacationing in EU countries other than their own?

(D) Intra-EU Trade and Investment: Should there be one single EU-wide regime governing the flow of goods and capital across the internal borders of the EU?

(E) EU Financial System: Should their be a single EU currency whose supply is centrally controlled by an EU central bank?

(F) EU Environmental Policy: Should there be an integrated environmental protection regime, formulated and enforced at the EU level?

(G) EU Security Cooperation: Should there be an integrated EU defense force politically controlled by the EU executive?

(H) EU Foreign Policy: Should there be a unified EU foreign policy in charge of, in particular, negotiating treaties and maintaining diplomatic relations with non-EU countries, regulating temporary and permanent migration (including asylum) into the EU, formulating and administering unified EU economic policies concerning trade and investment across EU borders, representing the citizens of the EU in international organizations and at international conferences, and responding in behalf of the EU citizenry to special events (wars, natural catastrophes, etc.) outside the EU?[26]

My proposal of these eight fields is illustrative and preliminary, because more thorough reflection and discussions might well show that some of these fields should be consolidated or subdivided, or that some further fields should be added or some listed fields deleted (to be handled, perhaps, according to the discretionary model).[27]

Once the list of fields is finalized, the corresponding list of binary questions can be presented to the citizens of the prospective member states for their judgment. Each prospective citizen of the EU is asked to answer about eight straightforward yes/no questions on the understanding

(i) that the citizens of each country will have a chance to reject membership in the EU through a referendum at Stage Two;

(ii) that fields of first-order political decision-making allocated to the EU will still be subject to the subsidiarity principle, so that countries — and, indeed, provinces and towns — would, for example, be free to formulate basic rights or economic-justice targets that go beyond those set by the EU (cf. note 26); and

(iii) that the powers reserved to the EU will be transferred carefully and gradually, once appropriate EU procedures will have been put in place.

After tabulating the results of the poll separately for each country, the outcome of Stage One can be represented in a two-dimensional grid, whose vertical axis lists the populations of the prospective member states and whose horizontal axis lists the eight fields with the corresponding binary questions. Each box within the grid might contain a percentage figure that represents the proportion of yes-votes received by a particular question in a particular prospective member state.

---

26 Affirmative answers to (A), (B), (G), or (H) should be understood to mean that the EU would be at least partly in charge. Some additional functions in these fields might remain at the national level (or even below), if this is mandated by the subsidiarity principle.

27 Many less important fields could obviously be added, but I believe that, at Stage I, citizens should focus on the most important issues (*basic* scope) Within the institutional framework of the EU, less important fields can be democratically decided later on — for example, whether there should be an EU-wide police force, an EU-wide vaccination program, EU-wide standards for food safety and quality, and so forth.

2. Stage Two: The Democratic Determination of the Domain

It is possible, of course, that the judgments returned by the people are highly unsystematic. It is much more likely, however, that these answers would cluster in such a way that some national populations would be more pro-EU than others across most fields and some fields would elicit more approval for centralization across the prospective EU populations. The main trade-off will then be one between scope and domain: The more fields of first-order political decision-making are included in the scope of the EU, the fewer states are likely to decide to join up. The results of the Stage One poll can help decide how this trade-off might best be made: Countries whose preferences are strongly anti-EU compared to the average should be dropped from consideration, with the understanding that they might join later. And fields with regard to which there was low approval for centralization even in the remaining countries should also be dropped, again with the understanding that they might be added later on. This procedure shrinks the grid in both dimensions, leaving a core of at least moderately pro-EU countries as well as a core of fields that were approved for centralization by most of these countries. Looking at this core grid, we may find that most of the remaining countries are likely to approve the list of the remaining fields, if this list were presented as a package deal. Should this not appear likely (from the Stage One approval figures), then the least approved field(s) may have to be dropped in order to arrive at a plausible package. This package can then be presented to all prospective member states (the full initial list) for a simple binary referendum: Do you approve of your country joining an EU whose scope is defined by the following fields?

Things may become a little more complicated at Stage Two, because a country's decision about joining the EU may depend on the decisions made by other countries. Perhaps the Portuguese want to join only if Spain also joins, or only if Iceland does not join, or only if the EU will have some critical minimum size. These problems might be solved by holding the referenda in some appropriate order or by adding a suitable conditional to some countries' referenda ("Do you approve of your country joining an EU whose scope is defined by the following fields, provided that ...?"). If there are enough such interdependencies of preferences, or if approvals of fields are not strongly clustered, then it is possible for a plurality of unions to emerge from the set of potential member states. The politicians actually produced such a plurality after World War II with the formation of the EEC, EFTA, and COMECON. Though much less likely, it is possible for democratic decisions to produce a similar result.

This is how it might happen. Suppose that the pro-EU core countries by and large prefer the scope of the EU to include the field of economic justice, but that the more affluent countries of Western Europe want to join such a union only if it excludes the poorer countries of Eastern Europe, which are equally pro-EU and equally in favor of including economic justice in the EU's scope. Under these circumstances, two separate unions might emerge. But it would be preferable, I think, to try other resolutions first: The Western countries might approve the package deal because they care a great deal about achieving a wider centralization in other fields ((**A**), (**F**), (**H**)) or because they are confident that they can use their influence within the EU to define the goal of economic justice modestly or to set a slow pace toward this goal. I believe that some such resolution would probably work in contemporary Europe, and I will thus set the problem aside.

Stage Two fixes then the domain of the EU to be created by producing democratic commitments from some of the European countries to participate in the formation of an EU, whose scope is defined at least vaguely in terms of general fields of centralized political decision-making.

3. Stage Three: The Democratic Determination of Procedures

The democratic determinations of Scope and Domain are easier than that of Procedures, where we are faced with a multi-dimensional array of innumerable options. This complexity must be reduced by politicians and experts to a few main options, or to a few straightforward and mutually independent issues, which can then be submitted to the EU electorate.

This reduction of complexity can start out from the idea that, while the features of Scope and Domain raise entirely new institutional questions, our questions with regard to Procedures are close analogues to ones that already have answers on the state level. To be sure, these answers vary from state to state. Still, the democratic procedures practiced in the EU member states will turn out to have a great deal in common, and reproducing these common features, at least, on the EU level would presumably be widely approved by the EU electorate.

Among the most important common features are the following:

(1) The powers of government are separated into three largely independent branches: Legislative, Executive, and Judiciary.

(2) The main legislative organ is an assembly or parliament, directly elected by the entire electorate whose votes have approximately equal weight.

(3) Candidates for parliament are nominated by political parties, which compete with one another by formulating alternative political programs (and by fielding alternative candidates).

(4) At least half of all parliamentary seats are tied to electoral districts and filled by the candidates winning a plurality of votes in such districts. Thus, every locale within the domain has a personal representative in parliament.

(5) Parliament has the authority to pass and rescind laws as well as the authority to block or approve appropriations.

(6) The main executive organ is a cabinet, consisting of the heads of various ministries — whose functions may coincide roughly with those fields from among **(B)** through **(H)** which were approved in Stages One and Two — and chaired by a prime minister.

(7) The cabinet is bound by the laws and appropriations passed by parliament and can be dismissed by parliamentary decision (which may require a supermajority).

The existing EU truly fulfills only features (3) and (4) and with respect to features (5)-(7) departs quite dramatically from the procedures practiced in its member states. The present European parliament is extremely weak and the governments of member states have inordinate powers to block concerted action at the EU level. These governments would argue, no doubt, that they must have these powers because they are, after all, democratically elected to represent their constituencies while decision-making at the EU level has only very weak democratic legitimacy (conferred by those EU citizens who have chosen to take part in EU parliamentary elections). But the question is: Whose fault is this? The very governments who have denied the EU citizenry a chance to approve (or disapprove) political decision-making on the EU level are now adducing the lack of such approval as a justification for the extraordinary powers they claim to gum up the works. On my proposal, EU-wide collective decision-making would have been explicitly sanctioned by the electorates of the member states, and there would then be no more reason for special veto powers than there is on the national level — if Scotland lacks the power to block British policies or legislation, why should Britain have the power to block EU policies and legislation?

I have proposed one method of reducing complexity in Stage Three: present to the EU citizenry the option of reproducing for the EU the procedural features that its member states share in common. Here is another proposal that would reduce complexity a good deal further. This proposal provides that Stage Three be split into two phases. The first phase is mainly concerned with the constitution of the European legislature, with how its members are elected and how it operates once it is constituted. It will be relatively easy, for politicians and experts, to develop a few main options or a few straightforward and mutually independent questions for this limited subject matter. These options or question can then be submitted to an EU-wide referendum, and an EU parliament can then be constituted pursuant to the winning procedures. The parliament so constituted could then, in the second phase, work out a proposal, or a few, concerning the precise structure of judicial and executive organs and the precise relations between the three branches of government.[28] When this work is completed, the EU electorate would, once again, have the last word — approving the parliament's proposal, or one of them, or else rejecting it (them) and requiring the parliament to rework it (them) for resubmission.

Since I am proposing to leave the work of the second phase to the new EU parliament, let me here say no more about it (though I might have some further ideas, of course, about how members of this inaugural parliament ought to proceed). But I should say just a little more about the first phase of Stage Three. I understand the fundamental idea of democracy as the moral imperative that political institutions should maximize and equalize citizens' ability to shape the social context in which they live. Let me here leave aside two obvious questions about this imperative: What is its weight in relation to other moral requirements and desiderata? And how should we trade off the two maximands stipulated within the imperative? I will briefly focus, instead, on the idea of political equality. This idea should be understood as requiring, I believe, that it be possible for all social groups of any kind (and especially for minorities) to gain something approaching proportional representation in the legislature. Ideally, any group that constitutes *n* per cent of

28 One may object to this idea that the parliament will be inclined to give itself excessive powers vis-à-vis the other two branches of government, thus undermining any genuine separation of powers. I do not believe this is a great danger, because many members of the first EU parliament will be plausible candidates for the executive and judicial position they create and circumscribe.

the electorate should be able to determine the composition of *n* per cent of the legislature.[29] Of course, it is up to the members of the group whether they, or some of them, choose to form a coalition for the purpose of filling a proportionate number of parliamentary seats. But the political process should be so designed that, if (some or all) members of a group choose to form such a coalition, they should be able to send a proportionate number of representatives to the legislature.

This ideal strongly favors institutional designs that involve proportional representation or multi-delegate constituencies. It is much harder to approximate the ideal in a system with winner-takes-all territorial electoral districts — as exemplified in the US and Great Britain — because one must then engage in a highly deliberate, and thus often divisive ("gerrymandering"), shaping and reshaping of electoral districts on the basis of elite anticipations of what groups voters will particularly wish to identify with. Forming a legislature through random sampling is likewise a bad way of implementing the ideal, because most persons do not want to be legislators and would not be good at it anyway (though random sampling might work better than the status quo in many so-called democracies, where legislative corruption is endemic).[30]

I have space to address only two obvious objections to this argument. One opposes the idea of equal treatment for groups of all different kinds: Yes, if gypsies of Italians strongly desire parliamentary representation in proportion to their numbers, they should be able to achieve this goal. But what reason is there to make the same demand with respect to all ethnic, religious, linguistic, lifestyle groups and even with regard to geographically completely dispersed groups such as dentists, dog-lovers, stamp collectors, war widows, socialists, and Porsche drivers? My answer is that some of these imagined

29 It may be thought that this specification still fails to do justice to permanent minorities who, even with a proportionate number of seats in parliament, may still lose on all contested issues. Often, political decentralization, fair-mindedness of the majority, or legislative bargaining (where the majority is sometimes divided) can solve this problem. But I see no plausible institutional solution for cases in which these remedies fail.

30 These matters have been understood and debated for quite a long time — e.g. by Thomas Wright Hill (1821), Thomas Gilpin (1844), and Thomas Hare (1873), all discussed in BEITZ (1989), Chapter 6. Unrepresentative systems can nevertheless survive, of course, if those who stand to lose from reform can use the existing system to block reform.

possibilities are, for now, quite unrealistic. For the foreseeable future, a just political process may well produce parliamentary representatives of national, ethnic, and religious groups; but it will not produce parliamentary representatives of Porsche drivers and stamp collectors. But I think it is important that this divergence should occur because of the distribution of deep identifications among the citizenry and not because the structure of the political process advantages citizens with some types of deep identifications over citizens with other types of such identifications. If enough citizens share a certain identification and are willing to form a coalition for the sake of securing representation for themselves in the legislature, then they should be able to gain such representation, irrespective of the type of their identification (and of whether they are geographically concentrated or dispersed). If, for some as yet quite unimaginable reason, citizens did develop a desire to be represented in parliament as drivers of a particular type of car, they should be able to implement this desire. This equal treatment of diverse deep identifications is, I believe, required by the ideal of political equality.

The other objection points to the need for a functioning legislature. If parliament is often dysfunctional because it contains too many odd-ball parties and groupings (late Weimar Republic, present-day Poland), then it will not maximize citizens' ability to shape the social context in which they live. This is why, in many social systems, the ideal will not be attainable *fully*, even with the help of fancy(ful) computer systems. But this problem does not require discriminations among types of groups, because there are neutral ways of reducing the number of represented groups. A society could, for instance, require a minimum number of votes (as exemplified by the German five-percent hurdle) for parliamentary representation, with the threshold set only as high as necessary to ensure its objective.

IV. Concluding Remarks

It will surely be said that the procedure sketched in this essay is excessively cumbersome and greatly overtaxes the interest and abilities of the average European. My response is that, if it does, the reason is not any genetic liability of the average European, but the simple fact that Europeans, and citizens generally, have never yet been allowed truly meaningful political participation. They have been excluded from such participation by their rulers: by politicians and judges, for whom democracy seems to have little to do with people shaping their own social environment. I am fully convinced that European citizens, if allowed a say, would rise to the occasion, would deliberate carefully about the options presented to them and make good decisions. The project of the EU presents an excellent opportunity for attempting a democratic shaping of democratic political institutions, because there is no pressing emergency demanding quick and decisive action.[31] The European elite has wasted an inordinate amount of time on intransparent horse trading and inefficient bickering. It would have been much better to spend this time on public deliberation and a gradual and careful shaping of our future political institutions, which could have given the EU the kind of birth that we and our progeny would have been able to look back upon with pride. In any case, it is worth reiterating that the complexities involved in my proposal are by no means unmanageable. Citizens would be called upon to participate in about five decisions: The poll about the scope of the projected EU at Stage One, a possible referendum about fields of discretionary centralization, the referendum about the domain of the EU at Stage Two, the referendum about the legislative institutions of the EU in the first phase of Stage Three, and the referendum about the judicial and executive institutions of the EU in the second phase of Stage Three.[32]

It may also be asked: What is the point of discussing how things should have gone, given that things have already transpired quite differently? To this question, I have three answers. My discussion is relevant to the attitude we should take toward the existing EU institutions and to those who have been shaping and are continuing to shape them. Pointing out the opportunities they foreclosed should make us more skeptical about their projects and intentions. My discussion is also relevant to the question where we should go from here. The EU is by no means finished yet, and while some of the roads I have sketched may now be closed for good, others are still open. Thus it is quite possible to submit future changes in the scope of the EU to a referendum, for example, or to reshape the European Parliament so that it accords

31 Such emergencies were typically present, of course, during the most important events shaping modern political institutions — in the wake of the French Revolution (with the threat of reactionary intervention) and during the shaping of the United States (with the War of Independence).

32 Insofar as options might have to be resubmitted, more than five decisions might be necessary.

better with what I have called the fundamental idea of democracy. My discussion is also relevant, finally, to future integrative enterprises in other parts of the world, or even in the world at large. Given the ever-increasing incidence of transnational externalities, significant supranational integration seems a practical necessity.

References

ACKERMAN, BRUCE: *We The People — Volume 1: Foundations*, Cambridge MA (Harvard University Press) 1991.

BEITZ, CHARLES: *Political Equality*, Princeton (Princeton University Press) 1989.

BLICHER, L. and SANGOLT, L.: "The Concept of Subsidiarity and the Debate on European Cooperation: Pitfalls and Possibilities", *Governance: An International Journal of Policy and Administration*, 7 (1994), pp. 284-306.

CASTIGLIONE, DARIO: "Contracts and Constitutions", in: R. BELLAMY, V. BUFACCHI and D. CASTIGLIONE (Eds): *Democracy and Constitutional Culture in the Union of Europe*, London (Lothian Foundation Press) 1995, pp. 59-79.

GUSTAVSSON, SVERKER: "Defending the Democratic Deficit", in: A. WEALE and N. NENTWICH (Eds.): *The Political Theory of European Constitutional Choice*, London (Routledge) 1997, forthcoming.

KYMLICKA, WILL: "Federalism, Nationalism, and Multiculturalism", typescript of a lecture delivered at the 1995 Annual Meeting of the American Political Science Association.

ROSSITER, CLINTON (Ed.): *The Federalist Papers*, New York (New American Library) 1961.

WEALE, ALBERT: "Democratic Legitimacy and the Constitution of Europe", in: R. BELLAMY, V. BUFACCHI, and D. CASTIGLIONE (Eds): *Democracy and Constitutional Culture in the Union of Europe*, London (Lothian Foundation Press) 1995, pp. 81-94.

Part C

Political Theory for the European Union

Chapter 8

The Problem of Autonomy and Democracy in a Complex Polity: the European Union

KNUT MIDGAARD

I. Analysing the EU as a Complex Polity Under Ideal and Non-Ideal Conditions[1]

Analyses pertaining to "Democracy and the European Union" may be more or less comprehensive: the purpose may be to gain a better understand-

---

1 The author has received financial support for the research on which this paper is based from the *Institute of Humanistic Research* (Lifo) and the programme ARENA under the *Norwegian Research Council*. A sabbatical year in the stimulating milieu at the Centre for Advanced Study under the Norwegian Academy of Science and Letters has been decisive for my work, which has so far led to an essay in Norwegian, "Mot en bedre organisert verden: Momenter til en teori om legitime og gode styreformer" (Towards a better organized world: Elements of a theory of legitimate and good forms of government), published as *ARENA Working Paper* No. 7, July 1996. - Thanks are in particular due to Andreas Føllesdal, Raino Malnes, Thomas W. Pogge and Martin Sæter - for discussions, comments and kinds of help which, more or less directly, have made progress possible.

ing of some specific aspects of the organisation or its practices; or it may be to attain a better general understanding and characterisation. In either case both theoretical, normative and political interests may be operative. In the case of a more specific focus, the inquiry may, e.g., be due to an interest in developing more satisfactory indices of power, i.e., a better theory of power. As to normative and political interests, the inquiry may be due to a wish to improve the organisation on points where improvements are possible and important, or the aim may be to get a better basis for advising non-members on the question of joining, or not joining, the organisation.

In the case of a more comprehensive approach, the aim may be to acquire a better understanding of the ways in which various principles of democracy are met, or not met, in the organisation; this may be both a theoretical and a normative enterprise. As to political - and normative - objectives, there may be a wish to contribute to reforms which in a balanced way take into account the different institutional elements characteristic of the organisation - and the social, economic, cultural and political realities which both underlie the organisation and are influenced by its decisions; or the purpose may, once more, be to advise non-members on the question of joining, or not joining, the European Union.

The present contribution is due to a theoretical and normative interest primarily triggered by the debate on the European Union, and the advisability of joining it, which took place in Norway before the referendum of November 1994. Attending this debate, and to some extent participating in it, I found that the following propositions had to be my point of departure if I were to undertake more than very limited analyses related to democracy and the EU:

(1) The set of properties which are closely associated with democracy at the local and national level, need not be realisable to the same degree and by the same methods in an organisation which is set up, and developed, to solve problems which are common to a rather high number of nations, including several hundred million people, characterised by different conditions, traditions and languages. There is, indeed, reason to warn against rash generalisations.

(2) On the other hand, aspects of the European Union which are portrayed as constituting deficiencies from a democratic point of view, are not *necessarily* consequences of the complexity and size of the community and of the problems to be solved; or if they are, they need not be *necessary* consequences of this complexity. It *may* be that principles associated with democ-

racy can be met to a higher degree than is done at present, and to a higher degree by the same methods.

(3) As was emphasised in antiquity by Aristotle (and Plato), it is fruitful, or necessary, to distinguish between two questions: the question as to what would be a legitimate and good form of organisation under *ideal* conditions, and what form of organisation may be so under various *non-ideal* conditions (Aristotle 1946: IV, 1, 1288b). Thus, in Europe of today, there probably are deficiencies in political culture, and in a common understanding of the problems and concerns of different countries, which may be overcome over time.

(4) Care should be taken, however, not to identify "ideal conditions" with homogeneity or uniformity. The European variety of conditions and traditions, including languages, should be considered an asset to be taken care of.[2]

Some examples may elucidate this set of propositions.

On the one hand, it seems clear that immediate improvements can, and ought to, be made with regard to *transparency*, and with regard to making the *subsidiarity* principle decide the level on which problems are dealt with. Neither under ideal conditions nor under the present non-ideal conditions can the present pattern be considered a necessary consequence, if at all a consequence, of the complexities of the organisation and its basis.

On the other hand, the question of *accountability*, which goes beyond the question of transparency, is a more complex one. Under the present non-ideal conditions an attempt at reproducing the national pattern of legislation by a directly elected parliament would, from the point of view of central democratic principles, probably be clearly inferior to the present set-up. Will directly elected legislators be a necessary consequence of democratic principles under ideal conditions? It may seem so. The problem is, however, that it is not *a priori* clear what ideal conditions would look like in the European context, with the richness of conditions and traditions to be taken into account. In any case, it seems clear that the institutional structure, and the patterns of influence, will have to be more complex than in small unitary democracies. Democracy will be more of a "distant" democracy, and there will be more ambiguity with regard to both formal and real political equality.

2 A similar concern is submitted in JOSEPH H.H. WEILER (1996).

II. Criteria of Democracy and Normative Principles

The above considerations suggest that an evaluation of the European Union from the point of view of democracy should systematically take into account what the consequences of different set-ups would, or might, be under different conditions. More is needed, however. It is also necessary to distinguish between different *criteria* of democracy, and these criteria should be seen in the light of the values or *principles* that may justify democracy in one or more of the senses in question, or are relevant for other reasons.

Since Aristotle, *political equality*, in the sense of equal political obligations and rights, including equal political weight (one man, one vote, one value), is a central criterion of democracy (cf. Aristotle 1946: III, 9, 1280a). Another central criterion is *majority rule*. A third one is *accountability*.[3] (For all three criteria, cf. Lively 1984, p. 8-51). The three criteria, of course, are not mutually exclusive. A person may indeed find that all three, and other criteria as well, should be met. Nevertheless, he or she may give the various criteria different rank, or weight, or salience.

If majority rule is made the central criterion in an evaluation, all occurrences of *unanimity* requirements will be examples of democratic deficit. If, on the other hand, political equality is made the central criterion, unanimity requirements will probably be seen in the light of the central value to be served by political equality, that of *autonomy*; unanimity requirements may be seen as serving the *end* of democracy.

If accountability is made the central criterion, there will be a strong tendency to look at legislation by representatives who are only *indirectly* responsible to the citizens as constituting a deficiency, whilst the criterion of political equality, in combination with its justifying principle, that of autonomy, will make for more conditional conclusions. On the other hand, whilst *federations* like the United States and Switzerland will stand out as unproblematic examples of democracy if accountability is made the central criterion, these complex systems, which include an influential second chamber where small subunits (States, cantons) are overrepresented according to population

---

3 Accountability as a criterion of democracy is central in analyses of the European Union by both Sverker Gustavsson and Philippe C. Schmitter. Although the arguments submitted in this paper follow somewhat different paths from theirs, their penetrating analyses have been clarifying and helpful. (See GUSTAVSSON 1996, and SCHMITTER 1996a and 1996b.)

size, may create a problem under the perspective of political equality; there will be a need to justify this kind of inequality in terms of what serves autonomy.

If complex political systems may be considered democracies even if some subunits are clearly overrepresented, the question arises what kinds of inequalities, and how large inequalities, may be accepted. Moreover, the question arises what kinds of principles can be appealed to as arguments for one distribution of votes, as distinct from others, within the range of democratically acceptable structures. Is it acceptable, for instance, to refer to how much the various subunits contribute to the common budget?

Two conclusions should be drawn from the fact that central criteria of democracy may lead to quite different characterisations, and thereby evaluations, of a political entity like the EU:

(1) When characterising such an organisation with regard to democratic features, or democratic deficiencies, it should be made clear to what extent this characterisation depends upon one criterion of democracy, as distinct from others.

(2) Care should be taken to make clear how, and to what extent, basic principles or values are, or are not, served by the organisational characteristics in question. This should probably be our main concern.

In the subsequent sections, democracy will be defined as a form of government characterised by political equality, in the sense of equal obligations and rights; and democracy in this sense will be justified by the principle of personal autonomy, which again follows from respect for *the dignity and worth of the individual person*, to use the words of the Charter of the United Nations.[4] An attempt will be made to deduce organisational consequences from this principle. The arguments, which are rather elementary, will lead to some clear-cut conclusions; the main tendency, however, will be to go through a variety of considerations. Hopefully, these considerations may help attack the problem of characterising and evaluating an organisation like the EU in a rather precise and systematic way.

First, however, a broader set of principles and forms of organisation will be introduced, to ensure that our discussion will not be too narrow.

4 The principle of autonomy not only justifies equal political obligations and rights. It also entails a concern that differences in political influence, or in potential for such influence, due to differences in economic resources, access to decision-makers, etc., should be kept within bounds.

III. Political Equality and Inequality: Three Political Principles

As already indicated, since Aristotle *political equality*, i.e. the principle of equal political rights and duties, including the principle of one man, one vote, one value, is one central criterion, or definition, of democracy.

Those who favoured democracy in Greece, in particular the free-born poor, maintained, according to Aristotle, that reason, which is characteristic of all free-born, is the only attribute which is significant when it comes to assigning political rights and duties. This principle competed with two others: The well-to-do tended to assert that those who made significant financial contributions to the state should have more to say than ordinary citizens; and Aristotle maintained that those who contributed much wisdom to the *polis* should have even more to say (Aristotle 1946: III, 9, 1280a). We might altogether talk about three principles of constitutional justice: *the principle of basic equality*, *the finance principle of proportionality*, and *the competence principle of proportionality*.

All three principles, and principles akin to them, still play a significant role in establishing rights and duties in different kinds of organisation. More specifically, this is true of organisations established by democratic states, or within them. When it comes to the basic institutions of society as a whole, however, the principle of basic equality prevails in these states, the central justification being respect for the dignity and worth of the human person.

IV. The Principles of Autonomy and Political Equality: Institutional Consequences and Ambiguities

What political principles does respect for the dignity and worth of the human person entail?

One principle is obviously the classical one: political rule should aim at the good of all citizens/inhabitants, not only that of the rulers. To quote Kant, nobody should be considered just a means; everybody should be considered an end in himself or herself (Kant 1970).

More is at stake, however. It is not enough that political rule is not *despotic*; it should not be *paternalistic*, either. Respect for the dignity and worth of the human person implies the principle of *autonomy* (for the significance of the principle of autonomy in contemporary political philosophy, see, i.a., Rawls 1971, Pogge 1989 and Kymlicka 1995). According to Rousseau, everybody should only act according to rules or laws adopted by himself, which in his opinion meant that each citizen should have one and only one vote in the legislative body of the country (Rousseau 1752/1972: Book II, Ch. 15). Today it is generally accepted that autonomy can be taken care of through *representation*. Various conditions have to be met, however.

What is the opposite of autonomy? The immediate answer will be *heteronomy*, i.e., the condition of being subjected to rules or laws adopted by *others*, or more generally: the condition of being subjected to conditions established by others. There is another opposite, however, which should also be taken into consideration: that of *collective powerlessness*. In what follows I shall deal with both pairs of opposites.

Let us now consider how public decisions on general rules, or laws, *can* be made, and how they *should*, or *may*, be made, given the principle of autonomy.

The first question is: *Who should make the decisions?* The principle of autonomy implies that the set of decision-makers should be *identical* with the set of persons for whom the decisions apply (except for children, non-citizens staying on the territory, etc.), or they should consist of *representatives* of these persons. Heteronomy will result if this condition is not met. The principle of *subsidiarity* is therefore a significant one from the point of view of autonomy.

The next question to be dealt with is: How should different *decision procedures* and *decision processes* be evaluated from the point of view of autonomy? Both in direct and in representative democracy, decisions can in principle be taken *unanimously* or through a *vote*. Let us consider these two possibilities.

Unanimity may mean different things: agreement based on a common set of normative and factual premises; agreement based on partly different premises; agreement due to a compromise out of mutual respect; agreement based on logrolling; agreement based on a certain distribution of bargaining power. In the three first of these five cases decision-making will hardly give rise to any element of heteronomy. Decisions due to distributive bargaining, on the other hand, may easily do so; it may even give rise to an experience of collective powerlessness. Logrolling may be due either to constructive discussions or to tough bargaining.

Attempts at reaching agreement may take too much time or may fail. *Majority decisions*, through a vote, can be a relatively easy way out. Where basic interests are not at stake, and in particular where the losing minority expects to win in other votes, there may be no serious element of heteronomy. Where either of these conditions is not met, however, the losing minority may experience heteronomy. In cases where the constellation of preferences is such that tactics, in particular with regard to voting procedure, is decisive, the arbitrariness of the outcome may lead to both heteronomy and a feeling of collective powerlessness (cf. Riker 1982).

To sum up, autonomy is best taken care of in a political community where there is so much common understanding and mutual good-will that major decisions can be taken on the basis of genuine agreement or a compromise out of mutual respect, rather than on the basis of tough bargaining or through a vote. Under favourable conditions, majority rule may indeed lead to little heteronomy or powerlessness, and votes certainly have an important role to play. From the point of view of autonomy, however, it is hardly justifiable to *identify* democracy with majority rule. The concept of *consociational democracy*, or *consensus government*, is a significant reminder of cases where another approach is needed (cf. Lijphart 1984).

Now, for a given polity, the question may arise whether in all major issues it is possible to identify one rule, and institutional arrangement, which would be acceptable to all parties if adopted as a common one. If this is not the case, there will be major issues where agreement on a common rule, and institutional arrangement, cannot be reached, and where a majority decision would hardly be acceptable from the point of view of autonomy. What solutions are possible? A drastic one is to dissolve the polity, or split it in two or more polities. Another would be to give up the principle of only adopting rules, and institutional arrangements, that are common to the *whole* community. (Cf. the concepts of 'variable geometry', and 'consortio' and 'condominio' (Schmitter 1996a and 1996b).)

What was said above about decision procedures and decision processes requires some elaboration.

First, a reasonable degree of *transparency* is a necessary condition for citizens to experience autonomy; this applies to both direct and representative democracy. It should be kept in mind, however, that by going very far in demanding transparency one may make constructive negotiations difficult, and thereby effect collective powerlessness or heteronomy rather than autonomy.

Second, in representative democracy transparency must be supplemented by *accountability*. Any representative system depends upon methods of making representatives accountable to their electors. More specifically, autonomy depends upon representatives being accountable to the citizens whom they represent. It does not go without saying, however, what institutional arrangements will be adequate, or optimal, in different contexts. To some persons, *recall* is the ideal method. This method, however, is irreconcilable with methods of proportional elections, which many find preferable from the point of view of autonomy. Moreover, it may give too much power to activists and make constructive work difficult for the representatives elected. Today, the kind of accountability implied in directly electing legislators for a *limited period*, e.g. four years, is by most people found to be sufficient. The question arises, however, whether such a method is appropriate and necessary in all possible contexts. More generally, the question arises for what polities, and political communities, it is possible to develop a system of accountability which can secure autonomy, and, moreover, what systems are appropriate where some are.

Take a polity like the European Union. The possibility is there that accountability will be too indirect, and therefore too weak to secure autonomy as distinct from heteronomy, if legislation at the union level is left to a council of government representatives, in particular when decisions are made through a vote. At the same time it may be impossible to carry through the constructive negotiations which are necessary to reach jointly acceptable solutions, if national parliaments are to take direct responsibility; collective powerlessness may be the result rather than autonomy. Finally, a majority decision by a directly elected common parliament might be based on too little common understanding and concern to secure a general experience of autonomy; heteronomy or even collective powerlessness might be the result.

I have indicated a negative possibility, linked to simple solutions. It may very well be, however, that the apparent impossibility of an adequate method of accountability may turn into *possibility* when various combinations of methods, and perhaps social and political developments, are taken into consideration.

The principle of accountability does not only apply to *legislators*. *Executive authorities*, and the *judicial system*, must also in some way be accountable to the citizens. The central question is how, and to what extent.

It pertains to the essence of legislation, and the rule of law, that the law should be interpreted and applied in an *impartial* and relatively *stable* way. If *judges* were accountable to the citizens in the same way as members of legislative assemblies are, this condition would not be met. Accountability here must mean *transparency*: verdicts and their motivation must be made public so that adjudication is always in the public eye. As to autonomy, which is the value to be served by accountability, it is also furthered by the possibility of appeals within a hierarchy of courts. Similar considerations apply to the *prosecuting authority*.

Legislation should be constitutional. Where a supreme court, or a constitutional court, has the authority to rule on the constitutionality of legislation, there is a guarantee against heteronomy due to arbitrary legislation by the majority. A balance must be found, however. A supreme court, or a constitutional court, may, in its interpretations, assume a political role which goes beyond its field of competence, or by many is found to do so. Then heteronomy ensues, due to arbitrary adjudication, or to adjudication that is perceived to be arbitrary.

In presidential systems where the president is elected by the citizens the highest executive authority is accountable to the people just as members of the legislative assembly are. In parliamentary systems, the highest executive authority, the government, is only indirectly accountable to the people; its direct accountability is to the parliament. In both kinds of system, authority is delegated to different kinds of agencies. How, and to what extent, should these be accountable?

The purpose of the agency must obviously be taken into account. Take the university, the purpose of which is primarily to do scientific and scholarly research and to carry out academic education. Public universities are financially accountable to the legislative, through its accountancy. They cannot, however, be accountable for the contents of their work in the same way; there must be a high degree of autonomy if the universities are to do their job properly. Other methods and mechanisms, like peer review, and the criticism of the students, are adequate.

The role and the status of central banks are of particular interest. Central banks normally have a responsibility for price stability. How much independence does this task require to be performed in a good way? A high degree of independence for the bank may mean *technocracy*, and thereby a significant form of heteronomy. On the other hand, insufficient independence may mean that different kinds of political pressure, in particular short-term pressures, may lead to interactions which undermine or destroy price stability, leading to economic suboptimality and to injustices, and perhaps even political crisis, which means that collective powerlessness and heteronomy ensues.

It goes without saying that these considerations are relevant to a discussion of the central bank planned in the European Union. (For a critical discussion of its degree of independence, see Gustavsson 1996.)

We have so far only touched upon the fact that a polity may be either unitary or complex, more specifically, federal.

This fact, of course, is significant in our context, because the European Union is a complex polity or organisation. The question we have to ask is under what conditions such a polity is consistent with the principle of autonomy.

Consider a polity which is divided into a set of sub-polities. Let us assume that on either level there is a one-chamber legislative: For each sub-polity there is a legislative assembly which is directly elected on the basis of political equality, and, similarly, for the polity as a whole there is a legislative assembly which is directly elected on the basis of political equality. Let us furthermore assume that the constitution assigns one agenda for the sub-polities and another, which does not overlap the former, for the polity as a whole. Under reasonable assumptions about the character of each of the two agendas and about decision procedures and processes, there is no reason to think that the principle of autonomy is not met in this complex polity. So, it can safely be characterised as a "democracy". (Cf. Dahl 1983 pp. 95-108, and Dahl 1989.)

Consider now instead a complex polity where there is a two-chamber legislative on the polity level, the second chamber consisting of representatives of the different sub-polities. Let us assume that the different sub-polities have the same number of representatives irrespective of the size of their population, or let us assume that the number or weight of votes is far from proportional to population size, the small sub-polities being favoured. Let us finally assume that the first chamber is elected directly on the basis of political equality.

This system does not meet the principle of one man, one vote, one value. So, it is not unproblematic to characterise the polity as a whole as a democracy. The question is whether the favouring of small sub-polities can be justified on the basis of democratic principles.

There may be a *historic reason* for the system indicated. Perhaps those entities that are now sub-polities would not have found it advantageous from the point of view of autonomy to join such a polity if they were not given this "advantage", and perhaps heteronomy and collective powerlessness would have resulted if the polity had not been formed. Afterwards, a change of the constitution has been politically impossible or would be considered a violation of established rights, and would therefore have implied heteronomy.

Another justification may have to do with *identity*. Only by being given more than a proportional share in power is the population of each of the sub-polities able to prevent a domination by the big sub-polities, and thereby have their identity respected, which is a condition for autonomy.

Closely related to this justification may be one related to the democratic *vitality* of each of the sub-polities, more specifically, the small ones, and thereby a political vitality in accordance with democratic principles on the polity level.

We have here dealt with federal systems. If, however, the kinds of justification suggested for overrepresentation of small subunits are accepted for federations, they must also be accepted for other complex polities, like the European Union. Where there is not a very simple rule, however, like equal representation for all subunits, two questions arise. First, how far can democratic principles, more specifically the principle of autonomy, narrow down the range of acceptable keys for distribution of seats or votes? Second, what role can be played by other principles when it comes to finding a key and, more specifically, for changing the key? We have already suggested that the Aristotelian finance principle of proportionality, or related principles, might come into the picture. The explanation need not be that those who contribute much to the common budget want to dominate. The possibility is there that those who receive more than they contribute, tend to dominate politically, and that they, in the eyes of the net contributors in question, do not demonstrate sufficient responsibility in decisions and implementations.

In the concluding section we shall have a closer look at these questions, among others.

V. Autonomy, Democracy and the EU: Some Concluding Remarks

The previous discussions have not been consistently theoretical although an attempt has been made to pursue some ideas systematically on a general level; we have to some extent been wandering back and forth between theoretical topics and concrete ones pertaining to the European Union. The function of this section, then, will be to emphasise some points rather than apply general conclusions in a systematic way.

The European Union is a complex polity in two respects:

(1) It includes both a national and a supra-national level.

(2) The set of nations included is characterised by a great variety with regard to conditions, traditions and languages.

Moreover, the various nations included exhibit a more or less complex structure with regard to identities associated with history, language, etc.

The first of the two kinds of complexity indicated makes it natural to compare the EU to federations rather than to unitary nation states. The latter kind of complexity, however, means that the institutions of federations can hardly serve as a model for the Union, especially not under the present "non-ideal" conditions but perhaps not even under "ideal" conditions. Thus, such institutions may be inferior to the present ones from the point of view of autonomy.

Since the EU is not, and hardly can become, a unitary "nation" state the following questions are unavoidable: How, and to what extent, should the distribution of seats and votes reflect the equality of the member states, and how, and to what extent, should it reflect the principle of political equality across nations? Moreover, to what extent should the distribution reflect other principles?

These are central questions today, in particular in connection with a further expansion of the Union. First, does there exist a wide range of keys of distribution that are acceptable, and fully satisfactory, from the point of view of democracy? Or, does there exist an optimum, either in one of the extremes or at some point in-between? The CDU/CSU parliamentary group in the German *Bundestag* in its "Reflections on European policy" early September 1994 seems to suggest that democracy or "equality" is a kind of mean between the two principles indicated: "With regard to the Council, democratisation means striking a better balance between the basic equality of all member states, on the one hand, and the ratio of population size to number of votes in the Council, on the other" (*Europe*, 7 September, 1994, p. 4). The suggestion, however, is rather vague although there can be no doubt that CDU/CSU want to increase the voting weight of the bigger member nations; it would be interesting to see how a concrete proposal would be justified.

French politicians have expressed concerns about possible outcomes of majority decisions. Thus, the then Prime Minister Edouard Balladur in an article in *Le Monde* on 20 November 1994 stated: "Thus, the five large states which represent four-fifths of the population and wealth could be placed in a minority, which they would not allow. How, for example, to imagine that a State be forced to send its troops to an external theatre of operation?" (*Europe*, 2 December 1994, p. 1). Jacques Chirac, after he became President, is very explicit: "France will show itself open to an increased use of majority voting, provided two conditions are fulfilled: i.e. that the possibility for a Member State to invoke its vital interests is maintained; that the weighting of votes is reviewed in order to take into account demographic, economic and financial realities." (*Europe*, 9 September 1995, p. 2)

Both French politicians refer to population size, or the demographic factor. So far they are in line with the CDU/CSU parliamentary group, whose concern was "democracy" and "equality". In addition, however, they refer to what is denoted as "wealth" and "economic and financial realities", respectively. In a clear although implicit way a principle closely akin to Aristotle's finance principle of proportionality has thereby been introduced to strengthen a reform proposal which is also justified by an implicit reference to the principle of one man, one vote, one value. It remains to be seen to what extent such a principle will be focused in the general debate, and how it will be received.

The discussion of how to characterise and assess the European Union from the point of view of democracy has to a large extent focused on the questions of transparency, accountability and subsidiarity. I shall not repeat the points of view presented in the previous sections with regard to these dimensions. My main concern has been, and is, to look at the totality of institutions, methods and practices from the point of view of autonomy. This has led to few sharp conclusions; my conclusions have tended to be that a balance has to be struck between different concerns.

These dimensions should certainly be focused on in future discussions. It seems to me, however, that the problems related to majority voting, and to the distribution of votes among member states, are equally interesting and important, both from the point of view of democratic principles and from the point of view of normative theory more generally.

References

ARISTOTLE: *The Politics of Aristotle* (Translated with an introduction, notes and appendixes by ERNEST BARKER), New York/London (Oxford University Press) 1946.

DAHL, R. A.: "Federalism and the Democratic Process", *Nomos* XXV, (1983) pp. 95-108 (= PENNOCK, J. R. & J.W. CHAPMAN (Eds.): *Liberal Democracy*, N.Y. & London (New York University Press) 1983.

DAHL, R. A.: *Democracy and Its Critics*, New Haven (Yale University Press) 1989.

GUSTAVSSON, S: "Defending the Democratic Deficit", in: A. WEALE and N. NENTWICH (Eds.): *The Political Theory of European Constitutional Choice*, London (Routledge) 1997, forthcoming.

GUSTAVSSON, S. & L. LEWIN (Eds.): *The Future of the Nation-State: Essays on Cultural Pluralism and Political Integration*, Stockholm (Nerenius & Santérus Publishers/Routledge) 1996.

KANT, I.: *Kant's Political Writings*, Edited with an Introduction and Notes by Hans Reiss. Cambridge (Cambridge University Press) 1970.

KYMLICKA, W.: *Multicultural Citizenship: A Liberal Theory of Minority Rights*, Oxford (Clarendon Press) 1995.

LIJPHART, A.: *Democracies: Patterns of Majoritarian and Consensus Government in Twenty-One Countries*, New Haven and London (Yale University Press) 1984.

LIVELY, J.: *Democracy*, Oxford/New York (Basil Blackwell) 1984.

POGGE, T.W.: *Realizing Rawls*, Ithaca/London (Cornell University Press) 1989.

RAWLS, J.: *A Theory of Justice*, London (Oxford University Press) 1971.

RIKER, W.: *Liberalism against Populism*, San Francisco (Freeman) 1982.

ROUSSEAU, J. J.: *Du contrat social*, Oxford (Clarendon Press) 1752/1972. Cf. E. BARKER (Ed.): *Social Contract: Essays by Locke, Hume, and Rousseau*, New York and London (Oxford University Press) 1960.

SCHMITTER, P. C. (1996a): "If the Nation-State Were to Wither Away in Europe, What Might Replace It?", in: S. GUSTAVSSON & L. LEWIN (Eds.) 1996.

SCHMITTER, P.C. (1996b): *Is it really possible to democratize the Euro-Polity?*, (Unpublished manuscript) Stanford (Stanford University) 1996.

SMITH, E. (Ed.): *National Parliaments as Cornerstones of European Integration*, London, The Hague, Boston (Kluwer Law International) 1996.

WEILER, J. H. H.: "Legitimacy and Democracy of Union Governance: The 1996 Intergovernmental Agenda and Beyond", *ARENA Working Paper*, No. 22, November 1996.

Chapter 9

Individuality and the EU Project

RAFAEL ALVIRA

I may be permitted to begin with a few general ideas. Social order is order in the way we live together. In its first, smallest form it is expressed in the *peace* which reigns between people or peoples who have no relationship other than this. To establish or maintain peace it is not necessary to have a common organisation, only common good will.

The same is true for relationships which may come about through friendship or on the desire for cultural exchange in a generic sense.

Difficulties tend to arise when an attempt is made to share a *common system of ownership*, which is not the same as a *system of common ownership*. If everyone could own something and make that property grow, without this sparking conflicts with the other people he/she lived with, no legal system, and therefore no political counterpart, would be necessary.

But, in the human being, both the means of acquiring property and those of maintaining and increasing it are socially and culturally conditioned. Normally, the family, or some kind of organisation that fulfils similar functions, is the first place in which a human form of acquisition and ownership arises; and at the same time it is the first place in which socialisation and education in the broadest sense are to be found. It is, therefore, also the place where we start to form our own identity.

The human preconditions for acquiring and owning something are to have an *objective knowledge* of it and to *desire* it. It is relevant also in this respect to bear in mind the *social condition* and the *basic functional unity* of the human being. We develop learning (objective knowledge) and we desire things, always in our interwoven life with others.

A self-centred individual, who lacks profound social bonds, either is not interested in learning and owning –is more or less depressed–, or has some frenzy for wealth which does not generate a true sense of ownership.

Real ownership – acquired through learning and desiring– gives everyone his/her *identity*. A person that has nothing has no *identity*. We are, first of all, named by our first possession, that is, our parents; we are also *identified* by *our* city, profession, job, etc.

The more superficial our possessions are, the feebler our identity is.

Material property, on the other hand, is necessary and legitimate to the extent to which it is, at the same time, a true possession, that is, something which I take care of, and use in a social manner. This kind of property contributes also to form our identity.

As the home or family is not fully self-sufficient, it has to relate to others, thus broadening its basis for socialisation and education, and thereby enriching the possible *identity* of the members of that community.

***

It is here, however, that we come up against greater difficulties. It may well be the case that some people develop cultural styles that are more similar to those of people living in far-away places than to those of the people living closer together. Or that trading conditions are better with people a long way away than with immediate neighbours, and so on.

That is, as we can clearly see, when the system of property, culture and society is homogeneous, it is not very hard to organise political unity, as there is a sufficient basis for identity within the population. But if homogeneity is lacking, as is increasingly the case, especially in Europe, matters are not so easy.

Between the countries which are already members of the EU, or which may be going to join in the foreseeable future, there are considerable differences. There is often no homogeneity in the *subsystems* which underlie the way that a given society is constructed, and which, as I see it, are as follows in this order:

a) habitat
b) economy
c) law
d) politics
e) ethics

f) religion.

a) conditions b), b) conditions c) and so on. On the other hand, f) "governs" e), e) "governs" d) etc. [1]

Each of the member countries has a unit of territory (habitat), an integrated economic, legal and political system, and, up to a certain point, a common set of moral and religious values. As all this implies a certain cultural and social identity on the one hand, and serves to reinforce and strengthen this identity on the other, these countries have been able to form political units (states), thanks to the existence of such an identity, an identity that we generally call the nation. They are nation states.[2]

As we can all see, the problem facing the EU now is this: how can a new political unity be created out of the relative self-sufficiency of the national states, a self-sufficiency which is given the name of sovereignty?

If we want not just to reinforce peace or increase certain cultural contacts, but to achieve a certain political unity, then we have to accept that the key lies in creating a *common system of ownership*, and that this affects all the subsystems from habitat, economy, law, politics, etc., to ethics and religion. Spanish territory also belongs to the British, and French land to the Germans, etc. The Greeks will be committed to the defence of Denmark, and the Italians to that of Ireland. And the same will go for foreign policy. We shall have a common economy -market and currency-, common laws, politics, and so on, and the key point is that all that becomes a true possession - that it is felt to be so by all Europeans.

Up until now, progress has chiefly been made in the areas of the economy and law. However, because of what I have just explained, it seems to me to be structurally impossible to maintain and improve economic and legal unity without unification in the other subsystems. In my view, we need to get this clear from the outset: we may meet with difficulties, as is to be expected, we may fix on swifter or slower routes or methods to achieve unity, depending on the approach we adopt, but a unity that is only partial –that is, only economic, or juridicial, etc.– will either be extremely fragile, or merely temporary.

---

1 See R. ALVIRA: "Versuch die Vielfalt der gesellschaftlichen Subsysteme einzuordnen, mit besonderer Berücksichtigung des Rechts", *Jahrbuch für Recht und Ethik*, Band 1, Berlin (Duncker & Humblot) 1993.

2 For the problem of nationalism, see E. GELLNER: *Encounters with nationalism*, Oxford (Basil Blackwell) 1994.

General unity is not easy, and complete homogenisation is impossible as well as undesirable. But there has to be sufficient homogeneity in theory and, above all, also in practice, in the whole set of the above mentioned *subsystems*, to make it possible for us to live together. Consequently, there must be an *effective will* to achieve this, and a *minimum of agreement* as far as ideas are concerned.

***

At this point the subject of the individual arises[3]. Faced with such complicated problems, we can feel a certain relief when we realise that there may be a ready-made solution. The idea of democracy as a social and political formula based on the fundamental respect for the individual as such seems to offer us a route which eases the task of integration. The universality proper to reason, which is expressed in human rights, provides us with the definitive support for this.

The simple logic of the relationship between *the pure individual and the universality of reason* undoubtedly eases the approach to the complexity of problems in the fields of economics, politics, etc. As has often been shown, however, both the individual taken in isolation from his/her circumstances, and pure universal reason, are *abstracts*, they do not *exist* as such in reality. This is why democracy is initially revolutionary as pure voluntarism, naturalistic cynicism, and disembodied mysticism are all in a certain sense "democratic" and revolutionary. Democracy is revolutionary in the deepest sense, because already in its pure definition it distances itself from reality -which steadily shows a great number of differences between individuals, due to their natural dispositions, and many shortcomings in the realm of liberty-, and then seeks to change reality itself.

But it is one thing to say that the pure individual and pure reason do not exist, that they are abstracts, and a very different thing to maintain that they do not exist in general. They do not exist purely or in isolation, but it is easy to see that in conjunction with other elements they play a leading part.

The advantage of a good revolutionary spirit is its analytical character. This brings to light an aspect which is perhaps neglected or which has passed

3 See S. LUKES: *Individualism*, Oxford (Basil Blackwell) 1990.

unnoticed. This is, in my view, the historical value of revolutions and, in particular, the great merit of democracy. Democracy has brought to light the importance of individual freedom and the essential equality of human beings. As a result, the need for respect and tolerance has been emphasised. What is more, and this is very important for all philosophers, democracy has raised social discourse to an *explicitly* philosophical level.

When all is said and done, democracy in its pure revolutionary form is nevertheless impossible to maintain; the "essential" fact that here are limits imposed by the actual variety of things, of that which is concrete and circumstantial, must be accepted. Democratic individualism cannot therefore constitute a *sufficient formula* for European unity, as it is not a sufficient formula for any political unity. The *universality* of reason and the pure individual can not be matched by a similar universality of sentiments and of the will. Therefore the plurality of political units is also unavoidable.

There are various indications that suggest this. For example, where are we to set the geographical boundaries of the EU, if every country on the other side of the frontier is also made up of individuals worthy of respect who accept human rights? Or, on the other hand, how can we integrate people living in the present EU territory who do not share our democratic philosophy (some Muslim fundamentalist, for example, or members of certain sects), or who share it but have lifestyles so different from those of most of the population as to hinder understanding? Not to mention the ambiguous issue of the present globalisation of the world economy: we can have many economic links and, as a consequence, many relations up to a certain social unity, with very different peoples and countries that can hardly claim to enter the EU.

In my view, homogeneity within a human group –which is the basic problem we are facing in the formation of the EU– is created through the confluence of a set of factors, which occurs differently in each historical case. The actual historical unity of every constituted human group has a *form*, and this form is the "result" of the synthesis of the different factors mentioned below. Sometimes not all the factors are present; at other times, their presence is nuanced and balanced in different manners. What I want to emphasize is that there are only five factors, and that there is a precise logic - the logic of the integration of the time dimensions in the unity of life - in their general relationships. As I see it, the main factors are as follows[4]:

a) The *past* –cultural aspect–: the *homeland*

material: { *space*: land, territory, *country*, "ius soli"
time: blood, *ethnic groups*, "ius sanguinis"

formal: { the set of languages learned: *Cultural tradition*.

b) The *present* –strictly political aspect–: the *State* or the *political unity*. The political system and the laws in force.

c) The *future* –moral/ethical aspect–: the *people*. The common aims and ends agreed on and pursued by a population group.

If factor b) is not present, there is no political unity. But if this factor is not sufficiently backed up by a) and c), then political stability is fragile and may be under threat. It is not easy, and above all it is not good, to maintain political unity through the sheer force of a politico-juridical system that has been imposed against the wishes of the members of the population. It is factors a) and c) which contribute by providing enough homogeneity and identity for good political unity.

The most rudimentary type of social identity is that based mainly on the "material" heritage from the past: land and blood. This is not just material, as it has been made human, but it is the most rigid, and consequently the one which has caused most conflicts in the course of history.

Its importance must not be underestimated. Although modernity has striven, in my view quite rightly, to relativise the territorial factor by declaring that all land can be bought and sold, by opening frontiers and removing barriers, and so on, it is still impossible to deny that the human being benefits from a certain element of geographical permanence. And indeed, everyone longs for secure and fixed "territorial" property, even if it is a small flat, in his/her born or adopted country.

4 R. ALVIRA: "Consideraciones sobre el criterio último de unidad política", in: F. FERNÁNDEZ (Ed.): *Estudios en honor de V.R. Casado*, Madrid (Ed. Asociación de la Rábida) 1988.

As far as ethnic origin is concerned, the Enlightenment continued the Christian tradition which rejects any differences on the grounds of inherited race. Of course, I agree completely with this view. But in spite of this, we cannot ignore the fact that "ethnic" differences do exist (they exist factually, also in the sense that people give them a real importance), and that therefore unfortunately it is not easy to suppress them. It is a hard task to integrate populations that feel "ethnically" very far from each other: history affords many examples of this.

It could perhaps be said that this "material" factor, despite being the most rudimentary, may well be the hardest to change, and the one which causes most problems. For the EU this is still today a problem - North and South European differences, for instance-, and the number of immigrants from other continents are beginning to threaten the relative European unity in this field.

***

Unifying the "formal" element of the past we have inherited, unifying languages and cultures, is no easy matter either, but it is simpler to achieve. Unification does not mean mixing things directly, but bringing about mutual enrichment which leads towards a good synthesis or at least a practical union of several cultures.

Fostering the understanding and deep comprehension of other peoples, countries and cultures, through the means of education, mass media and tourism is, of course, a very important task, as is well known. A growth of the general peace, and personal and social cultural enrichment are the inmediate consequences. But, above all, in this respect, learning to appreciate deeply the culture of other peoples is a principal basis to prepare for good political union in the future, here and now in the EU.

In any case, the unity which we call here "cultural", based on the *past* in the sense of inherited culture, is not enough to put a good political unity into practice. This type of identity is very important among young people, people who are still in education, and among the old, people who often no longer have many difficult tasks to fulfil. But in the whole "middle" period of life, the future unites more than the past: common projects are what draw us together and bring us closer. And as we are all adults, we can all *decide freely* whether we want to take part in these projects or not, or whether we wish to live together under certain conditions, or not. For this reason, I have called this an ethical or moral unity.

To sum up, the *identity* of a population group is similar to that of an individual person, consisting of a certain synthesis of *character* (the given "past", the psychosomatic material basis), *style* (the "present", the basic cultural form) and *ends* (the "future", the basic projects and intentions).

The EU will not be viable in the medium and long run if we do not begin work now to achieve a sufficient identity of this kind.[5]

In this context, it seems to me that even though Europe was the birthplace of the Enlightenment -with its primordial insistence on *reason* and *progress*-, the past still weighs us down too heavily, and this places serious obstacles in the way of our aspirations towards unity.

Within the limits of the possible, sufficient identity requires a good deal of homogeneity in all the factors we have outlined. But it is quite clear that the main factor in unity, if we are thinking of dynamic, open unity, lies in the future, in projects, in common ideas and tasks.

In his recent book, *The idea of civil society*[6], Adam B. Seligman brings out how the USA has a great advantage over Europe on this issue. American unity is not built on the past, but on the future. We still insist on saving the past at all costs. We think our nations should be sovereign – but the nation as the main political factor belongs to the dimension of the past. That is why unity is so difficult to achieve in Europe.

The USA has benefited from a historical experience that may well be unique, but which has facilitated its task considerably. The country was constructed on the move towards new frontiers. We cannot do the same.

Nevertheless, the American experience has not been capable of homogenising the past, the common culture, sufficiently, and therefore even if its unity is much more dynamic and open than ours, it is also under threat. The relative failure of the "melting pot" has given way to "multiculturalism", but this is a future experiment whose results can hardly be predicted.[7]

---

5 Pure *citizenship* is not sufficient without this kind of identity. For the idea of citizenship, see R. BEINER (Ed.): *Theorizing citizenship*, Albany (State University of New York Press) 1995.

6 A.B. SELIGMAN: *The idea of civil society*, Princeton (Princeton University Press) 1995.

7 See W. KYMLICKA: *Multicultural citizenship: a liberal theory of minority rights*, Oxford (Clarendon Press) 1995.

***

We have to learn what we can learn from both, from the reality of tense nationalisms closed in themselves, and from the inability to create a certain cultural unity. It seems to me that European unity is not just a project that is at once beautiful and useful, but also a voyage that we have already embarked upon, from which it would be hard to return, as it would be highly demoralising to have to accept defeat, to turn back.[8] This unity to underline some obvious but necessary points will be achieved:

a) trying to minimise the differences caused by "land and blood", by means of increased communication, interchange and the introduction of new "*imaginaires sociales*".

b) in cultural areas, pragmatically, through a progressive increase in contacts, exchanges, permanent dialogue, above all in the youngest sector of the population, among children and students.

c) in ethical matters, also pragmatically, by setting up common projects, especially directed towards the world outside. Generosity towards others is what unites people most. Excessive concern with one's own affairs makes people unhappy and ends up by eroding unity. Europe - each European nation - has spent too long gazing at its own navel. This is not the way forward.

d) Continuing the work of unification in economics, law and politics.

***

Each person's individuality is brought out, defines itself and forms itself in the relationships with other people. In an impoverished sense, it defines itself *against* other people; in a much better sense, it is formed by working *in favour* of others, and relating in many ways to others[9].

---

8 Even if the difficulties are great, as underlined by J. ATTALI: *Europe(s)*, Paris (Librairie Arthème Fayard) 1994. See also: N. GRIMALDI: "L'énigme européenne", *France Catholique*, nº 2211, Paris 1989.

9 See R. ALVIRA: "The philosophical analysis of social change", in: V. VÁZQUEZ & I. OLÁBARRI (Eds.): *Understanding social change in the nineties*, Aldershot (Variorum) 1995.

The great revolutionary idea of the democracy is the *defence* of just individual liberty and of the essential equality of human beings against unjust and even tyrannical social and political systems. But in achieving this task modern democracy has used an abstract idea of the individual and, at the same time, has emphasized the negative side, the vindictive.

It is already the moment to develop individual liberty more, leading it from the status of an empty entity - in which it remains revolutionary and unsocial - to a concrete cultural and morally formed liberty; and to realise more than the achievement of true concrete equality is the most difficult task, which requires -over and above the necessary legal measures- a profound cultural and moral education.

The great force of *individual freedom* becomes richer and more effective if it is able to lead -from the very origin of its life- its activities towards others. This spirit awakens the sense of legitimate ownership: everyone longs to have material and intellectual goods -cultural goods, as a whole- in order to share them with others.

It will be possible for Europe to form a cultural unity –rich in natural differences– if European individuals are neither nationalists with closed minds nor abstract individualists. That is, if they are able to accept that in order to have a common system of ownership that functions properly, it is necessary also to have something that takes hold of all of us together, a project to help others that can inspire us with enthusiasm.

As a set of countries, necessarily limited in number, which have opted to take this path, and which can be admitted to participate in this project, Europe will embody the spirit which some authors like Robert Spaemann[10] have attributed to it: it will become the centre from which there will radiate an increasingly powerful universal culture fostering human dignity and the material and moral growth of humanity.

Europe cannot be formed on the basis of nationalism or abstract individualism. This thesis does not seem to me to be either vague or general, even though it might at first appear so. In fact, I believe that this is the reality from which we have to work in order to build the European Union.

---

10 R. SPAEMANN: "Universalismus oder Eurozentrismus", in: K. MICHALSKI (Ed.): *Europa und die Folgen*, Stuttgart (Klett-Cotta) 1988.

Chapter 10

Fatherland Europe? On European and National Identity and Democratic Sovereignty

PETER KOSLOWSKI

I. Nation Europe or Fatherland Europe?
II. The EU as a Commonwealth with Limited Tasks and Power
III. Political Myth or Political Theology at the Foundations of the EU?
IV. The Need for a Restoration and Revolution of the Older Idea of a European Empire or Commonwealth

The philosopher Johann Gottfried von Herder presented a treatise in Riga in the year 1765 under the title "Do we have now still the public and fatherland of the ancients?".[1] Looking at the European Union we have to change the subject into "Do we have now still the national fatherland or do we have the Fatherland Europe?". Before the French Revolution and the era of nationalism following it, which should shape Europe up to 1945, Herder had answered: "We have not the political religion of the ancients any more, which would retain its value only up to the walls of a city, and which would change with the air of an other area. ... Do we have a fatherland whose sweet name is freedom? Yes! But we think differently about the word freedom as the ancients did. For them freedom was an untamed cheekiness, a daring to direct the wheels of the state by themselves. ... The character of our public is not

1 J. G. V. HERDER: "Haben wir noch jetzt das Publikum und Vaterland der Alten?", in: J. G. V. HERDER: *Sämtliche Werke*, ed. by B. Suphan, Vol. I, Berlin 1877. (All translations from Herder's German text are by P.K.)

the bold wildness of the ancients any more; it is a finer and more restrained freedom. ..."[2]

The Fatherland of the ancients, the republic of the city states, the *polis* of the Greek or the republic of the Romans was at the same time political religion and safeguarding of the freedom of their members, but in its particularism and through its wild freedom it was also a republic aggressively attacking others. On the other hand the Christian state before the era of nationalism has no political religion, but a universalistic religion and a more restrained freedom as the nationalist state of the modern age. The Christian kingdoms - like France, England, Spain or Sweden at the time of Herder - and the Holy Roman Empire had no political, particular religion, but a common religion and the freedom of their citizens was one under the sovereign and meant the right to be able to do one's own business - not so much to participate in the government of the state. Only with the French Revolution the fatherland of the ancients and of the ancient city states returned. So the Swiss canton Waadt (Vaud) bears the stroke "*Liberté et Patrie*" (liberty and fatherland) on its coat of arms. The *nation* of the French Revolution drapes itself in the costumes of the Ancient Roman Republic and tries to reintroduce the political religion of the "highest being" as the national religion of reason. The bourgeois revolution against monarchy, church and nobility dresses itself in the garments of the restoration, the restoration of the Roman Republic, which reestablishes the old freedom after the wrong tracks of the Roman principatus, of the Roman empire, and after the Christian empire and kingdoms.

I. Nation Europe or Fatherland Europe?

Where can we, the citizens of the European Union, whose passports are already written out for the European Union and which we do not even need as long as we travel within the magic country "Schengenland", find our fatherland with the soul? Is it the country, the landscape, in which, like the name fatherland - "patria" - says, our father's house stood? Is it the nation our father belonged to, the nation, which is the fatherly, strong and superego form-

2 *Ibid*, p. 22 ff. Cf. P. KOSLOWSKI: *Gesellschaft und Staat. Ein unvermeidlicher Dualismus* (Society and State. An Inevitable Dualism), Stuttgart (Klett-Cotta) 1982, pp. 12.

ing cultural ground of the social birth of our "Self", which stands beside the motherly ground of the biological and family birth?[3]

Europe might not become the fatherly landscape for its citizens since it is too much an artificial and rationally built entity and it is also probably too large a creation. But can it become the fatherland of the social and cultural birth of our "Self"? Can it become a nation? For a congress on Europe at Hannover in 1991, I had asked the French political scientist Joseph Rovan to speak about the question "Europe of the Fatherlands or Nation Europe".[4] He gave a brillant lecture by pointing out - among other things -, that during the period of Nationalsocialism a journal existed, in which the Nationalsocialists wanted to impart the European neighbour people, that "Großdeutschland" is just doing the building up of the Nation Europe, and the name of this journal was "Nation Europa". As a host I was, as one can imagine, a little bit embarrassed for formulating the title in that way because I had had no knowledge of this journal. Interestingly enough, however, Rovan did not reject the term "Nation Europe" completely, he thought that the development of the European Union into one Nation is possible and even desirable.

Is therefore our fatherland the Nation Europe, if it cannot be the fatherland Europe, the sphere of the paternal origin? Is the Nation Europe, which does not yet exist today, the political idea we should strive for? About the Fatherland Europe and the Motherland Germany Thomas Mann wrote in 1930: "Germany, the people, the nation - sure, that is the state of mind of the past, that are the roots, is the motherliness, the intimacy, the individuality and the eternity, it is the kingdom of the soul. Europe, that is the social and rational idea, it is the future, it is the fatherly principle, it is mind. As long as people

---

3 The father-house of my father stood in a country, which does not even exist anymore today; but in spite of the loss of his native landscape of "Ostpreußen" (East Prussia) my father never felt like a person without a fatherland, because his fatherly, social birth was carried out in a larger country, which had not been extincted.

4 Cf. J. ROVAN: "Europa der Vaterländer oder Nation Europa?" (Europe of Fatherlands or Nation Europe), in: P. KOSLOWSKI (Ed.): *Europa imaginieren. Der europäische Binnenmarkt als kulturelle und wirtschaftliche Aufgabe* (Imagining Europe. The European Single Market as a Cultural and Economic Task), Berlin/Heidelberg/New York (Springer) 1992, pp. 55-69. French translation: "Europe des patries ou Nation Europe?", in: P. KOSLOWSKI (Ed.): *Imaginer l'Europe. Le marché européen comme tâche culturelle et économique*, Paris (Les Éditions du Cerf) 1992, pp. 61-75.

fear, as long as one lets people fear that they betray their soul, if they say yes to Europe, because mind and soul are irreconcilable contrasts, as long Europe will not be. Through the falsly warm-hearted concern with this contrast one exposes oneself to the danger of isolating oneself from the development of the world and from the direction of its evolution."[5] For Thomas Mann the nation in the broader sense is the motherland, is motherliness, soulness; however Europe is the fatherly principle, is rational mind. But Thomas Mann does not forget to add, that mind and soul must not be considered as antagonists, that mind and soul are complementary to each other.

The German and also the English language do not have the great paradox semantic of a "female fatherland", which the languages of the *Romanitá*, like Spanish, Italian and French have with their word "*La patrie*". *La Patria* is the fatherly landscape, the masculine-female origin of the human beings in his or her nation, which makes the "patria" to be an androgyn, masculine-female ground of the social birth of human beings. Perhaps therefore the Romance mind does not get in the aporias and contradictions of soul and mind in the term "nation", since *patria* is at the same time soul and mind, the emotional and the mental, the motherly and the fatherly, for it.

But what is Europe for us? Rational idea or individual experience of the soul? And what *should* Europe be for us, the citizens of the commonwealth most rich in population behind China and India in the world, a commowealth which is on its way to become a single federate state? Will Europe be Patria, Fatherland, Nation, State, Commonwealth or Empire? It is contended here that the European Union is and must be an Empire and Commonwealth[6]

5 TH. MANN: "Die Bäume im Garten. Rede für Pan-Europa" (1930) (The Trees in the Garden. A Speech for Pan-Europe), in: TH. MANN: *Werke. Das essayistische Werk. Politische Schriften und Reden*; Vol. 2, Frankfurt/M. (Fischer) 1968, pp. 173-179, here 178 f.

6 The terms "commonwealth" and "empire" are used here as synonymous. This is particularly the case in the Germanic languages like Dutch, Swedish, and German in which *Rijk* or *Reich* has more the connotation of commonwealth than of empire. The European Union must be a commonwealth-empire. It might be noted here that the usual English rendering of the National Socialist term "Das Dritte Reich" as "the Third Reich" is not correct and does not do justice to the old Empire or *Reich*. In English, the translation should be either "the Third Empire" or "the Dritte Reich". The reduction of the concept of the *Reich* to its Nazi perversion is very questionable since the Weimar Re-

which can develop later into a Nation Europe. But it is not the task of politics to render the European Union to be one "Nation of all Europeans" because a nation is something that rather grows and is born in spite of being made. The uniting of people and nations to a new nation cannot be constructed by politics - not even by the majority-will of a democraticly legitimized supranational European Parliament -, because the minority-will who decides for retaining the original nations must not be easily passed over. The Nation Europe can only be born by historically prolonged processes of the non-political, rather cultural and personal interchange of the citizens of the different European nations.

The model for the Fatherland Europe for the next years to come cannot be the Nation Europe, the model must rather be the European Empire, the European Commonwealth, which *can become* later the Fatherland for all Europeans. The historical example for the European Union, which can give elements of advice, but which - like all historical models - cannot be imitated or be taken over, is the Holy Roman Empire as a supranational state, not as a state that is sovereign and centralized in the modern sense. The characteristic of the model of the Holy Roman Empire is that it gives us not positive directions but directions through negations which tell us, how the Fatherland Europe should not look like. The model of the Holy Roman Empire protects us from wrongly organizing the European Union as a centralized nation state in the way the sovereign nation-state of modernity was conceptualized and organized. It will protect us from following the Jacobin model of the nation. The European Union can only be organized supranationally, in a non-centralized and confederate manner and with restraint sovereignty.

What the European Union could learn directly for its instititions from the institutions of the Holy Roman Empire in Spain and Germany and after its end in 1806 from its follower-empire, the Austrian multinational state, should be pointed out by the historians and the law scholars. Political philosophy and the philosophy of history can point out, however, what may be adopted from the idea of an empire or commonwealth. Until the French Revolution and Napoleon, Europe was characterized in Central Europe and Spain by the idea of the *translatio imperii*, by the transmission of the Holy Roman Empire to the Franks and Saxons, and it was influenced in Eastern and Byzantine Europe by the transmission of the Eastern Roman Byzantine Em-

---

public also kept the concept. Article 1 of the Weimar Constitution stated: "Das deutsche Reich ist eine Republik" (The German Reich is a republic).

pire to the Slavonic peoples, to the Russians. Crucial is the idea of the limited task, the idea, that the Roman Empire is handed over as a task for a limited time-period and that the Roman Empire must be permanently renewed in a *restauratio imperii*, in a restoration of the empire. Limited task by transmission *(translatio)* of the Empire from one representative to another and restoration by renewing are the central ideas of the idea of a European Empire, on which the European Union must orientate itself.

II. The EU as a Commonwealth with Limited Tasks and Power

The European Union as the Fatherland Europe and as an empire of limited tasks means three things:

Firstly: The European Commonwealth or Empire is not based on a myth, which a group of people gives itself and which justifies this group as a nation for doing everything they want. The European Empire-Commonwealth is based on the historical, non-made, and non-contingent but almost so to speak God-given solidarity of the peoples of this area of the world in the continent of Europe. It is a very important, non-contingent fact that a nation must be in Europe, to be able to become a member of the EU. It is locus or site (*situs*) in the world that matters for the question whether a nation can join the European Union.

In the language of the religions, the European Commonwealth is a divine task, a task given by God. In the speech of history and economics the European Empire is the geographical-historical and economic task *to secure the common good* of the European nations.

Secondly: The Fatherland Europe as a supranational commonwealth has a limited task only: It is not its task to establish the sovereignty of one single European people or *demos*, through which - in the sense of the *volonté de tous* of Rousseau - the sovereign state-demos *(Staatsvolk)* can do anything politically that it wants and through which the people constitutes itself as the absolute subject in the Rousseauean sense.

Thirdly: The Fatherland Europe as European Commonwealth is not a political revolution, through which the nations of Europe separated themselves by a sovereign act of will completely from their past and from their history of having been nation-states. Rather, the Fatherland Europe is *restauratio* and *renovatio*, a restoration and a renewal at the same time. It is the restoration of the prenational Europe without intending the elimination of the nations, and it is, at the same time, something completly new, a renewal of the idea of a European Commonwealth-Empire without a precedent, because it bases this idea on a democratic foundation. The era of the Christian Kingdoms and of the Holy Roman Empire, the era of the modern empires of the emperors of France, Germany and Russia, and the era of the nation-states are followed by a People's Empire or a Commonwealth of Peoples, by the multinational Empire Europe, a democratically legitimized Empire-Commonwealth, which is different from the democracy of the nation-states. The Fatherland Europe stands in a dialectical tension with something, which existed once upon a time, the Roman Empire, as the renewal of it in the idea of a post-feudalistic and democratic Empire or Commonwealth.

The Fatherland Europe cannot consist in the concept of the *patrie* of the nation state that has become the dominant tradition since the French revolution. Its constitution is not based on the concept of popular sovereignty that has become essential for the nation states through the contingent history of France. The French *nation* formed the model for all nation states in modernity. The constitution of the Fatherland Europe is rather based on the voluntary surrender of rights of sovereignty by the European nations to the European Union. The European Union is not grounded, as Hermann Lübbe remarked[7], on the principle relevant for the sovereign nation state of modern democracies, namely the principle "one man - one vote", since the European parliament has no legislative power. The legislation of the European Union rather depends on the legislative power of the national parliaments and needs their approval.

Furthermore the fatherland Europe cannot be a Rousseauistic *patrie* and democracy because the principle "one man - one vote" is limited and modified by the principle of the overproportional representation of certain regional or national administrative bodies.[8] The often blamed democratic deficit of the European Union is to some extent unavoidable. One cannot ground the EU on the principle "one man - one vote" since this gave the nations with a larger population and particularly Germany an extremely strong influence on the

7 Cf. H. LÜBBE: "Geteilte Souveränität. Die Transformation des Staates in der europäischen Einigung" (Shared Sovereignty. The Transformation of the State in the European Unification), *Information Philosophie* (Lörrach/Basel), 3 (August 1994), pp. 5-13.

8 See also H. LÜBBE, *ibid.*, p. 13.

EU institutions. Indeed, one must assume that the principle „one man - one vote“ would drive the smaller nations out of the EU.

In federal states, the representation of the regional administrative bodies does not depend upon the number of votes of the population in each region, but is effected according to the principle of federal legitimacy, i. e. on the principle that all regional administrative bodies receive an adequate share of representation in the co-operation of the regional bodies (*Gebietskörperschaften*). The Grand Duchy of Luxembourg owns only two-hundredth of the population of the Federal Republic of Germany. Nevertheless it has an equal voice and equal vote in the European Council, and in the important council of ministers is has one fifth of the voting power of Germany.

The digression of the European Union from the norm of the sovereign nation state and of the democracy of competition is obvious, its divergence from the model of competition of political parties for the majority of votes, from the principle of a democracy of party competition (*Konkurrenzdemokratie*) is undeniable. The EU works more according to the model of the democracy of party concordance, the Swiss model of *Konkordanzdemokratie*, not the British or American model of democracy of competition. It deviates from the principle of "one man - one vote" and follows the model of a confederately legitimized, semi-sovereign, and concordance-democratic commonwealth. This divergence from the Rousseauean model of popular sovereignty in the EU should not be interpreted as a deficiency only but as a chance. It cannot be the aim of the Fatherland Europe to become a nation state in the sense of the concept of the nation of the French Revolution.

After all, the federal legitimacy of the European Union is founded on the insight in the deficiencies of the idea of the democratic nation state. The EU is the answer, found after World War II, to the failure of the nation of the Rousseauean popular sovereignty and to the desaster of the dictatorial nation state. The EU is not only a response to dictatorship but also to the deficiencies of the homogenous nation state of popular sovereignty. It would be wrong to assume that only the dictatorial nation state is a problem for Europa. Problematic for the peace of Europe is also the democratic nation state. In Eastern Europe, the region would be devastated if its countries followed Rouseauean principles as Ex-Yogoslavia has demonstrated. The confederate legitimacy of the EU can be seen as the corrective against the mistaken opinion that the majority of a state's people (*Staatsvolk*) constitutes the absolute and sovereign decision-making power or the popular sovereignty.

The philosophy of the state in the (Christian) natural law tradition has always considered the idea of popular sovereignty to be an error and there are good arguments for that position. The main argument is that popular sovereignty must be under the rule of law, and is not the "*Herr der Gesetze*", the Lord of the laws. The European Union, therefore, does not have to be embarrassed that it does not follow the model of nation state and that it does make progress towards the state of popular sovereignty since by its very nature the EU cannot be the holder of popular sovereignty in the sense of Rousseau.

Popular sovereignty contradicted and still is in tension with the rights of national minorities to being represented in those modern nation states that have no ethnic homogeneity - and those have been and are the majority of the states in the world. The unlimited popular sovereignty also contradicts the historical evolution of regional particularities and fails to acknowledge the contingency of the other commitments of humans. It fails to affirm the rights they have beside those derived from the will of the majority. This has always been the important and legitimate reproach of the English common-law-tradition against the French Revolution. This criticism had already been raised before the French Revolution against the Continental absolutism and its belief that the sovereign is the Lord of the laws. In as far as the English objections against the centralism of Brussels are in this tradition, they must be taken very seriously in a theory of the constitution and in the real constitution-making for a Fatherland Europe. Brussels should not become the Versailles of a European Empire.

III. Political Myth or Political Theology at the Fundaments of the EU?

The constitution and development of the European Union point to the fact that the interpretations of the history of the state that have become dominant in the European nation states are one-sided and do not do justice to the realities of European history as it can be demonstrated at the national philosophies of history. It is visible at the Jacobin philosophy of history in France which moves France to the centre of world history. It can be demonstrated at the "Whig Interpretation of History" which moves England to the centre of history and at the Germanocentric Hegelian philosophy of history which makes Germany and the Germanic people the centre of world history. Within a very small space one finds three nations claiming to be the centre and meaning of world history.

Neither the Jacobin interpretation of the history and constitution of Europe that Europe can only come to be herself by becoming a group of sovereign nation states nor the English "Whig Interpretation of History" that ever since the Magna Charta political liberty existed only in England, nor Hegel's concept of the consummation of world history in the Germanic world are adequate interpretations of the historical leads and lags in the developmental phases of the European nations. The Jacobin interpretation of history emphasizing the creation of the nation by popular sovereignty, by revolutionarily breaking with its past as well as by excluding the churches from the public realm[9] contradicts the historical continuity with the pre-Nationalist Europe. The English "Whig Interpretation of History" that England is the only historical force for liberty in the world constantly striving for the progress of liberty contradicts the fact that freedom has been sought by other nations as well. Hegel's concept of world history, in turn, that history is a progress in the consciousness of liberty that found its climax in the Germanic world did not do justice to the Slavonic nations.

The incongruencies in the images of the same historical event between the European nations can, for instance, be seen in the contradictory interpretation that the same historical personality receives in the different European nations. The English worship Sir Francis Drake as a hero of liberty, whereas the Spaniards see him as a pirate and international criminal who broke the law of the European nations. In the Fatherland Europe, these national philosophies of history will hit hard upon each other in their confrontation with the universalism of the EU as a European Commonwealth. A democratic European Commonwealth requires and tolerates more - and even contradicting - interpretations of history than a homogenous nation state with only one state people, that very often is too much of the same opinion about its mission in the world.

The Fatherland Europe is an empire with a limited mission, it is not a state in which the people has unlimited popular sovereignty. Consequently it does not need a founding myth to justify its sovereignty, as lately George

9 This thinking seems to be influential at Brussels where there are forces that contend that the churches should not play any public role at all in the European Union.

Steiner[10], has claimed. The myth as a political myth is the self-authorization of a people through fiction and poetry, through the invention of a history, that makes a people to be the master of a territory in a certain time. In the political myth, a people invents its legitimization as conqueror and master of a territory. It is obvious that the European Union which, according to its Charter, is open to all peoples and states in Europe that have a democratic government, cannot be built upon a myth, nor does it need one.

Here again, the comparison with the idea of the Holy Roman Empire is enlightening. This empire was not grounded on a myth, but on the idea of the limited and temporary mission by divine endowment, on the idea of the transfer of the empire, the *translatio imperii*. A divine endowment or order is different from a mythological self-authorization and empowerment. An order limits the discretionary power of the recipient of the power and it can be withdrawn and given to someone else being more deserving if it is not fulfilled properly. Such a delegation of power is not derived from one's own empowerment or from a self-invented myth, and thus again from oneself. Rather, it stems from someone else, to whom the order recipient is accountable. The idea of the *translatio imperii* as a limited authorization and fief does not retell the history like the political myth as the history of the winner only. It is not a history perceived from the perspective of the winner of history only. Its story and history is a history of continuity standing above the winners and losers of history and war that includes both, winners and losers.

Already the history of the heathen first Roman Empire starts with a *translatio imperii* from Troy to Rome: Aeneas carries his father from the burning Troy to become the founder of Rome and later the conqueror of his conquerors, of the Greeks. The idea of empire comprises the reminder and warning, that every conqueror will be conquered by the ones he conquered. The European idea of the empire includes the awareness that history is a history of renaissances and that in it there is only one order, the order to secure the common good of Europe. This one order includes the principle that the task of realizing the common good will be given to the one who fulfils it the best way. Aeneas received the order to build Rome out of the defeat of Troy, Charlemagne received the order of the *translatio imperii ad Francos*, to the

10 GEORGE STEINER: "Sind unsere Kräfte erschöpft? Europa ist müde, der Stier gefährlich geworden: Am Ende des Jahrtausends sucht der Kontinent einen neuen Mythos" (Are Our Powers Fading? Europe is Tired, the Taurus Turned Dangerous), *Frankfurter Allgemeine Zeitung*, Beilage "Bilder und Zeiten", 27. August 1994, No. 199, p. 1.

Franks, out of the defeat of the Roman Empire, the European Union received the order to form a new political entity out of the failure of the nation state.

The failure of the nation state was not only a failure of Germany, but had its origin in the injustice inflicted by the West European nation states on the entire Europe, on the European Commonwealth. In the 20s of this century, the Protestant theologian Erik Peterson who later converted to Catholicism contended that the West European nations had done injustice to the "Reich", to the Holy Roman Empire. In his analysis, Peterson criticized as well the Liberal nation states as the "theology of empire", the "*Reichstheologie*" of the Nationalsocialist "German Christians" (*Deutsche Christen*).[11] He contended that, from the 17th to the mid-20th century, France and England had not really been interested in Europe since they were occupied by their colonies. They put their national egoism and their raison d'état above the common good of Europe.

The idea of the *translatio imperii* implies that the holder of the empire's office has only a limited task, that he or she is not the Lord of Lady of this task, and that the task and the power to fulfil it will be taken away from him or her if it is not fulfilled in the right way for the common good of the commonwealth of Europe. One can, therefore, guess that there will be a further translatio imperii away from the EU. On some distant day, a world federation of states will receive the delegation to take over the politcal task and the commonwealth from the European Union since the idea of a confederation and alliance confined to one continent only will be defeated and outdated.

IV. The Need for a Restoration and Revolution of the Older Idea of a European Empire or Commonwealth

The European Commonwealth has the order to secure peace and the common good in Europe and is founded on the idea that this task is conducted in a series of renaissances and not in a series of revolutions. In this sense of renaissance, Europe can be described as the continent of renaissances that se-

11 Cf. B. NICHTWEIß: *Erik Peterson. Neue Sicht auf Leben und Werk* (Erik Peterson. A New Perspective on his Life and Work), Freiburg i. Brsg. (Herder) 1992, pp. 764f. and 774ff.

cures continuity and change through the consciousness and practice of reassuming the original heritage of Antiquity and Christianity in a sequence of renaissances, as Rémi Brague has shown in his book on the excentric identity of Europe.[12] The European Union is a renaissance of the European idea of the empire-commonwealth as *restauratio* and *renovatio imperii*, as renewing and continuation of the tradition of the Roman Empire.

The idea of the European Empire is not based on a single concept of the philosophy of state and of society. Its foundation is not popular or monarchic sovereignty, but the integration of elements of democratic legitimacy through equal elections and elements of confederate legitimacy by proportional representation of its member nations. In its bond with older traditions of Europe, the idea of the European Commonwealth is at the same time traditional and (post-) modern, and thus the contrary to being doctrinaire.

It cannot be the aim to create a new doctrine nor a new political myth for a European fatherland. For a European fatherland, it can only be the aim to unite the law of reason and the law of history by connecting the EU to the older common European tradition. The Germans have been called a people without a myth, without a founding myth. One does not need to interpret this as a deficit but can take it for an advantage. The nations of Europe and their politicians must see themselves as representatives with limited power not as the absolute holders of sovereignty empowered by mythological fictions. The myth is always particularistic, without being conscious of this fact, and so is the power that is founded on a myth, whereas the power that is founded on a limited task remains conscious of its fiduciary character, of its only being lended, and thus remains subject to the common good, and not subject to the absolute will of the sovereign only - and be it the popular sovereignty.

Tradition is a constraint that is freer and looser in many respects than the constraints of the doctrines. It is also a constraint against the hybris of politics. Also for this reason, the Fatherland Europe must relate itself to the idea of a European Empire. The tradition and the task of the idea of a European Commonwealth demand the "weak state", not the strong state of nations and of popular sovereignty. A democratic empire and commonwealth respects and protects the rights of its regional institutions and provinces, but also the

12 Cf. R. BRAGUE: *Europa. Eine exzentrische Identität* (Europe. An Excentric Identity), Frankfurt am Main (Campus) 1993. Original: *Europe, la voie Romaine*, Paris (Criterion) 1992.

rights of the supranational and non-governmental institutions in it like the churches and the multinational corporations. Such a democratic commonwealth cannot be a body politic tailored centralistically and monistically towards *one* center of sovereignty. The European Union as a European Empire is not a state that is weak because of weakness, but a state that is "weak" or restrained because of strength. It is weak in its exercise of power by restraining itself due to arguments of reason and tradition and due to its respect for the proper right of the regional institutions, churches and of that what in ancient Europe would have been called "the estates".

The European unification takes place after Europe's colonial period which has been closely connected with the egoisms of the European nation states. Or saying it the other way around: the egoism of the nation states and their turning away from the idea of a European Commonwealth supported national egoism and colonial expansion in the interest of one's own nation only. Paradoxically, the Europe's turning towards the Non-European exterior world produced its internal cleavages and the worst civil wars within Europe. In the very historical moment in which the European idea of "world-history" in the Hegelian and Whig-interpretation of history is coming to its end, in the historical moment in which the idea that it is the destiny of world history that Europe rules the lands and the waves and leads them towards liberty is becoming obsolete by the rise of East-Asia, in this very moment Europe is able again after a long time to become one empire and commonwealth like the other continents. By growing into one commonwealth, Europe is becoming like the other continents.[13]

The historian Herrmann Heimpel has written: "That the nations exist is historically the particularly European feature in Europe's character."[14] When Europe is becoming nowadays one Fatherland Europe it is this very European trait in Europe's character, the nation, and, therefore, the very "Europeanness" of Europe that is questioned. This is the deeper reason for the resistance against "Maastricht". It is a paradox that the more Europe finds its way to the unity of one empire and one commonwealth the more becomes like the other

13 E. J. HOBSBAWM: "Welchen Sinn hat Europa? Ein halbes Jahrtausend haben die Europäer die Welt geprägt. Damit ist jetzt Schluß" (Which Meaning has Europe? For Half a Millennium the Europeans Shaped the World. That has Come to an End), in: *Die Zeit*, Nr. 41, 4 October 1996, p. 40, writes: "At the end of the first post-European century (after Columbus) we need a newly imagined history of Europe." (translation by P. K.)

14 "Daß es Nationen gibt, ist historisch das Europäische an Europa".

continents. We should not consider this development as a loss but as an advantage. The exaltations of nationalism in Europe have been so closely connected with its colonial claims, conquests and rivalries that Europe was not able to continue with its nationalism.

Only when Europe is ready to acknowledge that it is in all its singularity *also like* the other continents it will be able to open itself for what - as Jacques Derrida has put it - "has never been Europe and will never be it".[15] What is to be learnt and to be experienced from this opening especially towards Asia, towards China and Japan, will exceed in value by far the loss of the singularity of the nationalist and colonial era of European history.

The Fatherland Europe will have to learn that it cannot only be the mother of revolutions and conquests but must also be the mother of conservation and protection. The European Union is a great example for a revolution that is at the same time the restoration of a great older idea. All real revolutions must be at the same time restorations as it has been demonstrated by the revolutionary opening of Japan towards the West in 1868, a revolution that entered history under the name of the "Meiji-Restoration". The Fatherland Europe is a revolution of the European national states that is, at the same time, a restoration of the older European idea of empire, commonwealth, or *Reich*. In this sense, there is no reason to be ironical about the wisdom of Adenauer, de Gasperi and Schuman who related the foundation of the European Economic Community (EEC) to the foundation of the Holy Roman Empire in Aachen by Charlemagne. It is rather the task to continue the „refounding" of the European Commonwealth in new renaissances.

Unifications are only possible as long as they remain partial wrote the Jewish-Habsburgian writer Joseph Roth.[16] The Fatherland Europe cannot be the one "Nation Europe" since its unification would then be total and the her-

---

15 Cf. J. DERRIDA: "Kurs auf das andere Kap - Europäische Identität" (Steering to the Other Cape. European Identity), *Liber* (German edition), Nr. 3 (1990), p. 13.

16 Quoted in R. SCHENK: "Redimentes tempus. Der Beitrag der Kirchen zur europäischen Einigung", in: P. KOSLOWSKI, R. SCHENK (Eds.): *Jahrbuch für Philosophie des Forschungsinstituts für Philosophie Hannover, Band 7, 1996*, Wien (Passagen) 1995, pp. 43-62, here p. 43: "Joseph Roth .... zeigt ... daß, soweit unsere konkrete Phantasie reicht, Einigungsprozesse nur dann gelingen, wenn sie partiell bleiben." (Joseph Roth... demonstrates... that, as far as our concrete imagination extends, processes of unification can only succeed if they remain partial.)

itage of the European nations would not be conserved. Such a political unification cannot stand since it is not partial but total. The European unification and the Fatherland Europe are only viable as a partial unification that leaves possibilities to the member states of the European Union to keep part of their own and particular features outside of the process of unification. The political form of this partial political unification with a limited task and empowerment cannot be the nation but only the empire or commonwealth. In this respect, the Fatherland Europe of the European Union will be for a long period of time not a "Nation Europe" but a European multi-national empire.

The post-modern period we are living in has been named the epoch after the end of the grand narratives, after the grand theories of "world history" and their "master stories". It has been called a period of exhaustion and even of decadence. A conservative concept of postmodernism as developed by the author[17] shares the judgment of the French anarchist concept of postmodernism that the grand narratives of modernity, Hegelianism and Marxism that have been closely connected with European nationalism and Europe's supremacy in the world have come to an end. In 1994, the Japanese philosopher Yaoshi Yamawaki told the author in Tokyo when one discussed the question of the end of the grand theories that there existed one grand narrative of the present age. To the following-up question: "Which grand narrative?", he answered: "... the process of the European unification". If one thinks about the question deeper one recognizes that we are already, without having noticed it, in a grand narrative and a great (hi-)story, in the story and history of the formation of a new fatherland, the Fatherland Europe.

If one applies the question of Herder raised at the beginning of this paper to our times, modifies it and asks: "Do we still have the public sphere and fatherland of the nations of modernity?", the answer can only be: "We do not have anymore the political religion of the nation state that keeps its value only up to the frontiers of a nation." If one continues to ask: "Do we have" -

17 Cf. P. KOSLOWSKI: *Die postmoderne Kultur. Gesellschaftlich-kulturelle Konsequenzen der technischen Entwicklung* (The Postmodern Culture. Societal and Cultural Consequences of the Technical Development), München (C.H. Beck) 1987, 2nd ed. 1988; and P. KOSLOWSKI: *Die Prüfungen der Neuzeit. Über Postmodernität, Philosophie der Geschichte, Metaphysik, Gnosis (The Trials of the Modern Times. On Postmodernity, Philosophy of History, Metaphysics, Gnosis)*, Wien (Edition Passagen) 1989.

to quote Herder once more - "a fatherland whose sweet name is freedom?"[18]
The answer is:
"We have a new kind of freedom, in a wider and greater country".

18 "Haben wir ein Vaterland, dessen süßer Zuname Freiheit ist?"

Chapter 11

Democracy and Federalism in the European Union

ANDREAS FØLLESDAL

I. Introduction

Currently small states play important roles within the federal elements of the European Union, but their future status is at stake. What powers should small states hold in the Union?

In a federation there are two tiers of government: a central unit and regional sub-units. Each tier enjoys final authority with regards to some functions, without reference to the preferences of the other (Riker 1993, p. 509). Moreover, regional governments are represented in the central decision-making processes (King 1993). In confederal arrangements sub-units can veto decisions, and even leave the confederation. Hence in federal procedures, both member states and directly elected representatives play political roles.

To be sure, the EU may never become a full federation: territorial and functional internal sovereignty is not forthcoming (cf. Schmitter, this volume). Nevertheless, starting with the European Coal and Steel Community, the European institutions have had strong federal elements. Historically, in the case of Europe as in other systems of pooled sovereignty, the prominent role of states is no doubt due to the actual "social contracts" among formally equal sovereign members. As an example, consider the High Authority of the Coal and Steel Community, not strictly an intergovernmental executive but responsible to a European Common Assembly. The High Authority was also checked by the intergovernmental Council of Ministers. Introduced by the Netherlands, this feature ensured the interests of smaller states within the community (Pinder 1993). As general economic integration followed in the EEC in 1958, the executive body — the Commission — continued to enjoy broad powers, yet clearly under the control of the Council of Ministers.

The Single European Act of 1985 introduced federal elements: majority voting in the Council enhanced its ability to remove market distortions, and the European Parliament gained in power. The 1992 Maastricht Treaty on European Union added to the central powers by increasing Community influence over currency, and by establishing the economic and monetary union (EMU) by 1999.

Thus the central EU institutions enjoy supra-national powers, authorized to enact laws and regulations even contrary to the will of individual governments. State governments have given up some sovereign powers, since central decisions may override them. All the same, states retain the power to block common decisions, sometimes through requirements of unanimity, and sometimes through qualified majority voting. And the Principle of Subsidiarity confirms a commitment to the sovereignty of member states, limiting the competencies of central institutions, albeit in unspecified ways.

1. At Institutional Crossroads

Should states keep such significant powers in EU institutions? This question might appear to be of merely theoretical interest, given the central role of the Council. However, the status of states is currently at stake, due to dual and possibly conflicting accusations against the EU institutions: inefficiency and democratic deficiency.

The current power of state governments often yield a deadlock with conservative effects. Whether this inefficiency — i.e. conservatism — is to be lamented or applauded is of course a judgment based on an implicit normative political theory, insofar as the legitimate role of state government is at stake. Consider: if the proper role of the government is limited to securing negative rights, federal arrangements should tend to prevent anything more (Montesquieu; Acton 1907; Hamilton in *Federalist Papers* 10). To a large extent this is what we presently see in the European Union: Negative integration proceeds far quicker than positive integration, yielding de-regulatory competition rather than re-regulation at the European level (Scharpf 1996, p. 143). On the other hand, if central redistributive policies are required for a just Europe, the four freedoms are not enough (Føllesdal 1997a). Insofar as state power hinders the development of redistributive institutions, such conservatism is to be lamented.

The so-called "democratic deficit" of the EU is partly a clamor for increased transparency. But this criticism also raises important questions about the proper political role of citizens and states in securing political accountability of the central institutions. Increased political power for citizens may best be secured by having representatives determine by majority rule. But it is important to determine who should be represented: Individuals, or states. Presently, EU member states with small populations enjoy powers beyond what the principle of "one person one vote" seems to warrant.

This outcome is typical of the bargain leading to federal elements: small formally sovereign units require pay-offs to consent to a union where they risk minority status. However, in later stages such pay-offs are often frowned upon by citizens of more populous regions (Pinder 1993, p. 101). Thus institutional changes in the EU may well reduce the influence of small member states in the union.

In order to increase the equal influence of citizens, institutional reform could increase the powers of the European Parliament, a 'federal' institution. Furthermore, the electoral bases of the seats should be reallocated to equalize representation, roughly reflecting the influence of the population of Spain. Thus the populations of Germany, the United Kingdom, Italy and France should receive seats from the rest. Likewise, this conception of equality suggests that state votes in the Council of the European Union should reflect population size. Thus the influence of states, in particular large states, should be reduced so that individuals gain more equal control over the conditions shaping their lives.

State	Population in million (1995)	Members in European Parliament	Citizens/ MEP (in 100 000)	Votes in Council of European Union	Citizens/ vote in Council (in million)
Germany	81.3	99	8.2	10	8.1
United Kingdom	58.3	87	6.7	10	5.8
Italy	58.2	87	6.7	10	5.8
France	58.1	87	6.7	10	5.8
Spain	39.4	64	6.2	8	4.9
Netherlands	15.4	31	5.0	5	3.1
Greece	10.6	25	4.2	5	2.1
Portugal	10.6	25	4.2	5	2.1
Belgium	10	25	4.0	5	2.0
Sweden	8.8	22	4.0	4	2.2
Austria	8.0	21	3.8	4	2.0
Denmark	5.2	16	3.3	3	1.7
Finland	5.0	16	3.1	3	1.7
Ireland	3.6	15	2.4	3	1.2
Luxembourg	0.4	6	0.7	2	0.2
Total	**372.9**	**626**	**Average : 6.0**	**87**	**Average : 4.2**

Table 1: Representation in EU institutions by population size

In order to increase the equal influence of citizens, institutional reform could increase the powers of the European Parliament, a 'federal' institution. Furthermore, the electoral bases of the seats should be reallocated to equalize representation, roughly reflecting the influence of the population of Spain. Thus the populations of Germany, the United Kingdom, Italy and France should receive seats from the rest. Likewise, this conception of equality suggests that state votes in the Council of the European Union should reflect population size. Thus the influence of states, in particular large states, should be reduced so that individuals gain more equal control over the conditions shaping their lives.

Alternatively, 'peoples', that is states, should be represented as equals. In this case reforms should bolster the intergovernmental or 'confederal' Council of Ministers, and possibly tie Commissioners closer to the interests of the various states. To ensure this version of political accountability, state powers should be maintained or even increased, keeping and perhaps increasing the right to veto or using qualified majority. From this perspective, small states should continue to wield power irrespective of population size. The question might be whether Germany's 10 votes in the Council are too many in comparison to Luxembourg's 2 and Ireland's 3, even though Germany has a population more than 200 times that of Luxembourg and 22 times that of Ireland.

2. Equality: of States or of Citizens?

The status of states raises fundamental normative questions for a theory of federalism (cf. Beam, Conlan, and Walker 1984, 249 in: Laslovich 1993, 191; Mclean 1991, 191). The normative issue of concern here arise in federal arrangements where member states differ in population size, as in the EU. The central decision procedures may accord all member states equal power, or make the voting power of all Europeans equal, but not both. Should states or citizens be equal?

A normative theory of federations must address two main topics. Institutions should recognize and authorize communities or states only insofar as such allocation of authority are sound ways of securing the interests of some individuals of these states. Standards of legitimacy must be developed, either to hold for all federations, or to serve as guides for the elaboration of specific criteria for each particular federation. Unfortunately, neither kind of principles have yet been developed.

Secondly, federal arrangements appear to run afoul of the norms of equal political rights and majority rule. Consider: by entrenching the equality of states, a minority of voters living in several less populated states may override a majority of the citizens in the federation. This clearly runs counter to the normative bases for majoritarian voting procedures, which insist that the vote of each individual should count the same.

Thus normative theories consistent with the European values of liberty, equality and solidarity hesitate to support a democracy of states, rather than of citizens. The equality of states seems to run counter to the central principle of normative individualism which holds that only individuals' interests count, and all count as equals (Barry 1991, p. 26). Furthermore, the tradition of liberal contractualism holds that social arrangements must be in accordance with principles which persons can reasonably propose as a basis for mutual, informed agreement (Rawls 1971, Scanlon 1982, Beitz 1989). The social order must in principle be justifiable at the tribunal of each person's understanding (Waldron 1987) In contrast, the equality of states appears to be based on an alternative normative conception, that of communitarianism. There the normative point of view is one where interests "of communities", or of select dominant citizens, are the fundamental objects of concern. This position is incompatible with normative individualism and liberal contractualism (Rawls 1993b, cf. Føllesdal 1997b) .

These conflicts notwithstanding, I shall sketch a contractualist defense for the equal political rights of states within federal arrangements. On this view it is consistent with liberal contractualism that small states in federal arrangements wield powers out of proportion with their population size. This contractualist argument is contingent on empirical claims which must eventually be supported by evidence beyond the auspices of normative political theory; the task here is only to sketch the argumentative strategy and defend it against certain objections.

Section II sketches some fragments of a contractualist normative theory, focusing on the motivational assumptions and the case for majority rule. To allow a better grasp of the normative implications of this view, section III considers some of the arguments traditionally offered in favor of federal arrangements. Section IV brings liberal contractualism to bear on the puzzle of federalism, and defends this view against criticisms.

II. Aspects of a Contractualist Account of Legitimacy

On the face of it, EU institutions are blatantly at odds with central ideals and values of European political theory. The lack of transparency of EU institutions, and the discrepancy between them and established categories such as federations, unitary systems, or confederations, hinder assessment of the union by standards of normative political theory. The current Grotian situation, a network of overlapping loyalties and polities (Bull 1977), threatens the very notion of self-governance. The feeble opportunities for political control by citizens might even suggest that normative assessment is futile. The question of whether institutions can be justified towards all affected parties appears to play no practical role. However, such conclusions are too rash, one reason being the intricate connections between normative legitimacy and compliance. Popular support — social legitimacy — depends on several factors. The member governments are acutely aware that European citizens must recognize EU laws as legally legitimate, i.e. enacted and exercised in accordance with constitutional rules and the like. Moreover, the subjects must regard the emerging European institutions as normatively legitimate, i.e. as justifiable and imposing a moral duty to comply (Beetham 1991, Flathman 1993). The jury is currently out on both counts (cf. Gustavsson and Bellamy and Castiglione in this volume regarding the German case).

1. Liberal Contractualism

The contractualist account of normative legitimacy takes as its subject the rules of practices and of social institutions in particular. We ask under which conditions citizens of Europe have reason to accept European institutions as normatively legitimate and hence binding on their conduct.

All European states hold that all citizens are worthy of equal concern and respect. The tradition of liberal contractualism provides a particular interpretation of this commitment. Institutions are legitimate only if they can be justified by arguments in the form of a social contract of a particular kind. A fundamental commitment to equal respect entails that all individuals must be served by the social institutions: Every individual's interests must be secured and furthered by the social institutions as a whole. This commitment is honed by the notion of possible consent, allowing us to bring the vague ideals of equal dignity to bear on pressing questions of legitimacy and institutional design. The principles of legitimacy we should hold institutions to, are those that the affected persons would unanimously consent to -- under conditions that secure and express their status as appropriately free and equal. Appeals to consent thus serve to recognize legitimate authority, even though consent does not generate the moral authority of institutions (Murphy 1994). The set of social institutions as a whole should secure the interests of all affected parties to an acceptable degree, including our interests in peace, stability, basic needs, and shares of goods and powers.

2. Motivational Assumption: A Sense of Justice

Contractualism of this particular ilk does not assume that individuals are primarily interested in satisfying all their self-oriented interests. In comparison, other contractualist traditions in moral philosophy, including David Hume and more recently David Gauthier (1986, 1990), seek to answer the question posed by the moral skeptic or egoist: "why be moral?" They explore the reasons rational egoists have for being moral — i.e. for constraining their pursuit of their self-regarding interests in ways matching what we ordinarily think of as moral constraints. Thus Gauthier seeks to "defend the traditional conception of morality as a rational constraint on the pursuit of individual interest" (Gauthier 1986, p. 2).

Liberal Contractualism of the sort explored here is concerned with other central tasks of moral theory. It assumes that individuals generally have an interest in being "able to justify one's actions to others on grounds they could not reasonably reject." (Scanlon 1982, p. 116). They "desire to act in accordance with principles that could not reasonably be rejected by people seeking an agreement with others under conditions free from morally irrelevant bargaining advantages and disadvantages" (Barry 1989, p. 8). This commitment to give reasons "manifests our respect for the reasonableness of others" (Macedo 1990). Hence the aim of Liberal Contractualism is not to justify morality, but rather to bring this commitment to justice to bear on our rules and practices. However, this motivational commitment renders a contractualist account of federal arrangements vulnerable to even further challenges. Federations appear to assume a conflict model of politics, which seems at odds with contractualist motivational assumptions. Some authors claim that federal models either assume or foster a conflict model of politics. Checks and balances are carefully set up to resolve conflicting interests among individuals and factions assumed to be at odds. Furthermore, the conception of the common good secured by such federal arrangements is challenged. Goodin (1996) suggests that the method of checks and balances among branches of government with veto powers assumes that the common good secured is only that which is common to all. Politics only allows for Pareto-like improvements, by striving to have as many different partitions represented. In federations this includes populations divided by state boundaries.

Federal arrangements which allow for blocking votes encourage politics of selfish interests, and maintain cleavages, rather than to foster shared deliberation about how to best pursue the public good. Federal arrangements prevent politicians from taking a comprehensive view, seeing things from everyone's perspective. Institutionalized vetoes are particularly problematic, as they

> miscue people - voters and politicians alike - to think in narrow terms of personal and sectional interests. A veto is a device designed precisely to protect one's particular interests against the designs of others. It is not a device by which a group of people can sensibly decide what they collectively want to do... operating through a system of internalized vetoes is no way to evoke those higher concerns -- indeed, quite the contrary. (Goodin 1996, pp. 339-340; cf. Cohen 1991).

If indeed federal arrangements assume and foster a particular conception of citizens, and of politics as selfish competition, this is at odds with a commitment to normative individualism. Furthermore, Goodin's claim that federalism is incompatible with an attractive account of the public good should give us pause. Goodin holds that the public interest is not merely that which is common to all, but "(1) It is an interest that people necessarily share (2) by virtue of their role as a member of the public (3) which can best or only be promoted by concerted public action. ..'highest common concern'" (Goodin 1996, p. 339).

We must take seriously the charge that federal checks and balances and the day-to-day conflictual politics prevent this sense of justice. Why, if people can have a sense of justice, should institutions be shaped on the assumption that individuals are primarily self-interested or act out of ill will, rather than simply aiming to secure deliberation among people of good will?

Three central responses can be sketched here. Firstly, the institutions must be set up so as to prevent standard threats to individuals' vital interests. Hence, institutions should seek to reduce reliance on the good will of others, if other arrangements are available. The point is not that such reliance should or must be avoided, but rather that institutions should economize on virtue in order to remove the risk of partial compliance.

Secondly, the motivational assumption of a sense of justice, while concerned to comply, is of a weak form. To be sure, the situation is not one of prisoners' dilemma, where non-compliance is preferred regardless of compliance by others. But compliance with just institutions is not preferred regardless of compliance by others; but rather holds that given that others comply, individuals will also prefer to comply. By sanctioning non-compliance, and by reducing the other potential gains of non-compliance, institutions serve an important role in providing public assurance that others comply -- hence increasing the likelihood that individuals' sense of justice comes into play.

Finally, a society must make a wide range of decisions on an on-going basis, including those where there are conflicts of interest. One important task of politics is to secure what Goodin calls "highest common concerns", where the task is to generate benefits for every citizen. However, another important task is to resolve distributive conflicts, where some stand to benefit while others lose.

3. Majority Rule

Majority rule is often used in democracies to settle distributive conflicts. Entrenched federal institutions limit the role of citizens' political control through majority rule in at least two ways.

a) Some object to constitutional entrenchments in general insofar as they reduce the scope of majority rule and opportunities for democratic control of the political agendas. More specifically, constitutions are said to be unalterable, and distanced from political debate (Bickel 1962, Bellamy 1995, Harrison 1993). Constitutional federalism thus subjects citizens to the dictatorship of past peoples. b) Some object to constraints on majority rule, in the belief that unbridled majority rule is essential to democracy. A satisfactory response to this criticism must draw on a normative defense of majority rule.

From the perspective of Liberal Contractualism the task of political arrangements is not ultimately to carry out the will of the majority, but rather to secure the interests of all affected parties. However, the latter is often best secured by majority rule, properly regulated and circumscribed. Such decision procedures secure that all affected parties' interests are taken care of acceptably well, as compared to other arrangements. A formally equal distribution of political control among all affected parties secure and further the relevant interests to an acceptable extent, compared to alternative allocations of authority.

> the central virtue of democratic forms is that, in the presence of a suitable social background, they provide the most reliable means of reach-

> ing substantively just political outcomes consistently with the public recognition of the equal worth or status of each citizen. Democratic forms succeed in achieving this aim, when they succeed at all, less because they aggregate existing preferences efficiently than because they foster a process of public reflection in which citizens can form political views in full awareness of the grounds as well as the content of the (possibly competing) concerns of others. (Beitz 1989, p. 113; and cf. Weithman 1995, p. 325).

Such arguments must rely on substantive empirical information about how democratic measures and alternative procedures are likely to work, including the likely abuses of power they are likely to foster. Thus liberal contractualism supports majority rule, but on its merits, both regarding factual outcome and its socializing effects on citizens, and only by a comparative claim: that alternative institutional arrangements are less acceptable. Such arguments rely heavily on empirical claims which may well vary among particular states.

Let us first consider the fundamental objections of dictatorship of past and distant peoples, before turning to other concerns about majority rule.

Some writers argue against entrenching some individual rights in a constitution, since a constitution is anti-majoritarian and non-representational. Thus a constitution appears to fly in the face of the principle of rule by the people. Now clearly, the constitution is anti-majoritarian. One function of constitutional protections through rights is precisely to secure certain interests of every citizen, even those of minorities, against day-to-day majoritarian politics. Some issues are placed off the political agenda. From the point of view of Liberal Contractualism, this is justifiable insofar at some such arrangement is needed to secure the vital interests of each citizen against standard threats. The important issue is not whether this should be done, but which rights should be entrenched in this way, and how to provide for adjustment and revision of the constitutional protections. For a constitution must also provide channels for changing the constitution by qualified majority, in light of changing circumstances and risks.

From the point of view of justice, this removal of some issues from ongoing political debate is not to be regretted. It is surely not conducive to allegiance if the elected representatives are regularly able to redefine the basic rights of all, or those of minorities. Furthermore, constitutional protections do not remove all issues from public debate, even though the issues are taken of the political agenda. Constitutional constraints on political debate, for instance by a constitutional court, serves instead to give notice to the public. The political powers that be, now take an extraordinary course; or the unintended systemic effects of political decisions now cross certain important boundaries. Such warnings do not stifle political debate, since the legislature can revise the constitution if the requisite safeguards are satisfied (Ackerman 1988, p. 192; and cf. Sunstein 1994, pp. 13-14 for a list of reasons for entrenching institutional arrangements).

When is majority rule legitimate? The actual effects of voting mechanisms may be poor by contractualist standards, depending on several factors here only to be mentioned in passing. Electorates may have little actual choice among candidates, and poor grounds for assessing and predicting past and future performance. Indeed, the election process may be a placebo for self-rule and accountability (Dunn 1993, p. 17). All the same, majoritarian institutions can avoid the flaws noted by Dunn and others. Better systems secure that the public is regularly provided with a range of candidates with clear positions, that opinions are informed by an independent media, and that citizens have opportunities for deliberating about what the issues are, how they are resolved in pursuit of the public good, and which of the candidates are best for these tasks. These preconditions for a functioning system of majority rule explain the importance of transparency and public reason (Rawls 1993). Indeed, public deliberation can often yield general agreement on many issues. However, such stable procedures assume that the institutions inculcate citizens with shared concerns through public discussion, forcing each to casts appeals in terms others can share (Goodin 1996; Weithman 1995).

A full defense of democratic practices must specify and justify the formal and actual role and powers of representative assemblies and elected executives. Assemblies cannot always be mere rituals, but also serve as a forum for deliberation about legislation and policy. Representatives in the legislature may take part in the actual formulation of laws or limit themselves to initiate and correct proposals (Mill 1861). Representatives may be in charge of government, set the direction of policy, or oversee the executive branch solely with the power to eject. For accurate normative assessments we must determine the benefits and risks likely to occur under the alternative distributions of power, and the likely effects on affected parties.

The scope for majoritarian procedures is also important. Thus Brian Barry, for instance, argues from within a contractualist perspective that the best case for such mechanisms is when there is only one decision, only two alternatives, when the constituency not open to doubt, and the outcome is not of vital importance (Barry 1991, p. 27).

Turning to the European setting, these brief comments indicate why we have reason to lament the poor prospects of majoritarian mechanisms. EU institutions hardly provide arenas for well-informed discussion and political choice at the European level. Moreover, the preconditions for peaceful problem-solving: a background of shared interests, is difficult to obtain and maintain in the absence of a shared culture or common identity (Scharpf 1988). Finally, there are no clear limits on the scope of joint central decision-making, because of the legal doctrines of Direct Effect and Supremacy of EU law. The lack of constitutionally embedded allocation of powers to member states increases the risk that permanent minorities become permanent losers, and that vital interests are threatened. However, we must consider whether states are the best loci for wielding power in the EU, if the concern is to secure the interests of all. Which interests are best secured through states?

III. Arguments for Federations

Several reasons can be entertained why states should continue to enjoy power in European institutions, maintaining federal elements in the Union. However, few of them seem defensible in the absence of substantive, empirically informed normative arguments.

Undoubtedly, the European Union has developed out of the perceived national interest of sovereign states. The historical bargains yielding the union are crucial for explaining why the curtailed sovereignty of member states came to be embedded in current institutions. However, our concern is not to explain how the European Union came about, but rather to assess and guide further developments. For such assessment the actual intergovernmental bargains among sovereign states are insufficient unless we can show that this is a case of just bargaining, confirming that bargaining positions and the process itself were acceptable. Bargaining power must have been exercised appropriately, the parties must have been sufficiently informed, and so forth.

We should also note that appeals to a historically shared European identity which recognizes sovereign states are unhelpful and insufficient for our purposes. They are unhelpful, as several writers have noted, because the essence of Europe in fact is diversity and complexity of localized societies (Kundera 1984; Enzenberger 1987), with competing attempts at (re)defining the concept of Europe (Wæver 1990). Thus the quest for shared values, identities and loyalties may be arduous and yield little in terms of where Europe should go. On this point, we should agree with Habermas' recommendation:

> ... our task is less to reassure ourselves of our common origins in the European Middle Ages than to develop a new political self-confidence commensurate with the role of Europe in the world of the twenty-first century. (Habermas 1992)

Moreover, such appeals to a shared conception of a people's Europe are insufficient. The claims to unrestricted sovereignty among equal states are themselves notoriously troublesome, at odds with norms of the equal worth of all individuals.

Hence for our purposes another approach is required: we must seek to determine through normative arguments how the overall set of European social institutions should distribute benefits and burdens, powers and obligations among individuals and groups of individuals. We must draw on other shared ideals and values in addition to those of the sovereign state, in order to assess both claims to sovereignty and the legitimacy of federal arrangements.

1. A Step Towards Cosmopolitan Government?

Normative individualism endorses the equal worth of all affected parties. This norm is universal with regards to the domain of individuals whose interests count. It might therefore seem that this position tends to support global institutions, holding out a world government as the proper goal of political development. On this account, federal arrangements are to be favored either as an intermediate phase or as the best stable solution. (Cf. Kant 1796, Ackerman 1988, 156).

However, the fundamental 'universalism' of normative individualism is one of range of individuals, not regarding scope of institutional jurisdiction. It insists that the interests of every affected party must count, but does not rule some institutional arrangements in or out by definition, in the absence of knowledge about their likely impact on individuals. Thus the normative case for federal institutions must still rely on complex comparative claims about the likely effects of such institutions for individuals' interests, as compared to other stable arrangements.

2. Drawing Legitimacy from State Parliaments?

Another normative defense of federal arrangements would hold that the best — or indeed the only — way to legitimately add a supra-national level of governance must build on existing normatively binding sites of political authority. States are the only loci where the wills of the peoples find expression, for instance on the basis of consent of the governed. National parliaments, themselves normatively binding, transfer some of their powers to central institutions which thus can legitimately claim compliance. Only some such transfers are compatible with the tasks properly allocated to domestic governments. Hence federal, rather than completely centralized institutions, are called for.

However, this justificatory strategy takes for granted several contested claims. State sovereignty of the proper scope must be defended in the first place. Moreover, it is highly contentious to hold that national parliaments are the place, and indeed the only place, where the 'common good' finds its expression. Finally, this argument appears to draw on an unwarranted analogy, from an incorrect understanding of legal legitimacy: since the only legally binding international norms are treaty based, normatively binding norms must likewise be consented to by governments. However, this analogy must be justified. Moreover, and as a matter of international law, there are non-treaty based legal obligations that apply to all states, namely customary law of nations (Schachter 1982). Thus the basis of the analogy is flawed: there might in principle be morally binding claims within federations that do not rest on treaties among the member states.

3. Protecting Important Interests

Heterogeneity of preferences suggests that government should be small-scale. Individuals differ in opinion, value and condition, hence they must be granted an interest in political controls, in influencing the institutions that shape their lives. This interest suggests that jurisdiction should be local except insofar as larger scale arrangements are required for coordination or externalities. Thus "Federalism ... reduces the number of topics on which is necessary to arrive at inter-regional and inter-community agreement." (Covell 1987, p.75). A fruitful defense along these lines must argue that federal arrangements allow states to protect their vital "national interests" through cooperation restricted by veto powers and blocking abilities.

A defense of this kind must indicate how a system of checks and balances serves these ends, and how it constrains the day-to-day political bargaining between tiers. The grounds for veto or blocking must be specified, perhaps through a list of individual and state rights. A definite list of the objectives of the federation, coupled with a Principle of Subsidiarity must provide further guidance. Such an account must draw on a theory indicating which interests are at stake, and what are the legitimate ends of state and federal institutions. From the point of view of Liberal Contractualism, it is important that the "national" interests are specified in terms of the interests of individuals.

However, this strategy in defense of the nation state also raises some further problems. Firstly, why allocate powers precisely at the level of nation states, rather than insisting that decisions must be local, perhaps placed primarily in the various regions of states?

Secondly, this argument fails to explain why states should be granted powers out of proportion with their population sizes. Standard accounts of individuals' interest fail to illuminate this issue. Thus, plausible arguments in favor of federal arrangements must draw on a normative theory of legitimacy and address these two questions.

IV. States as Units Controlling Cultural Change

Against this backdrop of normative theory, we now consider why states should be allowed to play an institutional role within federal arrangements. The arguments will depend on empirical evidence beyond the scope of this article, concurring with Riker's remark, that "One does not decide on the merits of federalism by an examination of federalism in the abstract, but rather on its actual meaning for particular societies." (Riker 1964, p. 152, cited in Burgess 1993, p. 104).

We need an account that does not merely regard states as loci for checks and balances within a federation-like arrangement. No doubt a careful distribution of votes may serve to prevent permanent minorities within small states. However, we must be clearer about which interests of individuals that are likely to be secured by this arrangement. Moreover, the protection of individuals' interests may be secured by granting states veto or qualified majority rights, but at the risk of opening up for inappropriate bargaining holdouts. There are other ways of securing vital interests, e.g. through human rights, or through limits on the Union objectives by enumerating the powers of central government such as national defense and the regulation of commerce (Sunstein 1994, p. 35). Alternatively, states may be allowed to determine the means for pursuing shared goals through the use of EU directives rather than regulations. Thus further reasons must be offered for insisting that states should enjoy formal powers within federal arrangements.

A more promising strategy is to hold that states represent views and interests. Representation of views may be important to ensure that the various views are expressed in the deliberative process. However, this plausible aim does not require mechanisms of veto or qualified majority mechanisms, typical of federal arrangements. Nor is it clear that state governments are the primary locus for shared purposes and goals: cultural and value pluralism within states tend to render them too large and heterogeneous. Frequent regional unrest and the flourishing of political parties competing for domestic control indicate that the unit of the state is too large.

Nevertheless, I shall suggest that states are important units for individuals' pursuit of their interest in exercising control over institutional change. The social institutions that surround us have a pervasive impact. They provide the backdrop for the distribution of important goods, powers, burdens and obligations. At the same time institutions shape our expectations and values. We have a strong interest in affecting these circumstances that shape our interests and plans. Furthermore, we have a strong interest in fulfilling our legitimate expectations. Our expectations are best secured when we can control or influence political decisions. This is one reason why the distribution of political authority is a central issue of legitimacy.

Institutional and cultural changes challenge our ability to maintain coherence and continuity in our lives. With changes in values, norms, institutions, history and language, new options for life choices appear, while others disappear. Among the important interests individuals have is the ability to forecast correctly about their own future, including likely options, attainments and needs. The structuring role of culture and institutions in identifying paths and options, and thus shaping our expectations is of little value if the signals are false. Thus, cultural and institutional changes should not be too abrupt: Members have an interest in revising their plans as options and consequences change.

We need not assume a voluntaristic conception of the person, that the individual values the ability to continually change plans and values independently of others. Rather, the claim is that one's expectations form on the basis of the surroundings, and therefore are prone to influence by social institutions — themselves under political control. We recognize the interest in forming correct expectations, and this is why individuals should have the power to regulate the speed and direction of institutional and cultural change.

This role of cultural membership supports claims based on the interest of members to have resources for governing change. Given the threats of alternative allocations of such control, it seems plausible for citizens of a state to insist that they should have the means to control the development of their culture. This interest thus supports claims to allocate the power of maintaining and developing one's culture within the nation state, rather than with agents of the state at large.

Note that this interpretation of the interest in controlling cultural change does not ground claims to maintaining a variety of institutions and cultures. However, it has implications for the speed and the authority to change, somewhat similar to Kymlicka's view (1995).

The interest in controlling institutional and cultural change supports the view that changes should as far as possible be consonant with existing life plans. The power to control institutional and cultural changes must be allocated in light of this concern. Sovereign states have traditionally been entrusted these powers. Citizens' expectations have to a large extent reflected domestic institutions and cultures, maintained by state governments.

This state dominance cannot be justified without bounds. Thus, within states the interest in controlling cultural change grounds the right of some cultural and ethnic minorities to control some aspects of their culture (Føllesdal 1996, and see Kymlicka 1995 for a related position). Within a federation of states, institutional and cultural traditions still cluster around nationality and state borders. I therefore submit that this interest in controlling institutional change justifies the claim that state governments should enjoy a range of powers.

In a system of governance consisting of somewhat sovereign states, geographically clustered groups of compatriots share institutions and culture. The interest of individuals in controlling the development of their institutions and culture may best be served by allocating the power to maintain and develop these institutions in state institutions. Individuals' interests thus support claims to allocate the power of maintaining and developing one's institutions and culture within a small unit, rather than placing those powers with a body that regulates a larger population.

Even though this interest justifies some measures of conservatism, this view does not support unbridled status quo. Unjust distributive arrangements may not be defended by this line of argument, insofar as such institutions give rise to illegitimate expectations, which standing is different. However, when distributive justice is secure, our interest in satisfying expectations support an allocation of powers at the state level within federal arrangements.

This defense of state powers also explains why small states may properly be overrepresented in federal decision-making bodies. The similar interest of all is appropriately secured by allowing small states to enjoy influence beyond what their population size should entail. That is, the same interest of all, accorded similar weight, allows institutional arrangements where their representatives have different weight in the decision-making process. There are two reasons:

Firstly, the similar interest of all in controlling cultural change is protected by having representatives in central decision-making processes. This allows the deliberating parties to consider the impact of their decisions on the expectations of various peoples. However, this interest is not in general properly secured by majority rule, letting representatives' votes count according to population size: the outcome may for instance be of vital importance. Thus the general case for majority rule would not seem to hold across the board for such issues.

Secondly, the interest of citizens of small states is threatened differently than the similar interest of citizens of populous states. If decisions were made by majority vote, small states would tend to be policy takers rather than policy makers. The risks against established expectations is thus faced to a larger degree by members of small states. The Liberal Contractualist view holds that similar threats to similar interests must be equally avoided for all affected. It therefore seems acceptable to allow small states to veto or block changes to compensate for this added risk.

We have considered a justification of embedded powers of states, and small states, within a federal arrangement, consistent with Liberal Contractualism and with Normative Individualism. Individuals' interest in controlling institutional and cultural change justifies the continued role of states within federal systems of governance, and explains why states may enjoy powers that do not reflect population size. This account may prove useful for further work in a normative theory of justice for Europe: the proper scope of such powers and the allocation of votes securing blocking coalitions, the substantive content of the Principle of Subsidiarity, as well as the legitimate scope of 'vital interests' which states may appeal to in vetoing EU decisions.

References

ACKERMAN, BRUCE: "Neo-federalism?", in: JON ELSTER and RUNE SLAGSTAD (Eds.): *Constitutionalism and Democracy*, Cambridge (Cambridge University Press and Norwegian University Press) 1988, pp. 153-194.

ACTON: "Nationality", in: J. N. FIGGIS (Ed.): *The History of Freedom and Other Essays*, London (Macmillan) 1907.

BARRY, BRIAN: *Theories of Justice: A Treatise on Social Justice*, Vol. 1, Berkeley (University of California Press) 1989.

BARRY, BRIAN: "Is Democracy Special?", in: *Democracy and Power. Essays in Political Theory 1*, Oxford (Oxford University Press) 1991, pp. 24-60.

BEAM, DAVID R., TIMOTHY J. CONLAN, and DAVID WALKER: "Federalism: The Challenge of Conflicting Theories and Contemporary Practice", in: ADAM W. FINIFTER (Ed.): *Political Science: The State of the Discipline*, Washington, D.C. (American Political Science Association) 1984.

BEITZ, CHARLES R.: *Political Equality*, Princeton, N.J. (Princeton University Press) 1989.

BELLAMY, RICHARD: "The Constitution of Europe: Rights or Democracy?", in: RICHARD BELLAMY, VITTORIO BUFACCHI, and DARIO CASTIGLIONE (Eds.): *Democracy and Constitutional Culture in the Union of Europe*, London (Lothian Foundation Press) 1995, pp. 153-175.

BICKEL: *The Least Dangerous Branch*, New Haven (Yale University Press) 1962.

BULL, HEDLEY: *The Anarchical Society*, New York (Columbia University Press) 1977.

BURGESS, MICHAEL: "Federalism as Political Ideology: Interests, Benefits and Beneficiaries in Federalism and Federation", in: MICHAEL BURGESS and ALAIN-G. GAGNON (Eds.): *Comparative Federalism and Federation: Competing Traditions and Future Directions*, New York (Harvester Wheatsheaf) 1993, pp. 102-114.

CENTRE FOR ECONOMIC POLICY RESEARCH: "Making Sense of Subsidiarity: How Much Centralization for Europe?", *Monitoring European Integration*, 4, London 1993.

COHEN, JOSHUA: "Deliberation and Democratic Legitimacy", in: HAMLIN and PETTIT (Eds.): *The Good Polity*, Oxford (Blackwell) 1991, pp. 17-34.

COVELL, MAUREEN: "Federalization and Federalism: Belgium and Canada", in: Herman Bakvis and WILLIAM M. CHANDLER (Eds.): *Federalism and the Role of the State*, Toronto (University of Toronto Press) 1987.

DUNN, JOHN: *Western Political Theory in the Face of the Future*, Cambridge (Canto) 1993.

ENZENBERGER, HANS MAGNUS: *Ach Europa*. (English Translation: *Europe, Europe: forays into a continent*, 1989), Frankfurt (Suhrkamp) 1987.

FLATHMAN, RICHARD E.: "Legitimacy", in: ROBERT E. GOODIN and PHILIP PETTIT (Eds.): *Companion to Contemporary Political Philosophy*, Oxford (Blackwell) 1993, pp. 527-533.

FØLLESDAL, ANDREAS: "Minority Rights: A Liberal Contractualist Case", in: JUHA RAIKKA (Ed.): *Do We Need Minority Rights? Conceptual Issues*, The Hague, London, Boston (Kluwer Academic Publisher/Kluwer Law International) 1996, pp. 59-83.

FØLLESDAL, ANDREAS (1997a): "Do Welfare Obligations End at the Boundaries of the Nation State?", in: PETER KOSLOWSKI and ANDREAS FØLLESDAL (Eds.): *The Welfare State Under Siege: Ethical Issues of Social Policy*, Berlin, New York, Tokyo (Springer) 1997, pp. 145-163 (= Studies in Economic Ethics and Philosophy, Vol. 12).

FØLLEASDAL ANDREAS (1997b): "The Standing of Illiberal States: Stability and Toleration in John Rawls' Law of Peoples", in: *Justice and Welfare in Society and World Order*, Wien (Verlag Hölder-Pichler-Tempsky) 1997 (= Schriftenreihe der Wittgenstein-Gesellschaft, Vol. 24).

GAUTHIER, DAVID: *Morals by Agreement*, Oxford (Clarendon Press) 1986.

GAUTHIER, DAVID: *Moral Dealing: Contract, Ethics, and Reason*, Ithaca (Cornell University Press) 1990.

GOODIN, ROBERT E.: "Institutionalizing the Public Interest: The Defense of Deadlock and Beyond", *American Political Science Review*, 90 (June 1996), pp. 331-343.

HABERMAS, JÜRGEN: "Citizenship and National Identity: Some Reflections on the Future of Europe", *Praxis International*, 12 (1992), pp. 1-19.

HARRISON, ROSS: *Democracy*, London (Routledge) 1993.

KANT, IMMANUEL: "Perpetual Peace: A Philosophical Sketch", in: HANS REISS (Ed.): *Kant's Political Writings*, Cambridge (Cambridge University Press) 1970, pp. 93-130. First published 1795 Königsberg (Friedrich Nicolovius) 1796, *AA* 8 341-86.

KING, PRESTON: "Federation and Representation", in: MICHAEL BURGESS and ALAIN-G. GAGNON (Eds.): *Comparative Federalism and Federation: Competing Traditions and Future Directions*, New York (Harvester Wheatsheaf) 1993, pp. 94-100.

KUNDERA, MILAN: "The Tragedy of Central Europe", *New York Review of Books*, April 26, 1984.

KYMLICKA, WILL (Ed.): *The Rights of Minority Cultures*, Oxford (Oxford University Press) 1995.

LASLOVICH, MICHAEL J.: "The American Tradition: Federalism in the United States", in: MICHAEL BURGESS and ALAIN-G. GAGNON (EDS.): *Comparative Federalism and Federation: Competing Traditions and Future Directions*, New York (Harvester Wheatsheaf) 1993, pp. 187-202.

MACEDO, STEPHEN: *Liberal Virtues: Citizenship, Virtue, and Community in Liberal Constitutionalism*, Oxford (Clarendon Press) 1990.

MCLEAN, IAIN: "Forms of Representation and Voting Systems", in: DAVID HELD (Ed.): *Political Theory Today*, Cambridge (Polity Press) 1991, pp. 172-196.

MILL, JOHN STUART: *Considerations on Representative Government*, 1861.

MURPHY, MARK C.: "Acceptance of Authority and the Duty to Comply with Just Institutions: A Comment on Waldron", *Philosophy and Public Affairs*, 23 (Summer 1994), pp. 271-277.

PINDER, JOHN: "The New European Federalism: The Idea and the Achievements", in: MICHAEL BURGESS and ALAIN-G. GAGNON (EDS.): *Comparative Federalism and Federation: Competing Traditions and Future Directions*, New York (Harvester Wheatsheaf) 1993, pp. 45-66.

RAWLS, JOHN: *A Theory of Justice*, Cambridge, Mass. (Harvard University Press) 1971.

RAWLS, JOHN (1993a): "Law of Peoples", in: STEPHEN SHUTE and SUSAN HURLEY: *On Human Rights: The Oxford Amnesty Lectures 1993*, New York (Basic Books) 1993, pp. 175-216

RAWLS, JOHN (1993b): *Political Liberalism*, New York (Columbia University Press) 1993.

RIKER, W. H.: *Federalism: Origin, Operation, Significance*, Boston (Little, Brown and Company) 1964.

RIKER, W. H.: "Federalism", in: ROBERT E. GOODIN and PHILIP PETTIT (Eds.): *A Companion to Contemporary Political Philosophy*, Blackwell Companions to Philosophy, Oxford (Blackwell) 1993.

SCANLON, T. M.: "Contractualism and Utilitarianism", in: AMARTYA SEN and BERNARD WILLIAMS (Eds.): *Utilitarianism and Beyond*, Cambridge (Cambridge University Press) 1982, pp. 103-128.

SCHACHTER, OSCAR: *General Course in Public International Law*, Recueil Des Cours 178 (5) 1982.

SCHARPF, FRITZ W.: "The Joint Decision Trap: Lessons from German Federatism and European Integration", *Public Administration*, 66 (1988), pp. 239-278.

SCHARF, FRITZ W.: "Democratic Policy in Europe", *European Law Journal*, 2 (July 1996), pp. 136-155.

SUNSTEIN, CASS R.: "Approaching Democracy: A New Legal Order for Eastern Europe - Constitutionalism and Secession", in: CHRIS BROWN (Ed.): *Political Restructuring in Europe: Ethical Perspectives*, London (Routledge) 1994, pp. 11-49.

WALDRON, JEREMY: "Theoretical Foundations of Liberalism", *Philosophical Quarterly*, 37 (1987), pp. 127-150.

WÆVER, OLE: "Three Competing Europes: German, French, Russian", *International Affairs*, 66 (1990), pp. 477-494.

WEITHMAN, PAUL J.: "Contractualist Liberalism and Deliberative Democracy", *Philosophy and Public Affairs*, 24 (Fall 1995), pp. 314-343.

Chapter 12

The Normative Challenge of a European Polity: Cosmopolitan and Communitarian Models Compared, Criticised and Combined[1]

RICHARD BELLAMY and DARIO CASTIGLIONE

I. Introduction: A Copernican Revolution?

Consider for a moment how odd the European Union's political structure is.[2] It lacks the chief characteristics of a sovereign constitutional nation state

1 Research for this paper was supported by an ESRC award for a project on 'Languages and Principles for a Constitution of Europe' (R000221170). We are grateful for the comments on earlier versions of audiences in Oslo, Bologna and Edinburgh and for the written observations of Andreas Føllesdal, Barry Jones, and Barry Holden. We are also indebted to stimulating discussions of these themes with co-participants in the ESRC sponsered research seminar series on Legal Theory and the European Union.

2 These opening reflections are inspired by SCHMITTER (1996), especially p. 219.

- namely, a congruence of territory, functional authority and identity; a monopoly of legitimate violence within its borders; exclusive control over the movement of goods and persons within its domain; a clear locus and hierarchy of authority and offices; offers little if any democratic accountability to those affected by its decisions; and has no pre-set limits to its area of competence. These features are largely loaned to it indirectly via the Member States, which also offer it the main source of its legitimacy. Yet this transferral of powers does not occur in the institutionalised and consistent manner of a federal system. It is achieved in a piecemeal fashion, either through the internal dynamics of Community decision making, or as a result of periodic pacts and treaties between the various governments concerned. *Eppur si muove!* It has a life of its own. The Treaties are not simple international agreements, they offer the basis for an independent legal system. The European agencies and bureaucracies amount to more than an inter-governmental organisation. They can generate and allocate revenue, regulate both public and private behaviour through legal and administrative directives, respond to pressure groups and organise elections, possess diplomatic status, and have the ability to conduct and conclude binding international negotiations on certain trade and security matters.

That an organisation that is not a state can nonetheless possess so many of its salient characteristics offers a challenge to much conventional thinking about politics. Indeed, we want to suggest that we need something like a Copernican revolution in our traditional political concepts if we are to comprehend the true nature of the European Union. In particular, the civic concepts of rights and democracy have to be related to those concepts associated with nationhood, notably state and popular sovereignty, in ways that do not assume a complete overlap or fit between the two groups. At stake is the normative underpinning of the respective claims of national and European legal and political institutions to be constitutionally superior within their distinct domains, and the issue of how far these spheres can be compartmentalized. Who has the authority to make decisions, about what, for whom, and how have become questions that can no longer be easily avoided.[3]

The two dominant views of the EU within current British political debate, namely that of the pro-European neo-federalists on the one hand, and of the Euro-sceptical neo-nationalists on the other, do not adequately capture this

3 See WALKER (1996) for a review of the growing impact of such issues in the recent legal and, to a lesser extent, political science literature on the EU.

normative dimension of the European Union and the questions of political legitimacy it raises. In section one, we shall attempt to offer a more theoretically nuanced approach by aligning different models of Europe with arguments stemming from the cosmopolitan and communitarian political moralities proposed by contemporary political theorists.[4] Each of these broad schools of thought represent ideal-types that can be associated with different versions of federalism and nationalism respectively. Each also offers a distinctive account of democracy and rights that we employ, in section two, to illuminate current debates over citizenship and judicial competences within the European Union. We conclude that when due weight is given to communitarian as well as cosmopolitan considerations then a less harmonious and more pluralistic view of the Union becomes both attractive and plausible.

II. The Communitarian Ghost in the Cosmopolitan Machine

Two complementary strands run through both the cosmopolitan and the communitarian accounts of rights and democracy: the normative and the socio-political. We shall examine each in turn for both theories. Although the two positions need not be as opposed as they are sometimes presented, important differences of emphasis are nonetheless present that have considerable practical implications for how we think about political institutions.

1. Cosmopolitan Globalists and Federalists

The normative basis of the cosmopolitan ethical thesis rests on a theory of human rights that combines individualism, universality and generality.[5] The moral implications of these rights can be cashed out in either interactional or institutional terms - in other words, either as pertaining to the actions of individual persons and agencies, or as applying to the rules and pro-

4 For an overview of the debate, see MULLHALL and SWIFT (1996). For the application of these two models to IR theory, see BROWN (1992). We have offered a preliminary sketch of their relevance to European constitutional debates in BELLAMY and CASTIGLIONE (1996b).

5 This paragraph essentially summarises the argument of POGGE (1994).

cedures of certain institutional schemes. In a number of respects, the interactional case is practically weaker than the institutional. The perfect obligations necessary to uphold negative rights of non-interference can be conceptualized in global terms reasonably easily, since in principle at least they are costless and simply require individual forbearance. It is much harder to assign a global responsibility for positive rights to care and welfare which appear to rely on special obligations. Indeed, in the absence of any causal relation for the potential or actual harms involved, it is difficult even to justify positive action to secure negative rights world wide, through the supply of peacekeeping forces and the like. The institutional view appears to fill this lacuna, since it potentially links us to a whole range of unknown others and provides a duty even to safeguard those negative rights we have not personally violated. The focus here is no longer on the direct relations between individuals, but on the justice of the practices and arrangements within which people are involved and jointly and severally responsible.

This institutional argument is contingent on the possible or actual existence of a global institutional scheme within which we all to some significant degree participate.[6] The socio-political strand of the cosmopolitan argument comes in here. Global socio-economic forces are held to have created a greater degree of interconnectedness within the world than ever before. Technological advances have internationalised production, distribution and exchange and transformed financial markets. Multinational Corporations (MNCs), even when they possess a regional or national base, are said to organise their affairs on an international scale and respond to global market pressures. This internationalisation of markets is even more apparent in the financial sector, where new information technology has radically increased the mobility of economic units and to a large degree tied the world's major banking and trading centres into a single integrated network. New communications systems have also rendered ordinary people more aware of these global developments than ever before. The media, according to proponents of this thesis, have altered the 'situational geography' of social and political life by giving people direct access to distant events and creating new experiences, commonalties and frames of meaning that do not require direct physical contact - popular reactions to Tiananmen Square and the plight of the Kurds in the aftermath of the Gulf War being good examples of this phenomenon. A

6 The exposition of this thesis in the next three paragraphs derives from HELD (1995), Chs. 5 and 6.

series of common cultural references - from the banality of soap operas through to greater popular awareness and knowledge of world events - have allegedly generated new solidarities as evidenced in transnational social movements such as Greenpeace and Amnesty International.

The above mentioned processes are claimed to have weakened in turn the capacity of nation states to provide for the security and welfare of their citizens, and led to the creation of a number of international power blocks, regimes and organisations to facilitate their continued ability to do so by managing various areas of transnational activity. These institutions range from collective security arrangements such as NATO, through a variety of other intergovernmental organisations of different degrees of formality aimed at controlling various aspects of economic and social policy, such as the G7, to a number of international non-governmental organisations, some purely technical, like the Universal Postal Union, others more politically contentious, such as the IMF. All these organisations modify to one degree or another the freedom of action of states and undercut their capacity to operate as sovereign units. Consequently, their title to act as the agents of the sovereign will of their people has been likewise eroded. Effective decision-making and the sources of identification has in many cases passed elsewhere, or so at least it is alleged.

Finally, this move beyond the sovereign nation state is reflected in the body of international law that has grown up in the wake of these developments. Here individuals are gradually replacing states as the main subjects of the law. On the one hand, it has been recognised that individuals have rights and obligations that are independent of and go beyond those duties and entitlements they have as citizens of particular states - a point made most strikingly in war crime trials. On the other hand, the legitimacy of states has come to rest as much on the justice of their rule as on their *de facto* hold on power. The post-war international declarations of rights have reinforced this shift from state to individual, as have challenges to the notions of 'immunity from jurisdiction' and 'immunity from state agencies' which have hitherto operated as central principles of international law.

This global positivisation of individual moral rights brings the normative and empirical strands of the cosmopolitan thesis together. At least two broad possible views of the European Union can follow from this perspective. One version holds that the forces described above have undermined the nation state, but that a centralised federal Europe, that is itself not unlike a nation state writ large, can fill the gap. Another, more truly cosmopolitan version, is not so much supra-national as post-national in orientation (Ferry 1992, pp. 179-89), viewing moves towards federalism as an alternative to, rather than a new form of, the unitary sovereign state (Beaud 1995). By and large, political scientists - especially those of a functionalist disposition - have been drawn towards the first position. They have advocated the strengthening of the Union's supra-national features - particularly the European Parliament and the Commission - and the phasing out of intergovernmentalism, and have welcomed the move towards common policies in the spheres of domestic justice and foreign affairs in addition to economic and social matters (e.g. George 1985 1991, Keohane and Hoffman 1991). Lawyers, by contrast, have been the principal advocates of the second position. They have drawn inspiration from the gradual development of a single legal framework by the European Court of Justice, noting with approval its increasing tendency to appeal to human rights and its claims of Supremacy over the domestic law of Member States and Direct Effect with regard to their citizens (Mancini 1989).[7] Needless to say, the reality falls far short of either version of the cosmopolitan ideal - a fact that communitarians are not slow in pointing out.

2. Communitarians, Nationalists and the Sovereignty of States

Communitarians question both the normative and empirical aspects of the cosmopolitan thesis. With regard to the first element, they dispute the universalist and individualist rights-based starting point of the cosmopolitan case. Rather than viewing rights as foundational principles presupposed by all legitimate societies, communitarians contend they are best conceived as components of particular forms of life and their related patterns of human flourishing (Sandel 1987). Moreover, different communities are likely to prioritise different kinds and sets of rights. Indeed, even within a given conception of rights conflicts between different sorts of rights involving incompatible and incommensurable values and interests tend to arise (Waldron 1989, Bellamy 1995). Such clashes can generally only be resolved by reference to the broader social picture of which they form a part. This wider social context is also important to motivate people to identify with rights and take on the burdens that upholding them usually entails. Finally, given their

7 For the contrast between the legal and political science paradigms, see WEILER, HALTERN and MAYER (1995), pp. 24-33 and WINCOTT (1995).

belief that the nature of our rights depend on the character of the society and the culture in which we live, communitarians tend to stress the priority of democracy over rights in the preservation of our liberty (Walzer 1981). A link is thereby established with national sovereignty. Nationality defines a common political culture and identity, that to be subjected to political control has to be tied to a democratic state (Walzer 1983, pp. 28-9; Miller 1995, Ch. 4).

Communitarians also contest the second, empirical, element of cosmopolitanism, questioning both the degree and consequences of the processes of globalisation and interconnectedness. It is possible to dispute, for example, the extent to which MNCs truly operate at a transnational level. As Hirst and Thompson have recently shown (1995), core capital, basic Research and Development, and management personnel and structures are mostly located within a main national base. The various political bodies and non-governmental agencies that have developed to cope with global problems of security and welfare tend to be inter-national and inter-governmental rather than supra-national. The UN, for example, far from representing a nascent form of cosmopolitan governance, as is sometimes argued (Held 1995, Part IV), remains very much an instrument of the sovereign states which compose it - not least the superpowers, whose hold on the security council effectively blocks any move that might damage their interests (Zolo 1995, pp. 27-8). Indeed, the major powers effective control over the purse strings enables them to manipulate most important, and hence costly, initiatives requiring inter-state co-operation, and to stop those that do not meet with their approval - witness the sabotaging of UNESCO by Britain and the United States (Jones, 1995b).

Cosmopolitans also overlook the differential impact of global forces on different countries and the imbalances in the degree and nature of the interdependence that they create. By and large the wealthier and more powerful nations are net beneficiaries from global market forces, for example, whilst poorer states are either locked out of many of the networks or are subordinate partners and often damaged by global trade, becoming sources of cheap labour and resources, rather than developing strong economies of their own. Global environmental, health, security and other dangers that are no respecters of state borders are said to bind the peoples of the world together as sharing a common fate. However, they rarely affect all of them to an equal extent. When joint actions have shared consequences, such as the depletion of fish stocks, then co-operative action may be possible, although here too the standard free rider problems that arise with all public goods and bads mean that many countries will attempt to evade their responsibilities. Because the advantages and disadvantages are not usually mutual even with shared activities or problems, the incentives for co-operative behaviour are usually lop-sided (Jones 1995a, pp. 75-7). Even within the EU, the substantial differences in economic performance, social standards and political interests between the Member States has rendered the formulation of common policies far from easy. Britain's acrimonious attempts to reduce the massive financial transfers to other EC states via the CAP reflect a genuine problem, that potentially weakens the commitment to the Union of all the main contributors (Hirst and Thompson 1996, Ch. 7, Jones 1993).

Although nations do form blocs for certain limited purposes, it is also important to note that these often have the goal of preserving state autonomy rather than diminishing it. Alan Milward's (1992) account of the European Community as a 'rescue' of the nation state is highly pertinent in this respect. The EU emerges from this analysis as being, in part at least, a reaction against the forces of globalisation. Indeed, many of its more 'social' corporatist and welfare elements are in a number of respects anti-cosmopolitan - reflecting a desire to preserve the standards of Member State workers against the effects of foreign competition. This feature has been highlighted by the exclusionary character of recent moves to create a European Citizenship, discussed below (Lyons 1996).

For related reasons, more homogeneous consumption patterns and a greater awareness of world affairs has not necessarily produced as much convergence in political identity amongst the general population as cosmopolitans assert. People distinguish a humanitarian concern with famine or other disasters in countries other than their own from the sort of formalised responsibilities they have for co-nationals. They may support initiatives such as Band Aid or give to Oxfam, but that is a long way from condoning increased taxation to expand the development aid budget, say. Television, faster communication systems, greater job mobility and the like, may have broadened people's horizons in certain respects and encouraged them to identify with a wider community, but the identification may not be so deep as the soldiarities of old, based as they were on continuous, direct contact and personal involvement. Later in the paper we shall produce some evidence from the EU to support this argument.

Just as we distinguished two different versions of the cosmopolitan ideal with regard to the EU, so two broad positions can be associated with communitarian thinking. On the one hand, there are conservative Euro-sceptics of the British variety who think in terms of narrow national interests and conceive the nation in quasi-ethnic terms, resulting in a particularly hard line position on immigration for example. On the other hand, there are civic nationalists. These tend to be more left wing and influenced by republican notions linking patriotism with democratic participation, as in the French tradition (Thibaud 1992, although see Miller 1995 for a British version, especially Ch. 6). For different reasons, both groups will be reluctant to see a dilution of the intergovernmental character of the EU. However, whilst the first would dispute any shift in a federalist direction, the second merely argue that until such time as a global identity and public culture develops, moral weight has to be given to the self-determination of different peoples. Attempts to force the pace will be seen as unjustified, but certain moves of a cosmopolitan kind are possible - even if the total transcendence of the nation state remains highly unlikely.

3. Two Views of Rights and Democracy

Cosmopolitans and communitarians hold two different views of the nature of rights and democracy and the way they relate to each other. Cosmopolitans see rights as essentially self-standing. Their justification is independent of their recognition by any given society or culture and do not rely on democratic endorsement for their validity. Their scope and application is uniform and universal with individuals as their subjects. Citizenship and sovereignty are regarded as largely antithetical to rights, since they link them to membership of a state rather than regarding them as attributes of human beings as such. Even if democracy to some extent embodies the notion of equal rights, its procedures cannot always be counted on to uphold them. At best, it operates as a mechanism of imperfect procedural justice. Within the governmental and constitutional system, therefore, democracy has essentially instrumental uses as a means of allowing individuals to voice and protect their vital interests by controlling the decisions, usually indirectly via influence over their makers, which affect their lives. To the extent that those decisions have passed beyond, or in certain cases below, the nation state, then so must democratic institutions. What defines the demos is largely functional, making the parcelling out of popular sovereignty theoretically unproblematic even though there are numerous practical difficulties. In cases where democracy fails to offer the best protection for rights, or even endangers them, non-democratic mechanisms, such as judicial review or regulative agencies, are to be preferred (Pogge 1994, Ferrajoli 1996).

Communitarians regard rights as socially grounded and as oriented towards securing the participation of individuals within certain worthwhile collective practices. Democracy plays an important role in legitimising and justifying a particular understanding and interpretation of rights within a given society. Consequently, its instrumental qualities are valued far less than its intrinsic ones. Communitarians conceive democratic decision-making more in terms of deliberation on the common good than as a mechanism for the aggregation of individual interests. Moreover, they contend that compromise and the avoidance of a purely self-regarding stance are far more likely amongst a people who identify reasonably strongly with each other. It is no accident in this respect that the two paradigmatic examples of constitution-making, namely France and the United States in the eighteenth-century, were simultaneously instances of nation-building. For democracy implies the existence of a people who feel bound together. It is this sense of a shared fate and mutual responsibility that leads minorities to accept majority decisions, for example, and, perhaps more importantly, motivates majorities to take into account the opinions and concerns of minorities rather than excluding them altogether (Miller 1995, pp. 96-99).

Judicial review tends to play a more subordinate role in this version of democracy to that accorded it in less communitarian accounts.[8] Majority tyranny, which offers a prime motive behind this legal protection of rights, is deemed less likely, and such judicial interference with the popular will be regarded as in any case illegitimate since the deliberations of the people provide both the rationale and the source of rights. Within this conception, democracy is itself a forum of principle that allows conflicting accounts and exercises of rights to be weighed and balanced against each other in ways that show equal concern and respect for the individual autonomy of others. There is no need, as some have argued, for judges to take on this role. Indeed, there are numerous disadvantages associated with their doing so. Politics mobilises public support and commitment for taking on the burdens that are often en-

8 The role of judicial review in relation to rights and democracy has been been debated most fully with regard to the part played by the Supreme Court in the United States. The case for has been made most forcefully by RONALD DWORKIN (1985), especially pp. 70-1, and that against by CASS SUNSTEIN (1993). See BELLAMY and CASTIGLIONE (forthcoming) and BELLAMY (1997) for a fuller examination of this debate, on which this paragraph draws.

tailed by granting particular rights. Moreover, the broader interests and values of diverse groups can be heard, and the defence of a particular right placed in the context of the whole range of policies being undertaken by the government and the wider needs and wishes of citizens. Judicial decisions tend to foreclose democratic involvement in policy making and thereby impair the identification of citizens with the rights they imply. Focus on the litigated case can also lead judges to ignore the knock on effects of legal intervention for other equally important programmes, overlooking the way spending in one area might withdraw resources from others. In these ways, reliance on the courts may have the grave drawback of impairing democratic channels of communication, and risks producing the very unprincipled politics that supporters of judicial review believe render it necessary. In any case, it is doubtful that the judiciary is capable of withstanding the influence of the wider community, no matter how independent it may seek to be. Like other parts of the political system, it needs a degree of popular legitimacy to be authoritative. The danger is that only highly selective pressure groups will be able to exercise such influence, so that the courts will become a prey to those very 'sinister' interests they are supposed to overcome.[9]

When rights and obligations are nested within particular political communities, their cosmopolitan reach will clearly be effected. To the extent that our understanding of basic rights is coloured by the culture of our community, there are likely to be conflicts between the priorities and publicly recognised needs of different societies. State support for certain religions or languages may be important in some communities and regarded as illegitimate in others, for example. Even when the same rights are acknowledged, variations in local context may lead them to being interpreted and balanced in contrasting and not always compatible ways. In addition, there will be a feeling that 'charity begins at home' that will set limits on how much people will commit themselves to helping outsiders when that clashes with programmes, also motivated by rights considerations, of a domestic character. Thus, communitarians regard it as legitimate that a more generous national social security system, say, might be established at the cost of less spending on foreign aid overseas (Miller 1995, Ch. 3 and pp. 100-103).

Support for national sovereignty need not entail a view of international relations as an anarchic and amoral Hobbesean state of nature. Claims to self-

9 For evidence to this effect with regard to the American Supreme Court, see MACKEEVER (1995).

determination for one group imply recognition of similar rights by others - including non-aggression and limited aid. To the extent that global interdependence does link states within institutional networks, then they will have the sorts of obligations cosmopolitans advocate. Nonetheless, the absence of agreed metrics as to the value of resources or the relative worth of various rights and liberties will make arguments for a global redistribution of goods and services hard to cash out in practice - especially as such schemes can conflict with as well as support the autonomy of national communities. Still, it is reasonable to suppose that globalisation will produce forms of inter-state co-operation in those areas such as defence, the environment and the economy where the capacity of states to act in autonomous ways has been seriously impaired. However, in most cases these co-operative schemes will be regarded as mechanisms for preserving rather than undermining national interests and self-determination, with transfers of decision-making power being largely conditional on the extent to which involvement in the relevant international body makes that possible (Miller 1995, pp. 104-108).

4. A Cosmopolitan Communitarianism?

In what follows, we shall argue that these two models shed light on a number of the debates and difficulties currently besetting the European Union. We have already identified four possible approaches to Europe - two stemming from the cosmopolitan and communitarian camps respectively. We wish to propose a fifth approach that combines one from each of the schools of thought: namely the cosmopolitan globalist and the civic nationalist. It would be mistaken to regard the cosmopolitan and the communitarian arguments as totally at odds with each other, with the latter anti-liberal, anti-rights and anti-individualist, as certain commentators have claimed (e.g. Holmes 1993). Rather, they offer contrasting but to some degree compatible accounts of how we should think about individuality, rights and their relationship to the societies that embody them. Our claim will be that cosmopolitan morality only makes sense to the extent that it is embedded within a communitarian framework: a position we dub cosmopolitan communitarianism.

Michael Walzer has recently explored the difference between the two schools in terms of a distinction between 'thick' and 'thin' moralities (Walzer 1994, especially Ch. 1). In his terms, universal human rights represent a 'thin', 'minimal' morality that all societies ought to uphold. But they do so in numerous 'thick', 'maximal' ways. Moreover, the individual rights bearers are similarly contextually defined. That is not to deny value-individualism, as is sometimes implied, but it is to reject those versions of methodological individualism that ignore the social dimension of personal identity and the development of autonomy (see Tamir 1993, Ch. 1 for criticism of such views). According to this thicker, more communitarian view of rights and the individual, a pure cosmopolitanism offers an inadequate account of moral agency. For the cosmopolitan universalist agents are supposed to act on the basis of rational considerations of pure principle that abstract from their sense of identity as persons holding certain convictions and possessing particular attachments. By contrast, the cosmopolitan communitarian believes that both the principles and the moral motivations and character of those who follow them need to be fleshed out with natural sentiments and 'thick' concepts such as courage, honesty, gratitude, and benevolence that arise out of specific ways of life. A pure cosmopolitanism cannot generate the full range of obligations its advocates generally wish to ascribe to it. For the proper acknowledgement of 'thin' basic rights rests on their being specified and overlaid by a 'thicker' web of special obligations. Welfare states, for example, have typically arisen in societies where there are strong feelings of social solidarity. These reinforce the formal obligations that arise from being members of an institutionalised scheme of political co-operation as citizens of the same state. Essentially, they create a sense of identification amongst a given group of people between whom it comes to be felt both legitimate and plausible that collectively binding decisions about the distribution of burdens and benefits should take place. That sense of commonness does not determine what its precise implications or content should be, but it does provide the basis on which such determination takes place. It defines the demos, as it were, for whom a form of democratic rule appears appropriate and plausible.

Nationalism has traditionally provided the ideological glue necessary to define a relatively circumscribed group of people and unify them around a set of shared institutions and practices that were sovereign over a well-defined territory. Political loyalty, accountability and legitimacy were tied in this way to state power and authority. Indeed, nationality was typically the creation of states and political elites seeking to consolidate their hold over their populations. Cosmopolitans deny the necessity and desirability of such attachments. They may, as Thomas Pogge (1994) does, grant them a certain empirical weight but not any moral significance. A mixture of voluntarist and utilitarian considerations of a broadly functional kind provide the only normatively relevant considerations so far as people's obligations to any particular polity are concerned (e.g. Simmons 1979). By contrast, our sketch of the communitarian argument has tried to suggest that largely unchosen commonalties of history, belief, geography and civic culture *do* have an ethical relevance. They supply the feelings of reciprocity, trust and commitment needed to supplement the ties of mere mutual advantage that result from individuals acting on the basis of rational self-interest alone. Such moral qualities have an important influence on the character of political life, since they increase people's willingness to engage in co-operative behaviour by raising their expectations and confidence in others. As David Miller (1995, Ch. 2) has recently argued, far from encouraging self-interested and partial behaviour, the lessening of the tension between personal and collective goals within a group is likely to make an impartial stance more acceptable.

On this account, the normative aspect of the cosmopolitan argument will only go beyond a 'thin' humanitarian concern for others to the extent we live in a relatively 'thick' cosmopolitan civil society with a corresponding public culture. So far as the EU is concerned, this result might be obtained in one of two ways. Either Europe itself will coalesce into a civic nation, or it must operate as a Union of nations involving a degree of variable geometry combined with a fair amount of consensus on central issues and even certain elements of a common identity. We shall defend the second option below. It represents an example of the cosmopolitan communitarian position outlined earlier, whereby nations demonstrate civic attitudes not only internally but also to a greater or lesser extent externally, with basic 'thin' cosmopolitan sentiments thickening in various ways depending on the nature and degree of their interaction and involvement with other nations and even international allegiances possibly developing in some instances. The civic nation varient of the communitarian argument is extended in this way to accomodate aspects of both the globalisation thesis and a universal cosmopolitan morality, whilst denying the normative or empirical possibility of a European, let alone a global, civic nation. This position involves a rejection not only of an unqualified cosmopolitan globalism and universalism, but also of the centralised federalist version of the cosmopolitan argument and the Euro sceptical version of the communitarian case. The neo-functionalist federalist line greatly overestimates the integrative potential of global forces and the capacity of people to transfer their allegiances. The Euro sceptical argument underestimates the new realities of global economic competition and has xenophobic overtones of a decidedly uncivic nature. In sum, they too are neither plausible nor desirable.

III. Whose Europe, Which Community?

1. The Challenge of Maastricht

It is commonly claimed that the European Union currently finds itself at a cross-roads. On the one hand, it operates as an intergovernmental organisation and its mode of governance is likened to a form of consociational confederalism. All four of Lijphart's consociational principles of grand coalition, segmental autonomy, proportionality and minority veto have typified deliberations in the Council of Ministers and negotiations surrounding the various treaties, for example. Moreover, these consociational mechanisms have had the aim and effect of rendering the integrative process consistent with the protection and, to some degree, the enhancement of national identities and interests (Chryssochoou 1994). These characteristics are basically compatible with a communitarian perspective. On the other hand, the EU embodies an extraordinary number of apparently supranational features - most particularly the European Court of Justice, and to a much less extent the European Parliament. The claim stemming from these bodies is that a new European constitutional order has gradually come into being possessing Supremacy over national law and Direct Effect upon individuals and agencies within the national jurisdictions of Member States. Increasingly the Court has justified its claims to judicial competence-competence as the authoritative interpreter of a 'higher' European law by reference to the protection of basic human rights. This development has been accompanied by calls for the European Parliament to have a greater role in the legislative process and the view that intergovernmentalism fails adequately to represent the interests of individual citizens - the so-called democratic deficit thesis (Mancini 1989). These arguments draw on cosmopolitan notions to underpin them.

Up until the Maastricht Treaty the tensions between these two dimensions of European integration rarely manifested themselves in practice. The jurisdictional and legislative expansion of the Court of Justice was largely controlled, and to high degree abetted by, the Member States - not least through a generous interpretation of Article 235 EC to allow a significant extension of the scope and powers of the Community. The shift to majority voting, combined with certain renewed worries on the part of national courts as to the integrity of their own position as guardians of their distinctive constitutional orders, has changed this situation and made governments far more sensitive to the Court's jurisdictional boundaries (Weiler 1994). These tensions are manifested in the Maastricht Treaty itself (Wincott 1994). Thus, while the Common Provisions in Title I, for example, emphasise the goal of an 'ever closer union of the peoples of Europe' (Article A), the Final Provisions in Title VII largely undercut them, not least by removing Title I from the jurisdiction of the Court (Article L). Another instance of this janus-faced character of the TEU is the way subsidarity is defined in both a devolutionary manner, to suggest that decisions should be taken 'as closely as possible' to the citizens (Article A and B), and in a potentially neo-federalist direction as a means for allocating different areas of competence that allows the Community to act even outside its 'exclusive' sphere when 'by reason of the scale or effects of the proposed action' it can achieve certain objectives more effectively than the Member States (Article 3B EC). Most significant of all are the various Protocols attached to the Treaty incorporating various derogations from common policies, such as the British opt out from the Social Charter and the possibility of opting out from EMU, the provisions for Danes to have privileged access to second homes in rural Denmark, and the protection of Irish anti-abortion law. These appear to threaten the central legal tenet of the Union, the *acquis communitaire*, and to open up the possibility of an *à la carte* Europe involving considerable variable geometry. Not surprisingly legal analysts have tended to be hostile to the Treaty, seeing it as reducing the capacity of the Court to produce a coherent legal order and denigrating the resulting constitutional structure as a patchwork of 'bits and pieces' . As one prominent legal commentator has put it, the Union displays 'more of a *bricoleurs* amateurism than a master brick-layer's strive for perfection and attention to detail.' The result, she continues, has jeopardised 'the cohesiveness and the unity and the concomitant power of a legal system painstakingly constructed over the course of some 30 odd years', threatening in the process 'the whole future and credibility of the Communities as a cohesive legal unit which confers rights on individuals and which enters into their national legal systems as an integral part of those systems' (Curtin 1993, pp. 23-24, 67).

Two issues bring out the conflicts between cosmopolitan and communitarian concerns in the Post-Maastricht climate particularly well - namely, the notion of European citizenship and the debate over the jurisdictional limits of the Union highlighted by the Maastricht decision of the German Constitutional Court. Both raise matters related to the contrast between the two models of rights and democracy discussed earlier, and indicate the problems of advocating democratic procedures in the absence of a demos and of assigning rights protection to judicial review. We shall examine each in turn, suggesting in the conclusion that resolving the tensions they reveal may be a matter of yet more *bricolage* rather than architectural design.

2. European Citizens in Search of a Nation

The establishment of Union Citizenship in Articles 8 to 8e of the amended EC Treaty has been taken by certain commentators as representing a first, albeit highly inadequate, step towards the creation of a European Demos. The chief criticisms from this cosmopolitan perspective have related to its limited nature and the huge anomalies that arise from its being tied to nationality as that is variously defined by the different Member States - especially with respect to immigrants resident within the EU (Lyons 1996). Conspicuously little thought, however, has been given to the more communitarian-minded issue of how many people actually desire this status (although see Weiler 1996). In fact, most of the empirical evidence, such as the findings of the Eurobarometer poll, indicates a very low level of identification with Europe. Even though a majority of Europeans are broadly favourable to integration it is largely on the grounds that it is a 'good thing' for their own country (an opinion expressed by 69% of those polled in 1990). Only 14% in a 1989 poll said they 'frequently' felt a 'citizen of Europe', whilst 48% responded that they 'never' did so. Indeed, the only group that appears to feel a higher level of European compared to national consciousness are those working in the various European institutions, who have a vested interest in fostering the European ideal (Wilterdink, 1990, p. 77-85; 1993, pp. 119, 128-129).

These findings reinforce some of the earlier criticisms of the globalisation thesis and suggest problems with the federalist version of the cosmopolitan argument, which seems to depend on the development of a strong European civic nation. In spite of a considerable degree of economic integration and a significant number of common political institutions, there has been comparatively little convergence in civic attitudes and allegiances. Although the intensification of trade, transport, and communication links, greater labour mobility, and an equalisation of social conditions were important elements in the development of national identities in nineteenth century Western Europe (Gellner 1983), they were never sufficient in themselves. In the case of the European Union, the crucial role played by centralised political institutions in unifying the economy is also missing, since the common market has been more the product of deregulation than regulation. Moreover, the growth of economic and social interdependence is not by any means centred solely on Europe, even if trade amongst the Member States has increased more than commerce between them and the rest of the world. The European Union is also a remarkably open-ended project in terms of geographical scope, and potentially might include the most varied cultural and political traditions. Earlier nation-state building projects usually had reasonably well defined territorial ambitions that were linked to certain pre-existing historical, linguistic and cultural boundaries. Although these sentiments were generally only shared by a dominant social group and had to be diffused amongst the rest of the population, there nevertheless was a sense of who was being united and where. No core cultural or geographical reference point seems to exist for the EU, however, beyond a vague commitment to certain unspecified 'principles of liberty, democracy and respect for human rights and fundamental freedoms and of the rule of law' (Preamble, TEU). Even the growing linguistic dominance of English, ironic given the general indifference of the British to the continent and the importance of French amongst the Eurocracy in Brussels, arises from its global significance rather than from its being a European language.

Post-nationalist cosmopolitans, of course, will regard the absence of a sense of European consciousness as highly desirable. A constitutional patriotism centred upon universal liberal democratic values ought to be enough to unite all peoples around common political institutions, and avoids the exclusionary connotations of a form of citizenship based on a territorially and culturally specific national identity (Habermas 1992). Communitarians, however, contend that a high degree of identification forms a precondition for democracy. Without a sense of Europeaness, increasing the powers of the European Parliament risks making the democratic deficit more profound rather than less. Unless voters feel an institution is socially as well as formally legitimate then they will be disinclined either to take part in its decisions or to accept them (Weiler 1993). As rational choice theorists have been forced to concede, self-interest alone cannot explain participation in elections since the rational voter will always stay at home. Voting is a practice involving a number of specific obligations that go with the role of citizen. I need a civic identity, in other words, to be inclined to vote, and that only comes through membership of a specific polis with appropriate traditions. Likewise, unless there is a single right answer, I will only accept a decision as valid if I identify in some respect with those who make it. Given the plurality of ultimate values and the complex ways in which they interact, it is unlikely that clear cut correct solutions can be discovered to many if any of the dilemmas that standardly confront governments over such matters as welfare, defence, health and education and the resources to be allocated to each of them. Rather, collectively binding solutions have to be constructed within specific contexts (Bellamy 1995). That entails involving those likely to be benefited or burdened by the outcome, and crucially getting those in the minority to accept the majority view. Once again, a feeling of belonging to a given community plays a vital part in legitimising the democratic process amongst those involved. It binds together a people and generates reciprocal ties that foster a disposition to consider the general welfare and to compromise where necessary.

Admission to citizenship for these reasons usually involves more than signing up to a set of abstract set of principles. Naturalised citizens, in particular, normally have to be inducted into a certain form of social and political life and declare a willingness to undertake certain duties. Education and the normal processes of socialisation provide a less formalised procedure for nationals. No such induction process exists at the European level, nor is it clear what it would entail. In this regard, it is noteworthy that in a 1989 Eurobarometer poll 59% preferred the idea that the European Parliament should be organised around national criteria rather than the current political ones, even though as yet no European-wide parties, as opposed to groupings of national parties exist. As Weiler (1996, p. 111) has pertinently remarked, at present there is as much reason for us to expect the Danes, say, to accept the legitimate authority of a German Bundestag to which they were given voting rights as that of the European Parliament.

3. Deutschland über alles? Das Maastricht-Urteil

Similar points emerge from the second issue to be considered, that of the respective judicial competences of the ECJ and national constitutional courts.[10] Recent attention on this question has focused on the 1993 judge-

10 The analysis here draws on MACCORMICK (1995) and GUSTAVSSON (1996).

ment of the German Constitutional Court in response to the challenge by Mr Manfred Brunner and others to the validity of Germany's accession to the Maastricht Treaty. Brunner had argued that Maastricht violated Article 79 section 3 of the Basic Law, which forbids amendments affecting the role of the Lander in legislation and, via reference to Articles 1 and 20, that curtail either basic rights or the 'democratic and social' character of the republic and the sovereign authority of the German people as exercised 'through elections and voting and by specific organs of the legislature, the executive power, and the judiciary.' This sort of challenge had already been partly anticipated by the insertion in 1992 of a new Article 23 on participation in the development of the European Union. However, this Article had been careful to assert how the EU was governed by the same principles as those guaranteed by the Basic Law and had insisted that the Bundestag and, where appropriate, the Bundesrat had to be fully involved in the legislative evolution of the EU. In this way, it was hoped not to fall foul of Article 79. Brunner's point was that the making of Community law through majority voting within the Council of Ministers, combined with the European Court's assertions of Direct Effect and the Supremacy of Community over national law, effectively undercut the right of Germans to control their own affairs. The Lander were particularly affected in this respect, since in spite of all the fine talk about subsidiarity there is no real involvement of the regions in Community decision-making. Although the Constitutional Court rejected this particular challenge, it chose both to reassert the continuing sovereignty of the German people and to deny that either the European Court of Justice or any other European organ could claim competence over its own competence. In other words, it remained for the German Court alone to decide whether or not a European measure or development infringed the German constitutional order.

German popular sovereignty, it asserted, remained intact so long as national parliaments not only limited the extension of European functions but states also retained 'sufficiently important spheres of activity of their own in which the peoples of each can develop and articulate in a process of political will-formation which it legitimates and controls, in order to give legal expression to what - relatively homogeneously - binds the people spiritually, socially, and politically together' (German Federal Court 1993, C I 2 b(2)). Their reasoning on this point was essentially communitarian - to be more than 'merely a formal principle of accountability', democracy had to be between a people who could influence each others opinions and have an impact on those who governed them (German Federal Court 1993, C I 2 b(1)). This condition, they noted, is not met by the European Union, which possesses neither a demos nor mechanisms for effective democratic control over its decision makers by any of its constitutive peoples, either severally or collectively. Consequently, the sovereignty of the German people required that 'functions and powers of substantial importance must remain for the German Bundestag' (German Federal Court 1993, C I 2 b(2)). To ensure that this situation persisted, the Court had to retain its prerogative to review legal instruments emanating from European institutions 'to see whether they remain within the limits of the sovereign rights conferred on them or whether they transgress those limits.' The 'Law of Accession' was provisional, therefore, on subsequent European developments continuing to be compatible with the German constitutional order as interpreted by the Court (German Federal Court 1993, C I 3).

A cosmopolitan perspective that sees national and popular sovereignty as matters of instrumental rather than intrinsic importance will tend to regard the German Court's arguments for defending a specifically German form of democracy as somewhat beside the point. The key question is whether liberal democratic values are defended, not their national location or colour. This issue might have been supposed to be resolved in the late 1960s and early 1970s, when the German and Italian constitutional courts obliged the ECJ to declare that the protection of fundamental rights formed 'an integral part of the general principles of law' it had a duty to uphold. [11] This declaration had been motivated by the European Court's desire to uphold the Supremacy of European law against scrutiny by national courts for its protection of human rights - a matter they were often pledged to uphold but the ECJ apparently was not. Since no European Bill of Rights has been formally adopted by the Community to which the ECJ might refer, the Court said it would be guided by the rights protected in the constitutions of Member States and international conventions - most particularly the European Convention on Human Rights.[12] Some commentators regarded this development as 'the most striking contribution the Court made to the development of a constitution for Europe' (Mancini 1989, p. 611). They have argued that 'there is hardly anything that has greater potential to foster integration than a common bill of

11 In case 11/70, *Internationale Handelsgesellschaft*, [1970] ECR 1125, 1134. See too case 29/69, *Stauder v. Ulm*, [1969] ECR 419, at 425 where the Court first stated that fundamental rights were 'enshrined in the general principles of Community law and protected by the Court'.

12 In case 4/73, *Nold (II)*, [1974] ECR 491, 507.

rights, as the constitutional history of the United States has proved' (Cappelletti 1989, 395). They contend that it ought to be possible to draw from the various national constitutions and international conventions a 'common bill of rights' for the Community that 'by encapsulating the nature of the legal order that it underpins ... would create an integrationist *culture* of rights.' Indeed, Article F (2) of the TEU, which refers to the European Convention and common constitutional traditions as offering 'general principles of Community law', might be regarded as a step in this direction, although characteristically it sits alongside F (1) with its insistence that 'The Union shall respect the national identities of its Member States, whose systems of government are founded on principles of democracy.'

The use of the language of rights by the ECJ since 1970, however, provides ample evidence of the difficulties with this thesis, and goes some way to explaining the German Court's reassertion of its prerogatives. The key problem relates to the distinction between cosmopolitan and communitarian views of rights and democracy that we made earlier: namely, that even if all the Member States endorse broadly the same set of rights and democratic principles, they have legitimately different views about their scope and their relative weighting with regard to both each other and other important values and interests that reflect valid cultural differences. The right to freedom of expression is accepted by all Member States, for example, but in certain countries it is interpreted as warranting the special protection of linguistic minorities or a national language on the grounds that a people's culture provides the necessary context within which they express themselves as possessors of a specific identity. However, these protections can place restrictions on the free movement of goods, services, capital and labour which the Community is pledged to uphold. This conflict has been at the heart of a whole series of key cases: notably, Cinéthèque, Groener, Bond and ERT. The reach of Community law has come to appear increasingly open-ended so that there has been a disturbing tendency for the ECJ both to extend the range of its jurisdiction and to interpret rights in a largely market manner that shows scant respect for national constitutional values (De Witte 1991, Coppel and O'Neill 1992).

4. A Right to Choose? Grogan

This process came to head in Grogan. In this case, the Society for the Protection of the Unborn Child brought an injunction against various office-holders of students unions in the Republic of Ireland to prevent them disseminating information about British abortion clinics on the grounds that it infringed Article 40 (3) (iii) of the Irish Constitution. The matter was referred to the ECJ under Article 177.[13] Notwithstanding the Irish constitution's proclamation of a 'right to life of the unborn', abortion was treated by the Court as simply 'a medical activity which is normally provided for remuneration [and] may be carried out as part of a professional activity'. Consequently, it constituted 'a service within the meaning of Article 60 of the Treaty', rendering the case justiciable under Community law. The only reason the injunction did not contravene Article 59, prohibiting any restriction by Member States on the freedom to supply services throughout the Community, was because the connection between the students unions and the British clinics was 'too tenuous'.[14] Had a formal relationship existed between the two, the ECJ might have decided very differently - a fact that led to a Protocol being added to the TEU expressly protecting the Irish clause. Whatever one's position on abortion, it is clear that the ECJ failed to consider the moral concerns underlying the Irish view (Coppell and O'Neill, 1992, pp. 685-9 although for a contrary opinion see Prosser 1996, pp. 73-4). In many respects, however, the Court had no alternative but to decide as it did. All it can legitimately refer to are the economic freedoms that provide the EU with its main *raison d'être*. Drawing on certain putative common European democratic principles would provide no help here, since the measure is unique to Ireland. Indeed, almost all the hard cases referred to above involve some national peculiarity. Moreover, they are morally grey areas in which the weighing up of the competing considerations involved proves hard in terms of pure principle alone, since at some point these become indeterminate. Popular legitimacy comes in here, either directly (as in a referendum such as the Irish held on abortion), or indirectly via political representatives or, even more loosely yet just as effectively and important, through the general prestige a national court has within the political system. Yet it is precisely this communitarian source of political legitimacy that the Court lacks and is unlikely to be able to obtain.

---

13 *The Society for the Protection of Unborn Children (Ireland) Ltd v. Stephen Grogan and others*, Case 159/90, 4 October 1991, reported in [1991] 3 CMLR 689. This analysis follows Coppell and O'Neill, 1992, pp. 685-9.

14 Opinion of the Advocate General of 11 June 1991, paras. 18, 21, 24.

Set against this background, we submit that the German Maastricht decision is unsurprising and defensible. Not everyone thinks so. Weiler (1996, pp. 530-532), for example, has suggested that it represents a declaration of Cold War - a stand off between the ECJ and national courts that, if either were to call the other's bluff, risks undermining the whole legal integrity of the Union. For the decision flies in the face of the ECJ's insistence that it alone has the authority to decide whether or not a community measure is *ultra vires* (Article 173 EC), and that within its sphere 'the validity of a Community measure or its effect within a Member State cannot be affected by allegations that it runs counter to either fundamental rights as formulated by the Constitution of that state or the principles of a national constitutional structure'[15] - a point emphatically reaffirmed by Grogan. However, the absolute supremacy of Community law over domestic constitutional provisions has never been accepted by all national supreme courts. In general, they have acknowledged the authority of Community law for reasons internal to the national legal order rather than, as the ECJ would have it, because of its intrinsic Supremacy, and have distinguished between alterations to basic principles of the national constitution and the transfer of certain powers. This picture suggests that a pluralistic and interactive, as opposed to a monistic and hierarchical, picture of legal systems might be the most appropriate frame of analysis for understanding the relationship of EC to national law (MacCormick 1995, 1996 pp. 143-150). It remains to examine the plausibility of this account.

IV. Conclusion: A Middle Way?

1. Mad Cows and Englishmen

What might be called hard line cosmopolitans and communitarians find the European Union something of a standing contradiction. The former argue that the EU requires a framework of legally binding legitimising constitutional principles and a system of supranational federal European political institutions that, within clearly demarcated spheres, are superior to either na-

15 Case 11/70, *Internationale Handelsgesellschaft*, [1970] ECR 1125 at 1134, [1972] CMLR 255 at 283, cited in De Witte (1991), p. 88.

tional or regional bodies. The latter argue that there can be no ceding of national sovereignty and that the EU has already gone too far. The British BSE affair offers a characteristic confrontation between these two positions. Federalist minded Europhiles saw the EU's action as a legitimate protection of individual interests in the context of a transnational market. It confirmed their image of the EU as a rational response to global economic and social forces that go beyond what national states can control, and that finds its justification in a growing liberal democratic consensus centred on the protection of human rights rather than state sovereignty. Sceptical Europhobes, in contrast, saw the EU's position as motivated by little more than the interests of rival producers in other Member States. For them, the event fuelled their conception of the Union as a centralised and unaccountable Leviathan, that served the cultural and economic imperialism of the Euro-elite and undermined the national self-determination of particular peoples.

Both perspectives possess an element of truth, as well as a good dose of hyperbole and misunderstanding. If few people are likely to man the barricades to defend some supposed British birth right to eat diseased cow brains, cattle farmers had legitimate interests at stake that needed to be addressed. If the health risks were real and could not be ignored, it would be naive to portray the EU as a totally benevolent institution representing nothing but the putatively higher interests of the states that compose it. Not just the British but all governments were faced with the difficult task of balancing the demands of producers and consumers within their respective national constituencies against both genuine concerns about health and the need to cooperate with their economic and political partners. There is no obviously right way of reconciling all the various elements in play. Moreover, the division of responsibility in the evaluation of risk between individuals, governments and expert regulatory bodies is a notoriously grey area for those of a liberal temper. Here we come to what is perhaps the central problem when thinking about democracy and the EU - namely the difficulty of deciding at what level such decisions should be taken and by whom. This fact suggests an alternative account of the EU as a somewhat messy composite arrangement that combines an uneasy mixture of national, intergovernmental and supranational elements that combine in *ad hoc* ways depending on the matter in play. Whilst Euro-federalists and Eurosceptics have a tendency to regard this middle way as inherently unstable and unsatisfactory, we want to argue that it might offer the most illuminating picture of the EU's largely *sui generis* nature.

2. Bricolage vs. Architecture

On this middle view, which draws on moderate versions of the cosmopolitan and communitarian arguments, it proves perfectly possible to acknowledge both the validity of certain general norms and obligations, and the need for supranational collective action in those areas where global processes have rendered it prudent to do so, without insisting that such acknowledgement need be of the same kind for all parties or require the adoption of a totally unified political system. Rather, it emerges from within the distinctive perspectives of the various participants and the dialogue that ensues between them.

It may be that increasingly common points of view, and hence a willingness to pool sovereignty, will eventually emerge. In an earlier article, we suggested that at such a time a 'democratic baptism' would still be necessary to provide the new institutions or constitutional framework with a thicker, more communitarian legitimacy than can be provided by principles of justice alone (Bellamy and Castiglione 1996b, and see too Weale 1995, which inspired this suggestion, and Walker 1996, especially pp. 280-3, who develops it). A somewhat similar and more detailed proposal is made by Thomas Pogge in his contribution to this volume, although we note that his more cosmopolitan orientation takes the existence of a demos somewhat for granted and he adopts a more instrumental view of the democratic process to ours. Nonetheless, we agree on the ultimate necessity of popular involvement in the constitutional process. The forms that it has so far taken have involved the systematic breaking of one of the principles of the separation of power, which assumes a distinction between the constituent power and the constituted powers. National governments are at present arrogating to themselves the powers to constitute a Union in which (it would seem) they themselves will have a fundamental role as institutional players. However, a word of caution is in order. Mass consultation on major constitutional issues can only take place in rather exceptional circumstances, otherwise the principles at stake risk being clouded by the relatively minor and transient concerns of 'normal' politics (Ackerman 1991), as the French Maastricht referendum illustrated. Such 'constitutional moments' are rare, and usually only appear when some disaster like a war has created a sufficient bond of solidarity amongst people to lead them to forget old differences and contemplate new allegiances. Such a moment gave rise to the European ideal in the first place, of course, but peace and prosperity have increasingly been taken for granted by subsequent generations, and their enthusiasm for the project has waned accordingly. Moreover, the integration process is in such a fluid state that there is a danger that any explicit attempt to legitimise the Union would ultimately back fire through being premature. New measures that people could claim not to have agreed to would be necessary - a complaint frequently made by British Eurosceptics, for example, to dispute the continued sway of the 1975 referendum on joining the then EEC.

Much more likely, is a continuation of the current piecemeal process whereby the Union develops through a mixture of *ad hoc* agreements, periodic major intergovernmental reviews, and certain internal dynamics of the Community itself. In keeping with the German Maastricht decision, democratic legitimacy within this set up comes largely from national parliaments and courts. The chief objection, fuelled by Maastricht, is that this mechanism leads to a fragmented *à la carte* Union of opt-outs and variable tracks. At some level, it will undoubtedly be necessary for Member States to agree what is and what is not optional. However, this cannot be decided *a priori* - as we have seen, conventional notions of what is or is not required for a political organisation to work are constantly challenged by the very existence of the EU. Rather, they have to be progressively negotiated. The normative foundations of this conception of the EU can perhaps be best characterised as a hybrid cosmopolitan communitarianism, in which different communities converge on a range of compatible perspectives on common goals and endeavours, rather than a communitarian cosmopolitanism, which assumes a universal consensus on principles and procedures. It suggests a civic Europe made up of different nations, rather than a homogeneous European civic nation. This approach may be more bricolage than architecture, but it has the great advantage of suggesting that the *status quo* may not be as unjustifiable and unstable as many have wished us to believe.

References

BEAUD, O.: "La Fédération entre l'état et l'empire", in B. THÉRET (Ed.): *L'État, la finance et le sociale,* Paris (La Decouverte) 1995.

BELLAMY, RICHARD: "The Constitution of Europe: Rights or Democracy?", in: BELLAMY, BUFACCHI & CASTIGLIONE (Eds.): *Democracy and Constitutional Culture in the Union of Europe,* London (Lothian Foundation Press) 1995, pp. 153-176.

BELLAMY, RICHARD (Ed.): *Constitutionalism, Democracy and Sovereignty: American and European Perspectives,* Aldershot and Brookfield USA (Avebury) 1996.

BELLAMY, RICHARD: "Liberal Politics and the Judiciary: The Supreme Court and American Democracy", *Res Publica: A Journal of Legal and Social Philosophy,* 3 (1997), pp. 91-106.

BELLAMY, R. and CASTIGLIONE, D. (1996a): *Constitutionalism in Transformation: European and Theoretical Perspectives,* Oxford (Blackwell) 1996.

BELLAMY, R. and CASTIGLIONE, D. (1996b): "The Communitarian Ghost in the Cosmopolitan Machine: Constitutionalism, Democracy and the Reconfiguration of Politics in the New Europe", in: BELLAMY (1996), pp. 111-129.

BELLAMY, R. and CASTIGLIONE, D.: "Constitutionalism and Democracy: Political Theory and the American Constitution", *British Journal of Political Science,* forthcoming.

BELLAMY, R., BUFACCHI, V. & CASTIGLIONE, D. (Eds.): *Democracy and Constiutional Culture in the Union of Europe,* London (Lothian Foundation Press) 1995.

BROWN, CHRIS: *International Relations Theory: New Normative Approaches,* Hemel Hempstead (Harvester/Wheat sheaf) 1992.

CAPPELLETTI, M.: *The Judicial Process in Comparative Perspective,* Oxford (Clarendon Press) 1989.

CHRYSSOCHOOU, DIMITRIS N.: "Democracy and Symbiosis in the European Union: Towards a Confederal Consociation?", *West European Politics,* 17 (1994), pp. 1-14.

COPPEL, J. and O'NEILL, A.: "The European Court of Justice: Taking Rights Seriously?", *Common Market Law Review,* 29 (1992), pp. 669-692.

CURTIN, D.: "The Constitutional Structure of the Union: A Europe of Bits and Pieces", *Common Market Law Review,* 30 (1993), pp. 17-69.

DE WITTE, BRUNO: "Droit communitaire et valeurs constitutionelles nationales", *Droits,* 14 (1991), pp. 87-96.

DWORKIN, R.: *A Matter of Principle,* Oxford (Clarendon Press) 1985.

FERRAJOLI, LUIGI: "Beyond Sovereignty and Citizenship: A Global Constitutionalism", in: BELLAMY (1996), pp. 151-160.

FERRY, J-H.: "Une 'philosophie' de la communaute", in: J-H. FERRY and P. THIBAUD: *Discussion sur l'Europe*, Paris (Calmann-Levy) 1992.

GELLNER, E.: *Nations and Nationalism*, Oxford (Blackwell) 1983.

GEORGE, S.: *Policy and Politics in the European Community*, Oxford (Oxford University Press) 1985, 2nd ed. 1991.

GERMAN FEDERAL COURT: *Ruling, Second Division, Dated 12 October 1993*, 2BvR 2134/92 2BvR 2159/92, English version.

GUSTAVSSON, S.: "Defending the Democratic Deficit", in: A. WEALE and N. NENTWICH (Eds.): *The Political Theory of European Constitutional Choice*, London (Routledge) 1997, forthcoming.

HABERMAS, J.: "Citizenship and National Identity: Some Reflections on the Future of Europe", *Praxis International*, 12 (1992), pp. 1-19.

HELD, DAVID: *Democracy and the Global Order: From the Modern State to Cosmopolitan Governance*, Cambridge (Polity Press) 1995.

HIRST, PAUL and THOMPSON, GRAHAM: *Globalisation in Question: The International Economy and the Possibilities of Governance*, Cambridge (Polity Press) 1996.

HOLMES, S.: *The Anatomy of Antiliberalism*, Cambridge Mass. (Harvard University Press) 1993.

JONES, R. J. BARRY: "The Economic Agenda", in: G. WYN REES (Ed.): *International Politics in Europe: The New Agenda*, London and New York (Routledge) 1993, pp. 87-110.

JONES, R. J. BARRY (1995a): *Globalisation and Interdependence in the International Political Economy: Rhetoric and Reality*, London and New York (Pinter) 1995.

JONES, R. J. BARRY (1995b): "The United Nations and the International Political System", in: D. BOURANTONIS and J. WEINER (Eds.): *The United Nations in the New World Order: The World Organization at Fifty*, Basingstoke (Macmillan) 1995, pp. 19-40.

KEOHANE, ROBERT O. and HOFFMANN, STANLEY: "Institutional Change in Europe in the 1980s", in R. O. KEOHANE and S. HOFFMAN (Eds.): *The New European Community: Decision making and Institutional Change*, Boulder Colo. and Oxford (Westview Press) 1991, pp. 1-39.

LYONS, C.: "Citizenship in the Constitution of the European Union: Rhetoric or Reality?", in: BELLAMY (1996), pp. 96-110.

MACCORMICK, NEIL: "The Maastricht-Urteil: Sovereignty Now", *European Law Journal*, 1 (1995), pp. 255-262.

MACCORMICK, NEIL: "Liberalism, Nationalism and the Post-Sovereign State", in: BELLAMY and CASTIGLIONE (1996a), pp. 141-156.

MCKEEVER, ROBERT J.: *Raw Judicial Power? The Supreme Court and American Society*, 2nd edition, Manchester (Manchester University Press) 1995.

MANCINI, G. F.: "The Making of a Constitution for Europe", *Common Market Law Review*, 26 (1989), pp. 595-614.

MILWARD, A.: *The European Rescue of the Nation-State*, London and New York (Routledge) 1992.

MILLER, DAVID: *On Nationality*, Oxford (Clarendon Press) 1995.

MULHALL, STEPHEN and SWIFT, ADAM: *Liberals and Communitarians*, Oxford (Blackwell) 2nd. ed., 1996.

POGGE, THOMAS W.: "Cosmopolitanism and Sovereignty", in: C. BROWN (Ed.): *Political Restructuring in Europe: Ethical Perspectives*, London and New York (Routledge) 1994, pp. 89-122.

PROSSER, T.: "Understanding the British Constitution", in: BELLAMY and CASTIGLIONE (1996), pp. 61-75.

SANDEL, M.: "The Political Theory of the Procedural Republic", in: G. BRYNER and N. REYNOLDS (Eds.): *Constitutionalism and Rights*, Provo, Utah (Brigham Young University Press) 1987, pp. 141-155.

SCHMITTER, PHILLIPPE C.: "If the Nation State were to Wither Away in Europe, What Might Replace It?", in: S. GUSTAVSSON and L. LEWIN (Eds.): *The Future of the Nation-State: Essays on Cultural Pluralism and Political Integration*, Stockholm (Nerenius and Santérus) 1996, pp. 211-244.

SIMMONS, A. J.: *Moral Principles and Political Obligation*, Princeton N.J. (Princeton University Press) 1979.

SUNSTEIN, CASS R.: *The Partial Constitution*, Cambridge Mass. (Harvard University Press) 1993.

TAMIR, Y.: *Liberal Nationalism*, Princeton N.Y. (Princeton University Press) 1993.

THIBAUD, P.: "L'Europe par les nations (et réciproquement)", in: J-H. FERRY and P. THIBAUD: *Discussion sur l'Europe*, Paris (Calmann-Levy) 1992.

WALDRON, J.: "Rights in Conflict", *Ethics*, 99 (1989), pp. 503-519.

WALKER, N.: "European Constitutionalism and European Integration", *Public Law* (1996), pp. 266-290.

WALZER, M.: "Philosophy and Democracy", *Political Theory*, 9 (1981), pp. 379-399.

WALZER, M.: *Spheres of Justice: A Defence of Pluralism and Equality*, Oxford (Martin Robertson) 1983.

WALZER, M.: *Thick and Thin: Moral Argument at Home and Abroad*, Notre Dame (University of Notre Dame Press) 1994.

WEALE, A.: "Democratic Legitimacy and the Constitution of Europe", in: BELLAMY, BUFACCHI & CASTIGLIONE (Eds.) (1995), pp. 81-94.

WEILER, J. H. H. with HALTERN, U.R. and MAYER, F. C.: "European Democracy and its Critique", in: J. HAYWOOD (Ed.): *The Crisis of Representation in Europe*, London (Frank Cass) 1995, pp. 4-39.

WEILER, J. H. H.: "Parliamentary Democracy in Europe 1992: Tentative Questions and Answers", in: D. GREENBERG et. al. (Eds.): *Constitutionalism and Democracy: Transitions in the Contemporary World*, Oxford and New York (Oxford University Press) 1993, pp. 249-263.

WEILER, J. H. H.: "Journey to an Unknown Destination: A Retrospective and Prospective of the European Court of Justice in the Area of Political Integration", *Journal of Common Market Studies*, 31 (1994), pp. 1-30.

WEILER, J. H. H.: "European Neo-Constitutionalism: In Search of Foundations for the European Constitutional Order", in: BELLAMY and CASTIGLIONE (1996), pp. 105-121.

WINCOTT, D.: "Is the Treaty of Maastricht an Adequate 'Constitution' for the European Union?", *Public Administration*, 72 (1994), pp. 573-590.

WINCOTT, D.: "Political Theory, Law and European Union", in: J. SHAW and G. MORE (Eds.): *New Legal Dynamics of European Union*, Clarendon Press (Oxford) 1995, pp. 293-311.

WILTERDINK, N.: *Where Nations Meet: National Identities in an International Organisation*, Florence (EUI Working Paper) 1990.

WILTERDINK, N.: "An Examination of European and National Identity", *European Journal of Sociology*, 34 (1993), pp. 119-136.

ZOLO, D.: *Cosmopolis: La prospettiva del governo mondiale*, Milan (Feltrinelli) 1995.

Part D

Conclusion

Chapter 13

Should the European Union Become More Democratic?

PHILIPPE VAN PARIJS

I. Can a Democratic Deficit Ever Be a Good Thing?

Does the European Union suffer from a democratic deficit?* The answer clearly depends on what exactly counts as a "democratic deficit", and hence also on what counts as "democracy".

Democracy is frequently linked to *accountability* (for example, in this volume, by Gustavsson and by Schmitter), roughly understood as the need for decision-makers to justify their decisions in a persuasive way, or more explicitly as the conjunction of transparency (the provision of all relevant information to the controlling party) and responsibility (the serious risk of being sanctioned by that party). But there can be democracy without accountability — as in direct democracy, where the people are themselves the rulers

* I am most grateful to the participants in the Oslo workshop on "Democracy and the European Union" and in the Louvain workshop on "The normative foundations of federalism" for stimulating exchanges, and to Renaud Dehousse for instructive written comments on an earlier version.

—, and there can be accountability without democracy — when the controlling party to whom accounts need to be given does not ultimately consist in the people of the entity concerned, but a foreign ruler for example. Leaving out the possibility — irrelevant on the scale of the EU — of generalized direct democracy, democracy should therefore be characterized, more specifically, as accountability *to the demos*, i.e. to the people expressing themselves through majorities emerging from free elections under universal suffrage.

If this is democracy, what is a *democratic deficit*? At the most abstract level, a democratic deficit is sometimes understood as less than maximal feasible democracy, and at other times as less than optimal democracy.[1] Under the former construal, it makes sense to ask whether a democratic deficit is a bad thing which one should attempt to get rid of. Under the latter construal, it does not, as a democratic deficit — on a par, presumably, with a democratic surplus — is by definition suboptimal. Whether there is a democratic deficit in the former sense is easily settled, as it is obvious enough that the complex amalgam consisting of the European Commission, the European Council, the Council of Ministers, the European Parliament, the European Court of Justice, the European Monetary Institute and their respective administrations is quite a bit less than maximally accountable to the relevant demos. The sheer opacity of many decision processes within the Commission's administration, the constant reliance on expert committees, the weakness of the democratic control over the activity of the European Council, the Council of Ministers and the European Commission — whether because of their mode of selection or because of the lack of a genuine arena for political debate — uncontroversially establish the existence of a democratic deficit understood as less than maximal democracy.[2]

---

1 For my purposes, these abstract definitions are more appropriate than the common characterization of the democratic deficit in the EU context as a loss of democratic accountability at the national level unmatched by a corresponding gain of democratic accountability at the European level (see e.g. DEHOUSSE 1995; SCHARPF 1995; GUSTAVSSON 1996). If there is a democratic deficit in this specific sense, it is nearly self-evident that there is also a democratic deficit in my first abstract sense ("less than maximal"), but by no means certain that there is also one in my second sense ("less than optimal").

2 See DEHOUSSE (1995, pp. 8-13) for a useful overview of the various dimensions of the "democratic deficit" in this sense.

But they do not *ipso facto* show that there is also a democratic deficit in the second sense — a suboptimal level of democracy. For whether there is such a deficit depends on what criterion of optimality one adopts, and this criterion cannot plausibly be, as a general rule, maximal democratic accountability. Why not? Let me just mention two possible sources of discrepancy. For reasons related to the general case for a separation between the judiciary power and the legislative power, it is arguably essential that the European Court of Justice should be sheltered from accountability to any demos. For reasons rooted in an analysis of the causes and effects of inflationary pressures, it is also arguably essential that the prospective European Bank should be an independent agency protected against political pressures. So, if optimal democratic accountability is not maximal democratic accountability, what is it? My answer is ruthlessly, unapologetically consequentialist.[3]

II. Ruthless Consequentialism

More explicitly, my claim is that the very existence of the European Union, the powers it is given and the way it is organized must be evaluated, criticized, shaped, on the basis of the conjunction of empirical conjectures about the likely consequences of alternative options and of a normative criterion for assessing these consequences. What should this criterion be? It should certainly incorporate considerations of security and prosperity — the two central concerns in the first two decades of the European Communities —, but also of sustainability, diversity and solidarity. Can these considerations be integrated into an explicit, coherent and plausible conception of the overall goal? I believe they can, and have tried to systematically spell out and defend such a conception in *Real Freedom for All* (Van Parijs 1995a). Being able to rely on a precise conception of this type presents great advantages. But only a recognition of the relevance of the broad set of considerations ar-

3 Unlike Midgaard's (1997), for example. His criterion of autonomy (everybody should be ruled by laws adopted by himself or his representatives) defines optimality by the extent to which the decision-making design satisfies some procedural feature, not the extent to which it fosters the achievement of some substantive goal. The purely instrumental approach to democracy on which I rely here is presented and defended more fully in VAN PARIJS (1996a).

ticulated in this conception, not the particular way in which it articulates them, is assumed in the argument which I am now about to present, by way of an answer to the question whether or not the European Union suffers from a democratic deficit.

The question can be rephrased as follows. If the overarching goal is the maximal feasible achievement of some substantive conception of social justice which incorporates the various considerations listed above, is there any strong reason to believe that the EU's current institutional situation is unsatisfactory and, if so, that enhancing the EU's democratic accountability would make things better, as far as the achievement of our overall goal is concerned.

III. No Option but Going Forward

Is the status quo satisfactory? Certainly not. Most fundamentally because the very existence of the single European market, added to the globalization of the economy, jeopardizes sustainability, the persistence of cultural diversity and, above all, the preservation and strengthening of solidarity.[4] To clarify what I have in mind, let me just briefly illustrate this last dimension. At the national level, we used to be able to exert our solidarity in a variety of ways. For example, when publicly run bus services needed new buses, they could self-evidently select the single bus-manufacturing firm on its territory, perhaps quite a bit more expensive than alternatives abroad, but providing employment to large number of workers, and hence the rational choice, since the cost of unemployment benefits would far exceed the premium paid to the local firm. Moreover, state-owned firms or state-protected monopolies used to contain massive pockets of unprofitable activities and to apply rigid wage scales largely disconnected from any assessment of worker's actual productivity, thus implementing a large, though implicit solidarity in favour of the low-skilled. As a result of the policing of public orders and the dismantling of monopolies by EU legislation, these two forms of solidarity are no longer available.

---

4 In comparison, the threat to security that stems from globalization (via the growth of the extreme right), as emphasized in Raino MALNES's "Hobbesian" contribution to the Oslo workshop, appears rather modest.

Never mind, you might say, all we need is replace these inefficient, untidy, implicit forms of solidarity by more efficient, systematic, transparent transfers to the unlucky and the less talented, through our tax and social security systems. But you then face another problem. For suppose that in order to finance unemployment benefits or employment subsidies you attempt to impose high taxes or social security contributions on those firms, or on those owners of financial or human capital who earn handsome incomes, among other things because of the opportunities offered by the Single Market and globalization you will then realize that many of them move out — or credibly threaten to move out — to places where they face lower tax rates, while retaining for their products unhindered access to the home market.

Consequently, both because of ongoing changes in the external economic environment ("globalization") and because of the gradual unfolding of the legal, economic and organizational implications of the single market, we cannot stop where we are. Since there is much to lose from going back to more autarkic economies, as well as from attempting to restore the inefficient and biased forms of solidarity illustrated above, we have no serious option but to move forward, by greatly increasing the powers of the European Union in matters that are directly and explicitly of a distributive nature. On the background of the diagnosis just sketched, this is required even in order to preserve current levels of solidarity within each member state.[5] It is obviously also required if one regards as desirable to strengthen solidarity across member states. And it is further required to secure sustainability — against downward

5 SCHARPF (1995, pp. 565-581) essentially shares this diagnosis, but he is rather pessimistic about the EU's political ability to remedy the national powerlessness brought about by the Single Market. His pessimism is rooted in the legal asymmetry between "negative integration" (the effective dismantling of discriminating legislation by the Commission and the Court) and "positive integration" (the laborious EU-level re-regulation by unanimous Council decisions), in the conflicting interests of member states with a developed and a rudimentary welfare state, in the ideological disagreement among the former group, and in the great institutional differences between social protection and industrial relations in the various countries. At the most fundamental level, I believe that these difficulties must be tackled through a combination of the political-institutional strategy sketched below and a basic-security approach to European social integration sketched elsewhere (VAN PARIJS 1996b). These need not be incompatible with the less radical, shorter-term measures favoured by SCHARPF (*ibid.*, 581-88).

environmental competition —, to generate sufficient human capital — against the downward spiral of free riding on the education and training provided by other countries — and even to protect diversity — against the homogenizing pressure of a mad dash for competitiveness.

IV. A More Democratic Union ?

Granted that we need a more powerful Union for the reasons just mentioned, do we also need a more democratic Union? Let me say at the outset that I do not believe that this issue can be settled on the basis of a simple dichotomy between efficiency-oriented policies, which require no democratic accountability and can therefore be left to the Union as it is, and redistribution-oriented policies, which do require democratic accountability and should therefore be left under the control of the national *demoi*.[6] Competition policy and monetary policy may be efficiency-motivated but they have massive distributive implications, and should therefore not be exempted, according to this very position, from democratic scrutiny. Deliberately redistributive policies, on the other hand, cannot be left, for the reasons just sketched, at the national level. Given this massive distributive relevance, should European policy-making, whether old and new, therefore be made more democratic than it now is? Not necessarily. From the consequentialist perspective sketched earlier, the real question is rather how all relevant actors — rulers, officials, representatives, pressure groups and even voters — can be given the powers and the incentives to do the right thing, i.e. to do what is needed (given what the others do) for the best possible decisions to be made, as far as the achievement of social justice is concerned.

In the case of monetary policy hinted at before, this may well involve shielding the governors of the prospective European Bank against democratic accountability. Such shielding would not be justified by some alleged distributive neutrality of monetary policy, but by the presumption that accelerating inflation and political business cycles would jeopardize the sustainable fostering of the fate of the worst off. But what about the deliberate redistributive policies, which I claimed the EU should take on far more than it

6 As in a rather rash interpretation of Giandomenico MAJONE's (1996) position.

does now? How should the relevant decision-making institutions be designed? Should they be any more democratic that EU institutions currently are?

One cannot offer a sensible answer to this question without first looking at how generous the redistributive policies of various existing polities are, especially federal ones, and reflecting on whether the observed differences have anything to do with the design of their respective political institutions. As part of this exercise, it will be important to think, for example, about the reasons why the U.S. welfare state is so much stingier that the typical West-European welfare state, despite comparable economic circumstances and a common cultural inheritance. Can this difference be attributed to greater internal heterogeneity, to the racial factor or to a greater openness to immigration, or rather to the presidential system, to the importance of money in the electoral process or to a majority system with large constituencies which prevents the underdogs from being represented in Congress?

From a casual exercise of this type, I derive the tentative conclusion that there is not much to expect from a European legislative body made up of representatives of the various governments — certainly if it is governed by a unanimity rule or by a wealth-weighted majority rule,[7] slightly less certainly if it is governed by some unweighted or population-weighted majority rule. Why? Fundamentally because each government's representative at the intergovernmental table would be expected to bring back home at least the *juste retour*, at least the equivalent of what (s)he is giving away, and the closer one gets to a purely distributive issue, the more likely possible moves are likely to be blocked by one (unanimity) or more (majority) countries whose interests are perceived to be damaged. Even if, under unweighted or population-weighted majority, there turned out to be enough countries to gain from the redistributive measure, they may well refrain from pushing their advantage for fear of creating alienation, frustration, indignation in the countries which stand to lose. It is only if the discussion could be sufficiently shielded from scrutiny by the national media, parliaments and electorates and/or if it could

7 As has apparently been suggested by President Chirac. Note that when the first European institutions were set up in 1951, Chancellor Adenauer was about to suggest that the weights in the European institutions should be determined according to the size of their coal and steel production, when Jean Monnet, immediately endorsed by Adenauer himself, proposed that each of the three larger countries (France, Germany, Italy) and the three smaller countries together (Belgium, Luxemburg, the Netherlands) should each have the same weight. (See MONNET 1976, pp.413-415.)

remain sufficiently ignorant or quiet about the transnational distributive consequences that the governments' representatives would not lose face (and by the same token a few points in the opinion polls) if they returned home with a bad deal. But if it can only be purchased at the cost of such a large "democratic deficit", this possibility would unavoidably remain shaky, as it would falter should media attention suddenly seize the issue.

V. Single-Constituency Parliament, Public Council, Elected President ?

Are things hopeless then? They need not be. But it is essential that the crucial legislative body should be made up not of the representatives of the various countries or their governments, but of subsets of their populations. The most obvious way of achieving this would consist in greatly extending the scope and strength of the legislative powers of the European Parliament, at least partly at the expense of the Council.[8] This preference for the Parliament is by no means based on the fact that each country's representation and weight at the Parliament is far more sensitive to the size of its population than it is at the Council. Not only could this in principle easily be done at the Council too, as is actually put forward in some of the reform proposals made in preparation of the Intergovernmental Conference.[9] But it is also, for

8 This could probably be done most effectively by giving the Commission the power to propose legislation in the relevant area and the Parliament the power to approve, amend or reject it. By introducing co-decision by the Parliament and the Council of Ministers on some acts, by requiring Parliamentary approval of both the President and the members of the European Commission, by synchronizing (at a six-month interval) European elections and choice of a new Commission, the Maastricht Treaty has already gone quite a long way in this direction.

9 For example in August 1993 by the German Member of Parliament Karl Lamers, who suggested that Council decisions be taken with a double majority of 4/5 of the member states and 4/5 of the populations they represent; or in February 1994 by the Institutional Committee of the European Parliament, who proposed a simple majority of both the member states and the populations represented by them. (See FRANCK 1995, p. 41 for a survey of relevant proposals.)

our purposes, of rather minor importance. What matters is rather, first, that the representation should be structured along ideological or social rather than ethnic or territorial lines, so as to allow for alliance or indeed party formation across the national borders. What also matters greatly is, next, that the representation should not be significantly affected by wealth, whether as a result of making the number of representatives (per capita) a function of a nation's GNP (or some other correlated variable), of allowing campaign expenditure to significantly affect election outcomes or of the *de facto* or *de jure* disenfranchisement of a significant proportion of the poor.

This may not prove enough, however. For one key factor in explaining the viable generosity of European welfare states is bound to reside in the existence of a nation-wide forum of political argument and competition, in which an appeal to the common interest, or to the interests of "the weakest among us all", can make sense. For something analogous to happen at the European level, despite linguistic barriers and cultural differences, more institutional help may be needed. One could, for example, imagine that a portion of the membership of the European Parliament, say 50 members, be chosen on Europe-wide lists, under a system of proportional representation with the possibility of multiple voting within each list.[10] Featuring on such lists would be attractive to major politicians, as there has probably never been as large an electoral constituency anywhere (not even for the US Presidential election). More importantly, such a system would force candidates to acquire a European profile, and hence to care about as much about their presence and image in the press of other European countries as in their own. It would of course also force them to collaborate closely across national borders on the programme and make up of the list. As a result, even the candidates for the remaining, nationally allocated, seats (more than 90% of the total) would be far more closely connected cross-nationally than they currently are. Above all, the politicians' and the media's discourse will gradually be reshaped so as to construct "our" interest on a Europe-wide scale.[11]

---

10 A (timid) step in this direction was made in Maastricht, when allowing each citizen of a member state to take part in European Parliament elections, whether as a voter or as a candidate, in any European country.

11 An analogous proposal is to be found in DEWATRIPONT & al. (1996, pp. 17, 165-167) and in ROLAND & al. (1997). One may object that this pan-European list system does not guarantee representation from all areas and involves a strong bias in favour of politicians from larger countries. One could think of countering this (1) by imposing constraints on the national make up

An alternative, less obvious and more hazardous way of pursuing the same objectives consists in modifying the other legislative bodies — European Council and Council of Ministers — in such a way that it can develop the same dynamic. One might think, for example of the radical conjunction of three changes: replacing unanimity by (not too qualified) majority, making the discussions public and adding, in the case of large or heterogeneous countries, representatives from their regional governments. This last element may be conceived in such a way that each country ends up with a weight that more or less reflects its population size. But this is not crucial.[12] What matters is that the combination of these three changes would take us quite some way from the diplomatic logic of hidden bargaining to the parliamentary logic of public argument, analogous to the one that prevails in the German or Austrian Bundesrat, or even in the US Senate or the Swiss Conseil général (with the significant difference, however, that in the latter cases it is the voters, rather than the governments, of the federated units that are represented). However, the key element of cross-national alliance would be far more difficult to durably and strainlessly achieve under this set up than under the Parliamentary scenario, as there would be a tendency for representatives from various parts of the same country either to systematically gang up together or to bash the traitors who defect to the opponents. Moreover, no electoral competition for votes from other countries would be put into place. Hence, the incentive to construct the interests one is mandated to defend as trans-national

---

of each list and attaching significant consequences to someone's position on the list, or (2) by making votes attracted from outside one's country count more heavily for the individual candidate (not the list). More wisely perhaps, one can simply rely on the nationally allocated seats to guarantee representation from all nations (and even most regions), with some overrepresentation of the smaller ones (as now) to compensate the disadvantage their politicians may have on the Pan-European ballot.

12 Indeed, making power a function of population size, for example by requiring a high qualified majority (4/5 as in the Lamers proposal mentioned earlier) of the populations represented, would be counterproductive from my standpoint, as it would give, or be near to giving, a veto power to the large countries, and thus take us back to the bargaining dynamics from which it is essential to break away.

would remain weak and the rise of a Europe-wide debate would hardly be fostered.[13]

In order to achieve these further objectives, one could think of supplementing the reform of the Council — while disposing by the same token of its unsatisfactory rotating presidency — by having the President of the Council elected through a pan-European election.[14] To prevent the contest from degenerating again into a divisive conflict between nations or groups or nations, one could restrict eligibility at each election to the citizens of particular countries, with a rotation among fairly equally populated groups of countries so that each of them has its turn, say, every 20 years. Here again, we would have major politicians forced to adopt a high European profile, enter a highly publicized Europe-wide debate, strengthen cross-national political alliances and above all compete with a platform that caters to the general interest (or to the interest "of the weakest among us all"), rather than to national interest. The experiment, however, may bring nothing but frustration if the elected President has no other power than to chair a Council that remains governed by inter-national bargaining, or even to appoint a Commission whose initiatives are entirely submitted to approval by such a Council. Hence, even with this addition of an elected President — which may be a de-

---

13 Note that it is precisely because of the lack of such a debate that Sverker Gustavsson finds it justified to give the same voting power or at any rate a fairly equal voting power to each nation at the Council level, as well as to secure a position in the Commission to at least one person from each member state. The underlying concern is with getting all arguments properly listened to, rather than with giving due weight to the interests of all. I can see the point of this argument (a variant of which also underlies Dehousse's position, to be discussed below). But the solution it points to must be viewed as a poor and transitional *Ersatz* to building a well-functioning European public realm — an admittedly difficult task for which electoral reform of the type sketched above for the Parliament and the uninhibited acceptance of English as the medium of debate provide two important preconditions. Moreover, an "alarm bell mechanism" (see DEHOUSSE 1994, pp. 121-123), which makes it possible for the veto of a number of countries to postpone the decision (so as to give them time to make their case), would probably be a better tool for screening out fair arguments from sheer interests.

14 As proposed, for example, by former French President Valéry Giscard d'Estaing (see FRANCK 1995, p. 41).

fensible idea in its own right —, the Council version of the strategy is far less promising that its Parliamentary version.[15]

VI. Demos-Cracy Versus Demoi-Cracy

Would the adoption of this strategy amount to making the EU more democratic? This is by no means obvious. For the crucial change that is being proposed in this policy area is not an increase or decrease in the level of democracy, but a shift from *demoi-cracy* to *demos-cracy*, a shift from accountability to the separate peoples of Europe (if redistribution were a purely national or intergovernmental matter) to accountability to the people of Eu-

15 DEHOUSSE (1995 p. 19-25) contrasts the partisan, majoritarian logic of parliamentarism, which is meant to provide "democratic legitimacy" to the EU, and the representative, pluralist logic of federalism, which is meant to provide it with "state legitimacy". He argues against a shift from the latter to the former on the ground that it would jeopardize the EU's authority and stability. In his view, an adequate balance between the two logics would rather require the Commission to remain non-partisan and accountable on all issues to the Council of Ministers turned into a real second Chamber. I have two main objections to his interesting analysis: (1) Authority, stability, legitimacy and the like do not form the ultimate objective — save perhaps for the rulers themselves — but only conditions for the pursuit of broader goals. All we need is "enough of them". This enough may be quite a bit less than is achievable but nonetheless better for the sake of what we ultimately need the EU for — which should be, as it is in the present contribution, the point of departure. (2) Which policies and institutions can be stable depends on how the interests are constructed, which in turns depends on how the institutions are structured. Highly centralized and powerfully redistributive national institutions can be stable when interests are not primarily constructed along regional lines, which in turn is powerfully affected by the way in which political institutions have been shaped. Put crudely, my point is that we should start with the policies we want, next ask which UE institutions we need to get them and finally scrutinize the conditions under which these institutions can be made sufficiently viable, rather than start with an analysis of current stability or legitimacy conditions and try to make EU institutions, whatever they are, as stable or legitimate as possible.

rope as a whole.[16] This shift is not justified because demos-cracy is always better than demoi-cracy, but because in the case of (much of) redistribution under contemporary economic conditions, raising the scale of the democratic game and changing its rules along the lines indicated can be expected to lead to far better decisions, as far as the overall goal of social justice is concerned, than those to which national governments would be driven by the interaction of economic and political mechanisms.

So, does the EU suffer from a democratic deficit, from a suboptimal level of democratic accountability? It is certainly not good in the long run that some officials in charge of decisions that deeply affect the citizens' lives should carry out their jobs unchecked by them or their representatives. But we have seen that there are ways in which increases in democratic accountability may make matters worse. The question whether there is a democratic deficit, whether we need more democracy, is therefore dangerously underspecified. For the key question concerns the type of democratic accountability we need: to start with, whether it is more *demoi-cracy* or more *demos-cracy* that is required.

---

16 On one definition of federalism, demoi-cracy would simply be democratic federalism, while demos-cracy would turn Europe into a non-federal, unitary state. (See for example KING's (1982 pp. 77, 143; 1993 p. 94) characterization of a federation by reference to the entrenched representation of the federated units in the legislative process of the federation.) But there is another conception of a federal system of government, that emphasizes the constitutional entrenchment of territorial decentralization, rather than of territorial representation. (See e.g. FØLLESDAL's (1997) characterization of federalism in terms of a sharing of final authority over different competences, or indeed Belgium's official claim to being a federal state, despite the absence of any explicit representation of the federated units in decision-making at the central level.) In this second sense, even if the Council were scrapped, even if the whole Parliament were elected in a single constituency, and even if Europe's fundamental law took the form of a Constitution to be approved and altered by the European Parliament alone (rather than that of a set of Treaties), Europe could still be a strongly federal state. Indeed, it would be of the greatest importance that it should remain so.

References

DEHOUSSE, RENAUD: "Community Competences: Are There Limits to Growth?", in: *Europe After Maastricht: An Ever Closer Europe?*, Munich (Law Books in Europe) 1994, pp. 103-125.

DEHOUSSE, RENAUD: "Institutional Reform in the European Community: Are there Alternatives to the Majoritarian Avenue?", *European University Institute: Robert Schuman Centre, Working Paper* N 95/4, 1995.

DEWATRIPONT, MATHIAS, GIAVAZZI, FRANCESCO, von HAGEN, JÜRGEN & al.: *Flexible Integration. Towards a More Effective and Democratic Europe,* London (Centre for Economic Policy Research) 1996.

FRANCK, CHRISTIAN: *Evolution institutionnelle de l'Union dans la perspective de la Conférence intergouvernementale de 1996,* Université catholique de Louvain: Institut d'études européennes, 1995.

GUSTAVSSON, SVERKER: "Preserve or Abolish the Democratic Deficit?", in: E. SMITH (Ed.): *National Cornerstones of European Integration,* London (Kluwer) 1996 pp. 100-123.

GUSTAVSSON, SVERKER: "Double Asymmetry as Normative Challenge", in this volume, pp. 108-131.

KING, PRESTON: *Federalism and Federation,* London (Croom Helm) 1982.

KING, PRESTON: "Federation and Representation", in: BURGESS, MICHAEL & GAGNON, ALAIN-G. (Eds.): *Comparative Federalism and Federation. Competing Traditions and Future Directions,* New York & London (Harvester Wheatsheaf) 1993, pp. 94-101.

MAJONE, GIANDOMENICO: *La Communauté européenne: un Etat régulateur,* Paris (Montchrestien) 1996.

MIDGAARD, KNUT: "The Problem of Autonomy and Democracy in a Complex Polity: the European Union", in this volume, pp. 189-203.

MONNET, JEAN: *Mémoires,* Paris (Fayard) 1976.

ROLAND, GÉRARD, VANDEVELDE, TOON & VAN PARIJS, PHILIPPE: "Repenser (radicalement?) la solidarité entre régions et nations", *La Revue nouvelle,* 5 (1997), forthcoming.

SCHARPF, FRITZ W.: "Demokratische Politik in Europa", *Staatswissenschaften und Staatspraxis,* 6 (4) (1996), pp. 565-591.

SCHARPF, FRITZ W., MARKS, G., SCHMITTER, PHILIPPE C. & STREECK, WOLFGANG (Eds.): *Governance in the European Union,* London (Sage).

SCHMITTER, PHILIPPE C.: "Is it Really Possible to Democratize the Euro-polity?", in: ANDREAS FOLLESDAL & PETER KOSLOWSKI (Eds.): *Democracy and the European Union,* Berlin & New York (Springer) 1997.

VAN PARIJS, PHILIPPE (1995a): *Real Freedom for All. What (if Anything) Can Justify Capitalism?*, Oxford (Oxford University Press) 1995.
VAN PARIJS, PHILIPPE (1995b): *Sauver la solidarité*, Paris (Cerf) 1995.
VAN PARIJS, PHILIPPE (1996a): "Justice and Democracy: Are they Incompatible?", *Journal of Political Philosophy*, 4 (2), 1996, pp. 101-117.
VAN PARIJS, PHILIPPE (1996b): "Basic Income and the Two Dilemmas of the Welfare State", *The Political Quarterly*, 67 (1), 1996, pp. 63-66.

List of Authors

RAFAEL ALVIRA is Professor of Philosophy at the University of Navarra, Pamplona, Spain.

RICHARD BELLAMY is Professor of Politics at the University of Reading, the United Kingdom.

DARIO CASTIGLIONE is Senior Lecturer in Political Theory at the University of Exeter, the United Kingdom.

ANDREAS FØLLESDAL is director of a research group on normative political theory at the Program on Advanced Research on the Europeanisation of the Nation State (ARENA), University of Oslo, Norway.

SVERKER GUSTAVSSON is Associate Professor of Political Science at Uppsala University, Sweden.

RUSSELL L. HANSON is Professor of Political Science at Indiana University at Bloomington, Indiana, USA.

MARKUS JACHTENFUCHS is a Senior Researcher at the Mannheim Center for European Social Research (MZES), Mannheim, Germany.

PETER KOSLOWSKI is director of the Forschungsinstitut für Philosophie Hannover and its Centre for Ethical Economy and Business Culture, and Professor of Philosophy and Political Economy at the University of Witten/Herdecke, Germany.

JANNE HAALAND MATLÁRY is director of the research group on policy change in the EU at the Program on Advanced Research on the Europeanisation of the Nation State (ARENA), University of Oslo, Norway.

KNUT MIDGAARD is Professor of Political Science at the University of Oslo, and an associate of the Program on Advanced Research on the Europeanisation of the Nation State (ARENA), University of Oslo, Norway.

MICHAEL NENTWICH is Senior Researcher with the Austrian Academy of Science, Austria.

PHILIPPE VAN PARIJS holds the Hoover Chair of Economic and Social Ethics at the Université Catholique de Louvain, Belgium.

LIST OF AUTHORS

THOMAS W. POGGE is Professor of Philosophy at Columbia University, USA.

PHILIPPE SCHMITTER is Professor of Political Science at the European University Institute, Florence, Italy.

ARENA is a research program under the Research Council of Norway, providing Advanced Research on the Europeanisation of the Nation State. The program seeks to describe, analyse and evaluate the European process of institutional, political and cultural changes.

FORSCHUNGSINSTITUT FÜR PHILOSOPHIE HANNOVER (The Hannover Institute of Philosophical Research), Hannover, Germany, is an institute for research in all disciplines of philosophy. It is funded by the Catholic Diocese of Hildesheim (Eastern and Northern Lower Saxony). One focus of its research is the process of European integration. Part of the institute is the Centre for Ethical Economy and Business Culture.

Index of Names

Page numbers in italics refer to quotations in footnotes or references

INDEX OF NAMES

INDEX OF NAMES

MIX
Papier aus verantwortungsvollen Quellen
Paper from responsible sources
FSC® C105338
FSC
www.fsc.org

If you have any concerns about our products,
you can contact us on
ProductSafety@springernature.com

In case Publisher is established outside the EU,
the EU authorized representative is:
Springer Nature Customer Service Center GmbH
Europaplatz 3, 69115 Heidelberg, Germany

Printed by Libri Plureos GmbH
in Hamburg, Germany